GENDER DEVELOPMENT DIMENSIONS AND POLICIES

GENDER DEVELOPMENT DIMENSIONS AND POLICIES

SIDDHARTHA SARKAR
Department of Commerce
Dinhata College, Dinhata
Cooch Behar, West Bengal, India

NETTEN NARAYANA
Department of Economics
Faculty of Social Sciences
University of Botswana, Botswana

SERIALS PUBLICATIONS
NEW DELHI

First Published - 2007

ISBN: 978-81-8387-112-9

Published by

SERIALS PUBLICATIONS
4830/24, Prahlad Street, Ansari Road
Darya Ganj, New Delhi-110002 (India)
Phone : 23245225. Fax : 91-11-23272135
E-mail: serials@satyam.net.in

CONTENTS

PROLOGUE

Gender is a development issue because social considerations are not easily incorporated into institutions such as policies, regulations, markets and organizations. This process is often referred to as the 'mainstreaming' of gender in development institutions. Escalating economic resilience of the poor is largely about enabling women to realize their socio-economic potential more fully and improve the quality of their lives.

The paper 'intra-household resource allocation and bargaining power of women using micro-credit in Bangladesh' looks at the relationship between intra-household decision-making and the impact of the women's income on household standard of living.

Mensah and Adamu argue that men-operated enterprises differ from the women-operated enterprises in some aspects of business operations in Ghana. Such differences could be explained by differences in gender roles, educational background, capital and other institutional factors.

Kiriti-Nganga finds that the poorest women in Kenya are discriminated against in access to micro-finance hence defeating the whole essence of poverty reduction through micro-finance. This study recommends an evaluation and revision on the terms and conditions of micro-finance if it has to succeed as a poverty alleviation strategy.

The objective of Wasim's study is to assess the continuation rates of injectable contraceptive and to examine differentials in continuity rate by geographic, social and demographic characteristics in Pakistan context.

The paper 'gender responsive national budget initiatives in Botswana' concludes that with a gender-blind budget, it is difficult for the government to attain gender equality and consequently meaningful positive impacts on economic growth and development.

The purpose of DiPietrot's paper is to use cross-country regression analysis to empirically assess whether across nations is there any association between differences in the value of family, the value of leisure, the value of religion, and the value of work and inequality.

'Dynamic and consequences of population ageing: a comparative inter-regional perspective of Asian economics' addresses emergence of ageing phenomenon in varying patterns, timings and with diverse effects.

Mmolawa's article looks at gender differentials in poverty and describes that women are found to be indeed poorer than men in most societies in many dimensions of capabilities such as education and health. Meenakshi utters that problem of child labour is not peculiar to India. It is due to the need of assistance in the struggle for survival of the poor families.

The study 'women access to online banking facilities' has been designed to understand the women customers' willingness to avail the Internet banking facility offered by Indian banks and level of satisfaction in present banking services.

Narayana stipulates that the high prevalence of HIV infection in most countries and especially in African continent is posing serious threat to the development process and destabilizing the economies.

Konar states that feminism accentuates social instability through the incorporation of lesbianism and gayism, which in turn threatens sustainability of the global society.

Kumar portrays that the programmes, which promote micro-enterprises operated by women, have to benefit those poor who are actually being ill served by credit programmes of financial institutions in developing countries.

Rathedi makes clear that gender analysis and perspectives should be systematically integrated into the trade policies. A comprehensive approach is essential to monitor the gendered impacts of trade policies and agreements and to hold governments accountable for their commitments to gender equality and women's empowerment.

The paper 'gender discrimination in West Bengal' finds that gender-discrimination persists in an increasing order in almost all the districts of the state in varying degrees.

Siddhartha Sarkar
Nitten Narayana

ABOUT THE CONTRIBUTORS

Shahnaz Taranuum Abdullah; Faculty, Economics Department, University of Birmingham, United Kingdom.

Munir Hassan; Associate Professor of Finance, School of Business, Claflin University, South Carolina, USA.

John V. Mensah; Senior Research Fellow at Centre for Development Studies, University of Cape Coast, Ghana.

Fatima L. Adamu; Faculty, Department of Sociology, University of Usmanu Danfodiyo, Nigeria.

Tabitha W. Kiriti-Nganga; Faculty, Department of Economics, University of Nairobi, Kenya.

Mohammad Pervez Wasim; Staff Economist, Applied Economics Research Centre, University of Karachi, Karachi.

Donatilla Kokwanguha Kaino; Faculty, Department of Economics, University of Botswana, Botswana.

Malebogo Bakwena; Faculty, Department of Economics, University of Botswana, Botswana.

William R. DiPietro; Professor of Economics, Daemen College, Amherst, New York, USA.

K. Muraleedharan; Project Director, ICSSR Research Project, Malapuram, Kerala, India.

Boitumelo D. Mmolawa; Faculty, Department of Economics, University of Botswana, Botswana.

R. Meenakshi; Reader, Department of Economics, Sri Sarada College, Salem, Tamil Nadu, India.

Siddhartha Sarkar; Faculty, Department of Commerce, Dinhata College, Dinhata, Cooch Behar, West Bengal, India.

Nitten Narayana; Professor of Economics, University of Botswana, Botswana

Arup Kanti Konar; Faculty, Department of Economics, A.M. College, Purulia, West Bengal, India.

M. Rathedi; Faculty, Department of Economics, University of Botswana, Botswana.

Kachiraju S. Kumar; Faculty, Department of Accounting and Finance, University of Botswana, Botswana.

Jayabati Gangopadhyay; Research Scholar, University of Calcutta, West Bengal, India.

R.K. Ghosal; Reader in Economics, Department of Commerce, University of Calcutta, West Bengal, India.

1

INTRA-HOUSEHOLD RESOURCE ALLOCATION AND BARGAINING POWER OF WOMEN USING MICRO-CREDIT IN BANGLADESH

Shahnaz Taranuum Abdullah and Munir Hassan

INTRODUCTION

The fundamental issue in household economics is to decide how to allocate scarce household resources to different uses. When the household members have some goals and objectives, this problem reduces to the standard consumer decision problem. Here a consumer maximizes his preferences over a set of attainable choice-options. Typically, the preferences are represented by a utility function, where the choice-options are forming the budget set.

If, however, the goods and objectives of the individual household members differ, the decision process within the household becomes relevant. The choice behaviour will not only depend on the goals and objectives of the household members but also on other determinants of the decision making process. One may think of the relative bargaining power of the individual household members or of the agreed procedure for taking decisions under disagreement, e.g., by transferring the right to decide to the winner of a game of Black-Jack. In precarious situation those where households have low wealth and limited choice options in labour, credit, and other key markets the household dynamics of resource allocation decisions may be especially crucial to basic welfare outcomes of family members (Kusago 2001).

So the basic question is 'how do decisions on household resource allocation come about?' Studies are showing that the pattern of allocation is changing depending on the person who is taking decisions. Recent intra-household theory has explored the conditions under which differences result in distinctive resource allocation outcomes (Carter and Katz 1997; Lundberg and Pollack 1993; Manser and Brown 1980; Mc Elroy and Horney 1981). Women can only exert individual preferences for resource allocation, if they have their own income and which they control. An increase in non-labour income for women result greater household spending on education, health and household service at about four times the rate that additional income for men increases similar expenditures (Thomas 1990, 1993). A number of studies around the world, especially in developing countries, have confirmed that shifts of income to women increases the children and family well being. Studies in Kerala, India by Kumar (1977); in Jamaica (Horton and Millar); in St. Lucia (Knudsen and Yates 1981); in Ghana (Tripp 1981); in Kenya (Carloni 1987); in Botswana (Carloni 1987); in Srilanka (Benson and Emmert 1977) and another multi village study in Guatemala (Blumberg 1986), strongly indicate a greater devotion of women's income than men's to everyday subsistence and nutrition[1]. A more recent study has shown the same trend in Bangladesh, where girls schooling, boy's schooling, total household expenditure and women's non-land asset increased with women's income (Pitt and Khandker 1995).

WOMEN IN INTRA-HOUSEHOLD RESOURCE ALLOCATION DECISION

In Bangladesh, in particular, women's access to earning opportunities is severely limited. The legal inheritance rights of the women are generally forfeited, their chances of becoming widows (because of age differentials between spouses at marriage) are a near certainty; their risk of divorce is moderate though emotionally salient; and their control by patriarchal structure is extreme (Dwyer *et al.* 1988). But the society in Bangladesh is changing with different economic development criteria and policy implications. Over the last thirty years, there has been a steady upward trend in the participation of women in the labour market in developing countries as well as in Bangladesh; they are coming more and more into the development frontier. The participation of women in the labour force has been increased both in the formal and informal market.

At this present context, it is expected that women in Bangladesh will be more conscious about their decision-making role as they are becoming a source of earning. Since the women are taking the role of direct contributors in the family as the wage earners, the household expenditure pattern is changing according to their priorities. Income earning capacity of women influences the intra-household resource allocation, which, in turn, influences the gender relations in the household.

IMPACT OF MICRO-CREDIT ON DECISION MAKING

Women in Bangladesh are becoming more involved in decision-making as they start being the active financial contributor in the family. Our study includes the women who are borrower of the MFIs'. The access to credit makes them more conscious about their preferences and their role in decision-making.

Table 1 shows the comparison of the incidence of male-female joint decision making for the past (1994) and present (2001). Here we use the IFPRI data (1994) and the data from our field survey (2001). In case of joint decision making our study is showing a slightly lower percentage than the study IFPRI (1994). The present study is showing 26% of the women are taking decisions without the consultation of their husband. 72% of the women under the current study are involved in decision making either alone or with their husband[2]. Table 1 creates the impression that the majority of the women under our study are involved in taking decisions in the household. Note that our sample covers only the women who have access to credit.

Table 1
Change in Decision Making

	Past	*Present*
	1994	*2000-2001*
Male-female joint-decision making for household expenditure	55.2%	46%
Female involved decision making without consultation	-	26%
Women involved decision making either alone or with consultation	-	72%

Source: IFRI data 1994 and author's own data derived from survey conducted [2000-2001]

The present study will examine the following questions:

- Whether household decision-making is following the unitary model where the husband and wife have same preferences for household expenditure or whether they have different expenditure preferences.
- Whether the income of the women from the micro-loan has any impact on the consumption expenditure of the household.
- When the women are direct contributors in the household, whether there is any change in their husband's treatment towards them.

In this present study, we found that women decision making and men decision making significantly differ over the use of the loan. We also found out that though the income from access to credit enables the women to spend more on household expenditure but they are not receiving any better treatment from their husbands in the household unless if they invest their money in productive assets, where their husband has equal interest.

MODELLING OF HOUSEHOLD BEHAVIOUR: A REVIEW

Intra-Household Resource Allocation in New Household Economics (NHE)

Intra-household decision making theory has started with Becker's seminal work on new household economics (NHE) extended the neo-classical model of individual consumer demand to households by assuming a single, well behaved utility function (Becker 1973,1974,1981).[3] Becker (1965) first introduced unitary household model where, in accordance of single set preferences, the household combines time, good purchased in the market and produced at home to produce commodities which generate maximizing utility for total household. This model offers a number of important theoretical perspectives on the question of intra-household distribution. But if individual household members have different preferences, the assumption of a household welfare function requires that these differing preferences be aggregated. So the question is how to aggregate these preferences. The first solution is that a welfare function should reflect the consensus among the member (Samuelson 1956). It does not indicate how to reach this point of consensus. Another approach applies Sen's (1966) model of co-operatives to the household. Here family welfare is the weighted sum of the net utility of all members. Firstly, this requires cardinal utility functions, which allows the trade-off of the utility obtained by one member against the utility obtained by another. Furthermore, it is not clear how the weights are to determine in the absence of a dictator.

Yet another approach, which relies on the altruism of the decision-maker, is given by Becker (1974, 1981), and is known as the 'rotten kid theorem'. Becker considers the case of a household with two members, a benefactor and a recipient. The recipient is selfish in that he or she derives utility solely from his or her own consumption. The benefactor, as an altruist, can increase the utility by transferring some of his or her own consumption to the recipient. Now suppose the recipient takes the action, which increases his own consumption but lowers the benefactor. The benefactor could respond by lowering transfers to the recipient, so much so that the recipient's new level of consumption is below his or her original level. Thus the preference of the altruistic and the preference of the household converge. But the problem of this theory is that the benefactor should be altruistic over all levels of the consumption of others. If consumption by others is either an inferior or a luxury good, the threat of reduced transfers may not be credible over all level of consumption.

The first point of departure of (NHE) from the orthodox economic theory is that it emphasizes the household and not the individual in the centre of the analysis. The second point of departure is the assumption that the household is a unit of production as well as unit of consumption.

The NHE model has been criticized by number of scholars. Obviously, this type of criticism applies to representative agent model in general. The application of social choice theory or mechanism design would seem to be the appropriate answer from the perspective of economic theory. From the applied / empirical perspective, however, this approach fails to be convincing. The followings are the most important criticisms among the others; first, the household is assumed to be a single decision making unit ignoring the complex economic and social relations. If the household is a polygamous household, which is structurally different from monogamous household, common preference model may not fit there. Secondly, the NHE model can only operate on the assumption that the consumption unit and production unit is unified, and that all choices are made by the same decision making unit. Empirical evidence indicates that production and consumption are a great deal more heterogeneous and shifting than the NHE model allows. In addition the decisions about what and when to produce and what and when to consume either impossible to separate or empirically or are carried out by different groups of people (Evans 1991). Thirdly, Folbre (1986) argues that the joint utility function removes the possibility of exploring conditions of unequal exchanges and exploitation between family members, and in particular between men and women. NHE approach often ignores the fact that the household choices can be motivated by anything other than prices and income. In fact research shows the societal norm and patriarchal culture may affect the maternal and paternal altruism (Chen *et al.* 1981, Henn 1983, Whitehead 1984)[4].

Presentation of Unitary Household Models

This type of model can be obtain in different ways, as a 'common preference model' or an 'altruism model' or 'a benevolent dictators' model, based on whether all the family members share the same preferences or there is a single decision-maker who is taking decision.

Assumptions

Household consists of two individuals, h and w.

All members of the household share the same preferences.

Household members derive a common utility from the consumption of a vector of individual commodities and labour supplied $(x_0, x_h, x_w, l_h, l_w)$, influenced by a vector of household characteristicsγ,

The household utility function is given by

$$U(x_0, x_h, x_w, l_h, l_w; g), \quad (1)$$

Which is maximised subject to an income constraint?

$$p \cdot x_0 + p_h \cdot x_h + p_w \cdot x_w = m_h \cdot l_h + m_w \cdot l_w + n_0 + n_h + n_2 \quad (2)$$

and non-negativity constraints

$$x_0, x_h, x_w \geq 0 \text{ and } 0 \leq l_h, l_w \; l_{\max}$$

Where $l_{\max}$ denotes the maximal individual labour supply.

Total household income is composed of wage income and the non-wage incomes joint income n_t, husband's individual non-wage income n_h and wife's individual non-wage income n_w.

Under this model, income is pooled and maximisation leads to a series of demands goods and supplies of labour, which are the functions of prices $p = (p_0, p_h, p_w)$, wage rates m

$=(m_h, m_w)$, total non-wage household income $n_t = n_0+n_h+n_w$, and household characteristics γ.

$$x_i = X_i(p, m, n; \gamma) \qquad j = 0, h, w \qquad (3)$$
$$l_i = L_i(p, m, n; \gamma)$$

Subject to the set of prices and pooled income, resources are allocated to the household, which maximises household utility.

Collective Models

In contrast to unitary models, which predict that household behaviour can be changed only by changes in prices and household incomes; collective models predict that a large range of policies can be used to affect household allocation outcomes. These include access to common property resources, credit, public works schemes, and legal and institutional rights. In this approach of the household, the analysis of decision making takes account of different characteristics, interests and resources, and therefore of different utility functions, on the part of household members.

In the traditional approach of micro-economic theory, households are considered elementary decision units. They are represented by a single utility function that is maximised under a budget constraint. The most important distinction between the traditional approach and collective approach is that the traditional approach assumes that the single consumers have single utility framework. The collective model recognises the existence of several decision-making units and potential different preferences, which do not systematically aggregate into a unique household utility function.

In single utility models, wages or non-labour incomes only affect behaviour through usual income and substitution effects, whereas much more complex influences can be taken into account within a collective framework. Collective decision making processes have outcomes that are Pareto-efficient; thus the central assumption is that households will never adopt a decision that is Pareto-dominated.

All collective models have two common features, first, they allow different decision makers to have different preferences, and second, they do not require a unique household welfare index as interpreted by a utility function.

Where decision-making is concerned, collective model have two subclasses. One refers to co-operative game theory and the other to non co-operative game theory.

Co-operative game theory models represent the household decisions as the bargaining process applying the tools of co-operative game theory. The vast majority of bargaining models rely on a Nash solution (Nash 1953). The division of the gains from marriage, then, can be modeled as a function of the 'fall back' or 'threat point' position of each member: itself a function of extra environmental parameters (EEPs) such as laws concerning property and prohibitions on women working outside the home.

Non Co-operative game theory model relies on the assumption that individual's actions are conditional on the actions of others. The conditionally of action implies that the outcomes of non-co-operative models may fail to be Pareto efficient (Carter and Katz 1997; Lundberg and Pollack 1993).

Bargaining Models

In economics of the household, approaches to the analysis of economic decision making that take account of different characteristics, interests and resources, and therefore of different utility functions, on the part of household members. Bargaining models are an alternative approach to the strict neoclassical view advanced by Becker, which argues that household behaviour is motivated primarily by a collective concern for economic efficiency. As in the collective model, the potential gains from making joint decisions are maximized and household production and consumption is Pareto efficient. Unlike the collective model, which only assumes that the outcome will be Pareto efficient, the co-operative bargaining model specifies which Pareto efficient point will be chosen.

Theoretical Framework of Nash Bargaining Problem

As before, consider two household members, h and w. Only now we assume that each household member has his or her individual preferences.

Their utility functions are

$$U_h\ (x_0, x_h, l_h) \text{ and } U_w\ (x_0, x_w, l_w) \quad (4)$$

Here, x_h is a private good consumed by h (such as food, water, or health care), x_w is a private good consumed by w, l_h and l_w denote supply of labour. Furthermore, x_0 is a public good within the household, consumed by both household members in the same quantity, whether they co-operate or not (such as schooling of their children). Let p be the vector of the prices of all goods, m be the wage rates of h and w, and n_h and n_w be the respective individual non-wage incomes. n_0 is the joint non-wage income which is only obtained if both household members co-operate. If h and w do not co-operate, their individual utility functions are each maximised subject to their individual full income constraints.

We can write their indirect utility functions as

$$V_h\ (p_0, p_h, m_h, n_h; \alpha_h) \ and\ V_w\ (p_0, p_w, m_w, n_w; \alpha_w) \quad (5)$$

The V's are interpreted as 'threat point', the utility obtained independent of co-operation, while the α's are referred to as extra-environmental parameters (EEPs)[5]. Suppose that these two individuals are considering co-operating in some activity. These are a number of reasons why this might be advantageous. For example, there may be economies of scale associated with the production of certain goods (household or non-household), or there may be some goods that can be produced and shared by couples but not by single individuals (e.g. children, in some societies). Denote utility values when co-operating in a joint activity as u_h and u_w respectively, where u is defined over the household public good and individual consumption of goods and leisure. The utility values of the corresponding 'threat point' are v_h and v_w.

Both individuals gain from co-operation when for a combination of price, wages, non-wage incomes and EEPs

$$u_i - v_i > 0 \text{ for } i = h, w \quad (6)$$

The outcome of this is a binding and enforceable agreement regarding the division of gains from co-operation. One approach uses the Nash utility gain product function, which takes the form

$$G = (u_h - v_h)\,(u_w - v_w) \quad (7)$$

This is maximised subject to a joint full income constraint yielding demand functions (food, water, health care) of the following form:

$$x_i = x_i\,(p, m, n; \alpha_h\, \alpha_w)_{;} \text{ where } j = 0, h, w \quad (8)$$

$$l_i = l_i\,(p, m, n; \alpha_h\, \alpha_w)\ \textit{where } i = h, w \quad (9)$$

In the Nash bargaining model two individuals are considered instead of one altruistic person. The Nash model maintains that these two individuals take joint decisions as to maximise the product of their individual gains from marriage. The Nash demand function includes the husband and wife's income effect individually. Thus it is possible to test empirically how the wife's income has different effects on the household than the husband's income.

According to Mc Elroy (1990) extra-environmental parameters are pure threat point shifters. In addition to own wages and non-wages income, the EEPs include measures of employability (for example, dummies for various degrees of prohibition on market work by gender) and measures of wealth of one's family of origin. (Mc Elroy 1997)[6].

In the Nash bargain model the threat point plays a key role. The threat point is the maximum level of utility that spouses can get outside their marriage. An improvement in the threat point for either spouse results in household demands that more strongly reflect the preferences of that spouse. In the bargaining models of Manser and Brown (1980)[7] and Mc Elroy and Horney (1981)[8] the outcome is determined by the feasible consumption set and a threat point that is interpreted as the utility of remaining single or getting divorced. The preference of husband and wife regarding the optimal allocation of resources among goods and services within the family need be the same and they are assumed to be independent.

For simplicity and to facilitate graphical illustration we consider a two-goods case- regarding food and investment in private assets. The individual indifference curves for husband and wives are shown in the Edgeworth box diagram (Figure 1). The locus of the tangency points of husband's and wife's indifference curves, for given other prices, wage rates and income, trace the contract curve as shown in the figure 2. All points on the contract curve are Pareto efficient allocations. From the contract curve from the correspondent pairs of utility levels for husband and wife, the utility possibility curve (UPC) can be obtained which is plotted in figure 2

The UPC forms the boundary of all feasible payoff pairs (u_h, u_w). Any point below the curve is feasible but not Pareto

Figure 1: Edgeworth Diagram

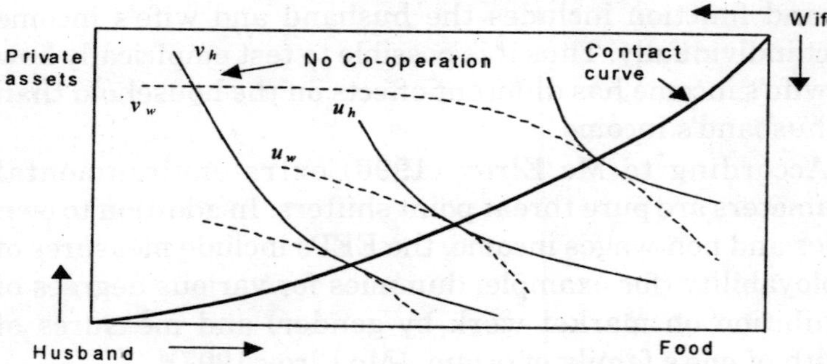

Figure 2: Utility Possibility Curve

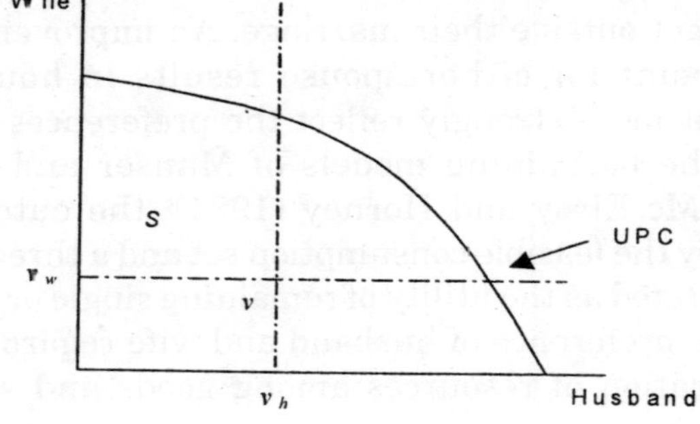

efficient. Let us denote the feasible payoff set as S. Note that points above UPC are unattainable. If the bargaining process ends without an agreement, then each individual obtains a disagreement payoff, which is also called the threat point payoff. The threat point v is always below the UPC (as shown in the figure) because of the gains from marriage to both partners.

Figure 3 shows the Nash bargaining solution. Like before we assume a family consists of two members: a husband and a wife. Each obtains a utility value: u_h for the husband and u_w for the wife. If agreement is not reached, then the payoff represented by a threat point (v_h, v_w) indicates the utilities associated with a divorce or, alternatively a non co-operative outcome within the marriage. The Nash bargaining model provides the leading solution concept in bargaining models of marriage[9]. Graphically, the Pareto efficient payoffs are indicated as a solid line connecting the points B and C in figure 3. The Nash bargaining solution is the tangency point of the utility possibility curve. If the husband has a higher bargaining power than the wife, then solution point is closer to point C and it would be closer to point B if the wife's bargaining power were higher.

The utility received by husband or wife in the Nash bargaining solution depends upon the threat point; the higher

Figure 3: Nash Bargaining Solution

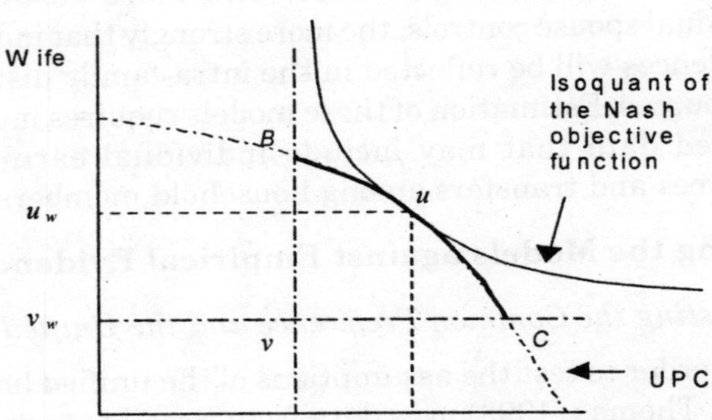

one' s utility at the threat point, the higher one's utility in the Nash bargaining solution. Household demands depend not only on prices and total household income but also on determinants of the threat point.

This Nash bargaining model is not out of criticism. Assuming the Nash bargaining solution is overly restrictive and does not yield easily testable restrictions unless premarital utility function is known.

In the Nash bargaining model two individuals are considered instead of one altruistic person. The Nash model maintains that these two individuals jointly allocate the commodity as to maximise the product of their individual gains from marriage.

Non Co-operative Bargaining Models

Non co-operative model assumes that income is not pooled explicitly, and this model shows how the levels of shared goods are chosen (Doss 1996).

Lundberg and Pollak (1997) advocates an alternative bargaining model named 'Separate- Spheres' based on two parent families.

A distinguishing feature of this bargaining model is that family demand behaviour depends not only on family resources but also on the resources controlled by each spouse individually. Individual control of resources matters because bargaining outcomes depend on threat point as well as on the feasible consumption set. The more resources an individual spouse controls, the more strongly that individual's preferences will be reflected in the intra-family distribution of resources. Estimation of these models requires much more detailed data that may include individual earnings and resources and transfers among household members.

Testing the Models against Empirical Evidence

A. *Testing the Common Preference and the Unified Model*

In order to test the assumptions of the unified household model, Thomas (1993) uses data from Brazil to test whether the distribution of non-labour income within the household has any impact on expenditure. Thomas's results indicate non-labour income controlled by women is associated with larger increases of the household budget share being devoted to human capital and leisure. Thus the unified household model is rejected. A consequence, though not a surprising one, is that differential control of income translates into different patters of expenditure. It is widely perceived that men spend a higher share of their income on goods for their personal consumption than do women, alcohol, cigarettes, status consumer goods, and even 'female companionship'. In contrast, women are believed to be more likely to purchase goods for children and for general household consumption. Guyer (1981)[10] is particularly noted for this observation, although a number of other researchers have commented on the phenomenon as well. In this context we can conclude unified model has been rejected by number of studies where the common preference does not prevail. Unitary model of the household has been rejected in a variety of country settings in both developed and developing countries (Haddad *et al.* 1997). One weakness of this model is that it considers all the incomes in the household are pooled. If preferences are not common to all household members, one household member must have the ability to monitor the others, which may create conflict of interests. Unitary models represent a special case of co-operative collective models where preferences are identical and, as a consequence, resources are pooled (Quisumbing 2000).

B. Factors Influencing Bargaining Model

Directly measuring one's bargaining power within the household is difficult if not impossible. The recent literature on intra-household resource allocation has focused on several factors that influence ones bargaining power and, thus, the ways in which resources are allocated within household. A body of recent micro-economic analysis has focused on command over economic resources, such as assets, unearned income, and transfer payments or welfare receipts (that is, factors that are 'exogenous or external to labour supply), as a major determinant of bargaining power.

Bargaining power determines the share of resources allocated to an individual within the household (Quisumbing *et al.* 2000). Quisumbing *et al.* (2000) identifies four sets of determinants that affect bargaining power. These are control over resources such as assets; influence, that can be used to influence the bargaining process; mobilization of interpersonal network; and basic attitudinal attributes.

Economic resources are the major determinants of bargaining power, these include assets (e.g. Doss 1996; Thomas, Contreras, and Frankenberg 1997; Quisumbing 1994), unearned income (Schultz 1990; Thomas 1997), or transfer payments and welfare receipts (Lundberg, Pollack and Wales 1997; Rabaclava and Thomas 1997) The proxy for bargaining power are public provision of resources to a particular member of the household and exogenous policy changes which affect the intra-household distribution of these resources (Lundberg, Pollak, and Wales 1997; Rubaclava and Thomas 1997); shares of income earned by women (Hoddinott and Haddad 1995); unearned income (Thomas 1990; Schultz 1990); Inherited asset (Quisumbing 1994; assets at marriage (Thomas, Frakenberg and Contreras 1997) and current Asset (Doss 1996).[11]

Legal rights, skills, knowledge, the capacity to acquire information, education can also influence decision-making power. In some cases domestic violence can be used to extract resources from spouse or their families (Rao 1997). Membership in organization and social capital may also influence a person's power to affect household decisions. Basic attitudinal attributes that affect bargaining power include self-esteem, self-confidence, and emotional satisfaction. The group-based micro-finance programs have been successfully includes empowerment approach as their major objective.

Quisumbing *et al.* (2000) undertook a study to test whether the assets brought to marriage by each spouse have different effects on intra-household allocation outcomes. In this research the authors focus on two types of outcomes:

household level income and individual level income. The survey has been undertaken on four countries e.g. Bangladesh, Indonesia, Ethiopia, South Africa.

Similarly, the extent of a person's social or economic fallback position influences the bargaining power. The members with more power often described in terms of 'voice' and 'exit potential' shape joint decisions. These terms voice means a family member's ability to bargain over the household resource allocation. Exit means the person's potential to exit the conjugal (familial) relationship (Katz 1992).[12]

Hoddinott and Haddad (1995) using non-co-operative model as a guide, they use two-stage least squares estimation with budget shares and women's predicted cash share of household income being treated as jointly endogenous. They find that doubling women's share of cash income within Ivorian households raises the budget share of food and lowers the budget shares of alcohol and cigarettes.

C. *Test of Income Pooling and Collective Models*

An additional perspective on income pooling is found in a study of informal credit programs in Bangladesh (Pitt and Khandker 1996). This study finds that credit affects household education and consumption choices differently if women rather than men obtain it. As the study employs a fixed-effect methodology that treats the availability of credit much as an experiment, it is able to control for the fact that credit choices reflect household preferences. A few recent studies use extra-household environmental parameters (EEP's) to support collective models. Pitt-Khandker (1996) their results are consistent with shifts in EEP's influencing intra-household distribution. They observe that communities where a credit program is in place have a higher demand for schooling than other communities. Although EEP'S may be one possible explanation for this difference, it could also be due to different expected returns mediated by economic impacts of credit or to pre-existing differences between communities for which they did not fully control.

One study undertook by Thomas *et al.* (1997) shows that income in the hands of women is associated with a larger increase in the share of the household budget devoted to human capital (household services, health, and education) and leisure goods (recreation and ceremonies). In addition of that, this study also confirms that the proportion of the budget spent on food (consumed at home and away) declines more if the income is in the hands of the women, although food composition also changes, with nutrient intakes rising faster as women's income increases. It appears that, as income under the control of women rises, more is spent on health and nutrient related expenses. The evidence from this study Thomas *et al.* (1997) indicates that child health outcome is consistent with this interpretation: maternal income has a significantly larger effect on the weight for height and height for age of children than parental income.

D. *Influence of Heterogeneity*

From the above discussion we can sum up that in most of the cases the unified household model has been rejected and there prevails preference heterogeneity among the men and women. Women and men have different systematic pattern of preferences, which shapes the household expenditure choices, based on who controls the income.

Kusago (2001) undertook a study on intra-household decision making in Malaysia which attempts to address two issues, preference differences from expenditure models and income control measures, by testing the role of preference heterogeneity and relative assets control in determining expenditure share decisions. According to the Kusago (2001) asset holding may be a good measure of the bargaining position of husbands and spouses over some types of decisions. The finding of this particular study has rejected the traditional single utility NHE model, advocating highly heterogeneous preferences at the household level and significant statistical evidence that women's preferences and power influence expenditure shares for some major items.

Lampietti *et al.* (1999)[13] introduced a new test of common preferences models, where a hypothetical preference test has been applied to the case of medical expenses to combat malaria among households in Ethiopia. They found that woman gives higher preferences than men to purchasing malaria vaccines.

Smith and Chavas (1999)[14] explore the effect of preference of heterogeneity on agriculture production decision, household income and household members' well being in the context of Burkina Faso. Their simulation exercises reveal that both the level of preference of heterogeneity and the associated power divergence within the family are likely to influence the impact of price liberalization on the household economy and household well being.

Resource Control, Bargaining Power and Household Allocation

Additional evidence on the gender-differentiated impacts of resource control on household level outcomes comes from recent micro-credit initiatives from Bangladesh. Two related studies examine the impacts of female and male borrowing from the Grameen Bank, BRAC and a government program called RD-2 on such outcomes as per capita household expenditure (income), girls' and boys' schooling and nutritional status. These studies find that the household level impacts often differ substantially based on the whether the borrower is a woman or a man and that, in a number of instances, the marginal impacts of borrowing are greater for women than for men.

For example, in the case of all three micro-credit programs, the impact of female borrowing on per capita household expenditure (income) is about twice as large as the impact of male borrowing (Table 2). As in the case of other form of resource control, female borrowing also appears to have a greater impact on child welfare than male borrowing.

For example, except in the case of BRAC, female borrowing has a greater positive impact on both girls' and boys' enrolment in school than male borrowing. At the same time, evidence indicates that male borrowing has a greater impact on household net worth than female borrowing. This suggests that while, at the margin, women seem to invest in the human capital of their children, men appear to invest more than women in physical capital.

Table 2
Impact of Female and Male Borrowing on Selected Household Outcomes
(Per cent change for a 10 per cent increase in borrowing)

Household Indicators	*Grameen Bank*		*BRAC*		*RC-12*	
	Male	*Female*	*Male*	*Female*	*Male*	*Female*
Per capita spending	0.18	0.43	0.19	0.39	0.23	0.40
Net Worth	0.15	0.14	0.20	0.09	0.22	0.02
Boy's schooling	0.07	0.61	-0.08	-0.03	0.29	0.79
Girls schooling	0.30	0.47	0.24	0.12	0.07	0.23

Source: Khandker [1998]

The evidence presented above indicates that the distribution of resources within household not just their total level matters to intra-household allocations and investments. More specifically, the evidence shows that increasing female command of resources plays an important role in improving the relative status of women as well as in enhancing family and child welfare.

Frankenberg and Thomas (2001) undertook a study based on the measurement of power relation between the household members, namely, husband and wife in Indonesia. This particular study (Frankenberg and Thomas 2001) throws the lights on the intra-household power relations, aiming to identify whether common preference prevails among the household members or one member dominates the preference over the other. Frankenberg and Thomas (2001) make an effort to identify the indicators of relative power in the household. The authors also try to identify the some common expenditure decisions in the household where joint decision-making is obvious. In this study (Frankenberg and Thomas

2001) has used three sets of questionnaire comprises of three different components. The first set of questionnaire focuses on how couples deal with money whereas the second set of questionnaire concerns how families make decisions about expenditure and use of time. The third set of questionnaire attempts to provide the insights into the relative status of husbands and wives within the household.

Another study has been undertaken in Mexico by Adato Michelle *et al.* (2000), which is based on intra-household decision-making patterns. In addition of intra-household decision making patterns, Adato Michelle *et al.* (2000)[15] also throws the light on how parental preferences for child schooling changes on the child's gender. The results of this study Adato, Michelle *et al.* (2000) found some interesting insights of intra-household decision-making. According to the study Adato Michelle *et al.* (2000) characteristics of husband and wife are the most consistent determinants of decision-making patters. This study confirms that the transfer payment to the women has increased the recognition of women's importance in the family and their degree of responsibility to ward the family relative to men.

Hellman (2000) studied on intra-household expenditure pattern in Bangladesh. This study has examined the effects of household asset ownership patterns on the morbidity status of male female pre-schoolers. In this particular study (Hellman 2000) asset control by each spouse has been measured by three different dimensions, one, by the current asset holdings of parents, secondly, asset brought to marriage by each spouse, thirdly, family background factors of each parent that help to determine the their current asset holdings. The findings of the study Hellman (2000) indicates that resource control in the household has noticeable effects on child health, and that the effects differ according to the sex of the child. The results of the study (Hellman 2000) clearly indicate that the unitary household model is not an appropriate description of household decision making, even in a setting such as rural Bangladesh. Using the different measures of parental assets, the study Hellman (2000) found that resources held by mothers have different effects on child health than those held by fathers; this leads to a rejection of the unitary model in favour of the collective household model. Asset brought to the marriage by each parent; a higher proportion brought by the wife reduces the morbidity of girl children (Hellman 2000). According to Hellman (2000) dowry (payments from the wife's to the husband's side at the time of marriage) most likely enhances the bargaining power of wives to make allocation decisions of marriage. The same evidence can be mentioned from other studies; namely, Russel *et al.* (1999) show that dowry is a strong determinant of child weight for age in Pakistan. Rao (1997) finds in India that smaller dowries increase wife beating and reduce child caloric intake later in the marriage.

Modeling for the Present Study

Based on Nash bargaining models as discussed before we can show graphically the income from micro-credit has increased the woman's threat point and the bargaining power. We interpret our hypothetical household consisting of two individuals' husband and wife. Previously the husband was the sole earner in that household. Assume now the wife has started using micro-credit.

The figure 4 is showing the treat point of the wife is shifting from u_w to u as a result of the change in their income[16].

Figure 4: Nash Bargaining Solution

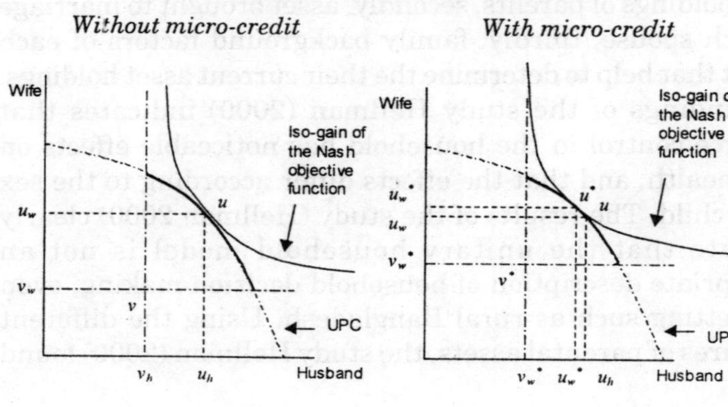

From the Nash bargaining model we know, wife's indirect utility function outside the marriage is

$$Z_w (p_o, p_{w,} m_{w,} n_w; \alpha_{w,})$$

If we consider the income from the micro-credit is the α_w which will shift the wife's threat point from u_w to u.

The change of income will shift the UPC curve outwardly.

Assuming the husband's indirect utility is unchanged, $Z_h (p_o, p_h, m_h, n_h; a_h)$

In order to fit an appropriate empirical model for the present study the following important consideration can be noted.

First, in contrast to the view traditionally held by economist and policy makers that household members pool their resources and allocate them according to a unified set of preferences, there is mounting evidence that household resources are allocated in the face of competing preferences and unequal bargaining power among members. One implication of this is that the distribution of resources within a household, not only their total level, matters. Policies that alter the distribution of resources among different members of a household shift the balance of power across those members, with potentially important implications for gender equality and family welfare. For example, in Bangladesh the evidence from micro-credit program indicates that access to credit is empowering the women. Female borrowing is not only associated with increased earning capacity and improved command over assets for women, but with increased autonomy, greater decision- making capacity within the home, greater household demand for formal health care for women and girls. Moreover, a growing body of evidence indicates that greater level of resources in the hands of women results, in greater household allocation to children.

Second, for choosing the appropriate model we shall consider the bargaining power concept in the household decision-making. We shall first test the unitary model; rejection to unitary model will lead to the acceptance of collective model. We shall take reinvestment choice as the dependent variable of two independent variables men taking decision and women taking decision, for testing the null hypothesis.

Third, if we can reject the unitary household model the question is still comes which alternative bargaining model we can use for our model. It is very difficult to find out a suitable bargaining model. Our model will examine whether the wife's income influences the household pattern of expenditure or not. If it does we can argue wife's has different expenditure preference than her husband.

Fourth, we already have shown in our theoretical model using Nash model that micro-credit increase the threat point of the women. It has been argued that the Nash bargaining assumption is overly restrictive and does not yield easily testable restrictions, unless the premarital (indirect) utility function is known. But we cannot empirically test it, as we do not have any premarital data. One empirical solution is given by Montalto (1995)[17] to estimate the indirect utility function of the single person households and then to assume that these represent the threat points for similar persons in two-person household. We shall consider this as our future research. We simply consider the income from the micro-credit as the extra-household parameter, which can influence the indirect utility of the women outside the marriage.

Here, in our model we shall consider access to credit and the ownership of or control over assets as the determinants of the bargaining power of the women and men in the villages. Why among the other determinant we choose these two factors? 'The significance of these two factors, namely command over property (especially land) and access to employment (through credit), is strengthening a rural person's survival ability outside power as a bargaining determinant (Agarwal 1997).

Again, In order to determine the intra-household relationship pattern after accessing to credit we use husband's treatment as a dependent variable to see the impact of the income and asset control over their behaviour towards their wife.

METHODOLOGY AND EMPIRICAL ANALYSIS

Data Collection

The survey for this research was conducted during 2000 and 2001 on 200 individual borrowers who are participating in the credit programmes of BRAC and Grameen Bank. 100 borrowers of Grameen Bank were randomly selected from three villages in the Comilla district and the other 100 were BRAC members randomly selected from five villages in the Jaidebpur district. The names of the borrowers were obtained from the offices of BRAC and Grameen in the mentioned districts. Semi structured questionnaire were used to gather information from the borrowers. This method made it is possible to obtain accurate and sensitive information on decision taking behaviour of the borrowers. All the 200 borrowers were used in the analysis were women. The practical experience of direct interview sometimes has given some insights of the actual use of the loan and the impression of the women regarding their own well-being and status.

Limitation of the Study

The following are the limitations that may prevent to get the reliable results.

(a) Limitation of the questionnaire. The questionnaire that is used in this study is not sufficient to understand all the dimension of the bargaining power of the women. Additional research is needed in this field.

(b) The present study is mostly based on refuting the concept of common preference model but did not provide enough idea of formulating an alternative bargaining model due to the limitations of the data.

Testing the Models against Empirical Evidence

Under the common preference model, expenditure patterns should depend only on total household income-not on who earns it. We shall reject the null hypothesis if we find that income of women after using micro-loan has any effect on household expenditure (Table 3).

Table 3
Tests of Intra-Household Resource Allocation Model

Null Hypothesis	*Common preference model*	*Collective model*
Women's income does not affect household expenditure	reject	consistent
Men and women decisions are the same for the use of the loan	reject	consistent

Source: The table is based on the analysis by Ross (1996)[18]

Econometric Specification and Operational Definitions of Survey Variables

For a test of the unitary model a dependent binary variable that states whether or not a decision has been taken to reinvest their profit from the loan.

If a unitary model held with common preference for household expenditure this variable should not be affected by a crucial variable on decision taking represented by two dummy variables against a base of joint decision taking.

Where D2 is variable representing women taking decisions on loan use, D1 represents men taking decisions on loan use and joint decision is a base.

The Control Variables are AGE which represents the age of the women borrower, which is a continuous variable. MAS represent the marital status of the women borrower, which is a binary variable where married is taken as 1 and unmarried as 0. NOC is the number of children of the borrower.

To evaluate our second question that woman's income has different impact on household expenditure pattern, the following are crucial variables.

LOG MONTH is the log of monthly income of women, OWNHOUSE represents whether or not woman owns any house. It is also binary. (If owns house then 1 and if not 0. PROASSET represents whether or not woman has any productive asset. (If owns any productive asset like land then 1 and if not 0. OTHTERASSET whether or not woman has other assets, which can be used in lieu of cash e.g. jewellery. It is also binary. (If owns asset then 1 and if not 0). ASSET represents whether or not woman has any savings in Banks. It is also binary. (If has any savings then 1 and if not 0).

We use income as control variables. We divide income variable into 3 different binary variables. Income from agriculture is AGRI. Income from trading is TRADING. Variable Y1 is the income from FARM, NURSERY, FISHING. Another control variable is education. Two education dummies are EDU1 education up to primary level. EDU2 is the education variable above primary level. No education is the base.

Result and Discussion

The results of the present study will be presented into 3 sections. In the first section we shall do the hypothesis testing for finding out whether the preference of men and women differs over a same expenditure decision. In order to test this we use two explanatory variables, men taking decision over the loan use and the women taking decision over the loan use. Here the dependent variable is reinvestment. This variable is a binary. Here the question was asked whether they use their profit for further reinvestment. If they say yes, we represents it as 1 and if they say no, we code it 0.

In the second section the evidences will be presented to show the effect of women's income on expenditure share. We segregate our dependent variables according to the expenditure, i.e. food expenditure, clothing expenditure, and other expenditure which includes children's schooling.

In the third section will show the impact of income from micro-credit on different consumption pattern. Here, we divide the consumption into three different types, i.e. food consumption (FOODCON), education consumption (EDUCON), consumption for medical (MEDICAL). Here the dependent variables are binary and we use logit regression model. We ask three different questions regarding this consumption. The questions were if they spend on food, education or medical from their income from micro-credit. If they say yes it is represented it as 1 and if they say no it is represented it 0.

In the last section will show the evidence whether the access to credit to women has changed their bargaining power with their husband[19]. Here our dependent variable is husband treatment (HUSTREAT). This is a binary variable as well. The question was asked here to the women whether after accessing the micro-loan their husbands are treating them better than before. If they say yes, we represent it as 1 and if they say no we represent it 0.

Section 1: Hypothesis testing for women taking decision and men taking decision over the loan use.

Table 4
Differences of Preferences over the Loan Use

Dependent Variable: REINVEST
Method: ML–Binary Logit

Variable	*Coefficient*	*Std. Error*	*z-Statistic*	*Prob.*
C	-2.334439	1.369748	-1.704283	0.0883
D2_WOMEN_01	-0.197175	0.533785	-0.369391	0.7118
D1_MEN_01	1.437178	0.589430	2.438249	0.0148**
CHIL	0.741546	0.824509	0.899379	0.3685
AGE	0.080829	0.033240	2.431664	0.0150**
MAS	1.028892	0.784376	1.311733	0.1896
NOC	-0.101203	0.191449	-0.528615	0.5971
Mean dependent var	0.885000	S.D. dependent var	0.319823	
S.E. of regression	0.302537	Akaike info criterion	0.679388	
Sum squared resid	17.66504	Schwarz criterion	0.794829	
Log likelihood	-60.93876	Hannan-Quinn criter.	0.726105	
Restr. Log likelihood	-71.36860	Avg. log likelihood	-0.304694	
LR statistic (6 df)	20.85968	McFadden R-squared	0.146140	
Probability (LR stat)	0.001944			

**Significant at 10% level

Our null hypothesis is that unitary household model will hold in Bangladesh where men and women have same preference for reinvestment.

From table 4 we can see that men taking decision and women taking decision differ over the reinvestment decision. Men taking decision is positively and significantly related to reinvestment decision whereas women taking decision is negatively related to reinvestment and it is not significant.

To sum up it indicates that if men are taking decision over the loan use they will prefer more reinvestment of the profit than that of the women. Why women are not interested for reinvestment? The reason could be two, one they may want to spend more on household consumption, second they want to keep the money for ownership of asset.

From the above table it is clear that women and men have different decision preference for the profit use.

Section 2: The following tables are regression results of the three expenditure items: food, clothing, schooling (other expenditure).[20]

The table 5 presents the impact of log of monthly income on different monthly household expenditures. The first dependent variable (LOG (EXA) is the total expenditure after taking the micro-loan. We then divide our expenditure as food expenditure (LOG (FEXP), clothing expenditure (LOG (EXP), and other expenditures LOG (OTHEREXP), which includes expenditure on schooling of the children. Each of these categories is taken as the dependent variable for each model presented above.

Here, the control variable, age of the women is not significant for total expenditure, share of food expenditure and other expenditure but only negatively significant for clothing expenditure. It means that as the women getting older they buy less clothing for theme-selves[21].

The second independent variable is whether the women have got any child (CHIL). It is a binary variable. It is not significant for any expenditure category.

The third variable is the number of child (NOC) of the women. It is positively significant with all dependent variables but not with clothing expenditure. It means that as the numbers of children are increasing, the women will spend more food and other expenditure, which is increasing significantly except the clothing expenditure. Clothing expenditure is not significant as it includes the expenditure on clothing of the borrower (women) only not for the children.

Here we use three sources of income for the women where they use their loan money as our control variables in this

Table 5
Impact of Log Monthly Income on Expenditure: OLS Regression

Dependent Variable:	*LOG (EXA)*	*LOG (FEXP)*			*LOG (CEXP)*		*LOG (OTHEREXP)*	
Variable	*Coefficient*	*t-Statistic*	*Coefficient*	*t-Statistic*	*Coefficient*	*t-Statistic*	*Coefficient*	*t-Statistic*
AGE	-0.00225	-0.40217	0.006714	0.878079	-0.0199	-2.09115*	0.008196	0.886481
CHIL	0.472737	2.295695*	0.275022	0.978249	0.042913	0.122648	-0.02353	-0.06264
NOC	0.074231	2.335289*	0.077025	1.774895**	-0.01534	-0.28401	0.169194	3.272871*
AGRI	-0.10773	-1.18596	0.07055	0.568884	-0.13984	-0.90602	-0.028	-0.19214
TRADING	0.059292	0.674484	0.288687	2.405431*	0.177769	1.190181	0.004011	0.02901
Y1	-0.079	-0.88684	-0.26578	-2.18549*	0.216387	1.42972	-0.20172	-1.38375
MAS	0.355163	2.480024*	0.73395	3.753894***	0.23065	0.947892	0.19028	0.84302
EDU1	0.064824	0.587059	0.0515	0.341616	-0.01945	-0.10364	-0.0792	-0.46013
EDU2	0.214038	1.503071	0.183337	0.943027	-0.11012	-0.45512	0.385803	1.708267*
LOG(MONTH)	0.099966	2.250748*	0.065365	1.077975	0.175426	2.324598*	0.175455	2.528039*
ASSET	0.226647	2.403954*	-0.05886	-0.45731	-0.18346	-1.14523	1.79534	1.199274
OTHERASS	-0.02549	-0.27756	0.038668	0.308386	-0.20461	-1.31116	0.031213	0.210618
OWNHOUSE	0.086293	0.891459	0.028213	0.213484	0.245142	1.490458	0.141838	0.948178
PROASSET	-0.09414	-0.93597	-0.01255	-0.0914	-0.19492	-1.14059	-0.2699	-1.69147**
C	6.297653	15.28626	5.66594	10.07352	4.193242	5.990325	4.462025	6.500143
R-squared		0.293674	0.226063		0.140896		0.275533	
Adjusted R-squared	0.232633	0.159179		0.066652		0.206064		
S.E. of regression	0.506582	0.691613		0.86074		0.764827		
Sum squared resid	41.57331	77.48917		120.0215		85.40428		

Dependent Variable:	LOG (EXA)		*LOG (FEXP)*		*LOG (CEXP)*		*LOG (OTHEREXP)*	
Variable	*Coefficient*	*t-Statistic*	*Coefficient*	*t-Statistic*	*Coefficient*	*t-Statistic*	*Coefficient*	*t-Statistic*
Log likelihood		-122.943	-178.05		-216.772		-177.412	
Durbin-Watson stat		1.849716	1.887926		1.379869		1.736859	
Mean dependent var		8.044861	7.625301		4.912651		6.584287	
S.D. dependent var		0.578293	0.754243		0.890944		0.858362	
Akaike info criterion		1.558677	2.181357		2.61889		2.390204	
Schwarz criterion		1.827843	2.450522		2.888055		2.677292	
F-statistic			4.811121	3.379946		1.89775		3.966248
Prob(F-statistic)		0	0.000085		0.029988		0.000009	

*Significant at 5% level **Significant at 10% level.
***Significant at 1% level

study. These are from agriculture (AGRI), from trading (TRADING) and from farm, nursery, fishing etc (Y1). Source of income, agriculture is not significant for any of the expenditure. Trading is positively significant for food expenditure and income from farming is negatively significant for food expenditure. It means that if the women use their loan money in trading, more likely that they will spend more on food expenditure. It is just reverse for income from farming etc; if the source of income is farming they will spend less on food consumption. It is quite obvious as they spend loan money on farming, fishing and poultry; they will buy less from outside and eat their own poultry, fish and milk.

Another control variable is marital status (MAS), which is positively significant for expenditure after taking the micro-loan and highly positively significant for food expenditure. This means that married women tend to spend more on food and total expenditure. This is not significant for clothing and other expenditure.

Another control variable is education of the women (EDU1), which is not significant for any expenditure category except other expenditure. Education above the primary level (EDU2) is positively significant with other expenditure. Other expenditure is the expenditure spend on the children's education and it is positively related to edu2 means as more women will be educated above the primary level they tend spend more on their children education as they will be more conscious about their children's education. Log of monthly income of the women is positively significant with total expenditure, with clothing expenditure and with other expenditure. This is not significant with log of monthly food expenditure though we found out that log monthly expenditure is positively related to food consumption. Consumption of food has been increased but not the expenditure on that, because the household may produce food on their own land and from their own farming, which may reduce the food expenditure but at the same time maintaining the increased consumption. Cash (ASSET) is positively significant with log of total expenditure but not with any other expenditure category. Keeping asset (OTHERASS) like jewellery and other semi cash item is not significant for expenditure. Ownership of house also does not have any effect on expenditure. Ownership of productive asset is negatively significant with other expenditure. Here in this category we use ownership of shop as the productive asset. It indicates that if the women own a shop by using their loan money, for either theme-selves or for their husband, they will tend to spend less for their children education. It may be the reason in rural area people needs another help to run a shop and the child could be used as the helping hand.

Section 3: In this section we shall discuss the impact of women's income and the asset ownership on different consumption pattern.

The table 6 presents four logit regression models showing the effect of monthly income and asset control of the women on reinvestment of income and different consumption pattern. We include here food consumption, education consumption, and medical of the household. Here the all the dependent variables are binary. The women were asked whether they spend their income on reinvestment for additional income or on food, education or medical expenditure. If they say yes, we assign 1 and if they say no, we assign 0. The control variable, age (AGE) of the women and having a child (CHIL) is not significant for any category of dependent variables. Number of child (NOC) is positively significant for education consumption and medical. It means that as the women have more children they will spend more for education and medical. If the income source is from agriculture, most likely the education consumption will be more, as the agriculture source of income is only significant for education consumption.

The source of income from trading is significant for reinvestment and education consumption. If the source of income is more farming, poultry and fishing (Y1) it is not significant for any type of consumption.

Marital status is negatively related to all the variables and only negatively significant for education consumption.

Table 6
Impact of Log Monthly Income on Reinvestment and Consumption Pattern: Logit Regression

Dependent Variable Independent	*REINVEST*		*FOODCON*		*EDUCON*		*MEDICAL*	
Variable	*Coefficient*	*z-Statistic*	*Coefficient*	*z-Statistic*	*Coefficient*	*z-Statistic*	*Coefficient*	*z-Statistic*
AGE	0.036477	0.625158	-0.04617	-1.58587	-0.04047	-1.44763	-0.03581	-1.46971
CHIL	1.615896	1.020046	0.676517	0.625856	0.660359	0.633232	-0.02156	-0.02328
NOC	-0.12394	-0.35223	0.290743	1.595865	0.301023	1.720005**	0.509928	3.315192***
AGRI	1.594734	1.493484	-0.25732	-0.54852	1.045709	2.155554*	0.123763	0.311993
TRADING	2.116341	1.886239*	0.674219	1.378146	0.911451	2.005704*	0.858608	2.215482
Y1	-1.05354	-1.13539	-0.74773	-1.44511	-0.30981	-0.66427	-0.06428	-0.16397
MAS	-2.16858	-1.41072	-1.03568	-1.35203	-2.1892	-2.22391*	-1.05257	-1.50409
EDU1	1.184307	1.336496	2.745769	4.656803	1.901872	3.483866***	1.228206	2.429773
EDU2	1.53213	1.185972	2.159541	2.989445**	1.215276	1.819003**	1.137056	1.767418**
LOG(MONTH)	0.928397	2.323088*	0.703585	2.831883*	0.531282	2.225548*	-0.01038	-0.05247
ASSET	-0.26105	-0.30702	-1.1411	-2.36934**	-0.95227	-2.10451*	-1.12922	-2.66312***
OTHERASS	1.386862	1.412877	0.328751	0.664814	0.192676	0.420548	-0.44682	-1.07742
OWNHOUSE	-0.71378	-0.7825	-0.88258	-1.70668**	-0.12837	-0.27223	0.333104	0.76693
PROASSET	1.482516	1.79391**	-0.22026	-0.42609	-0.32669	-0.65106	-0.0106	-0.02341
C	-6.55387	-1.805**	-4.03714	-1.84105**	-2.4294	-1.12789	0.253694	0.135954
Mean dependent var		0.932203		0.723164		0.689266	0.548023	
S.E. of regression		0.219772		0.400107		0.417239	0.471808	
Sum squared resid		7.824562		25.9339		28.20236	36.06164	

Dependent Variable Independent	*REINVEST*		*FOODCON*		*EDUCON*		*MEDICAL*	
Variable	*Coefficient*	*z-Statistic*	*Coefficient*	*z-Statistic*	*Coefficient*	*z-Statistic*	*Coefficient*	*z-Statistic*
Log likelihood		-29.3785		-78.582		-86.719	-103.968	
Restr. Log likelihood		-43.8786		-104.419		-109.685	-121.869	
LR statistic (14 df)		29.00016		51.67484		45.93128	35.80202	
Probability(LR stat)		0.01045		3.19E-06		2.88E-05	0.001117	
S.D. dependent var		0.25211		0.448704		0.464107	0.4991	
Akaike info criterion		0.501452		1.057424		1.149367	1.344276	
Schwarz criterion		0.770618		1.326589		1.418532	1.613441	
Hannan-Quinn criter.		0.610615		1.166587		1.25853	1.453439	
Avg. log likelihood		-0.16598		-0.44397		-0.48994	-0.58739	
McFadden R-squared		0.330459		0.247439		0.209379	0.146887	

*Significant at 5% level **Significant at 10% level ***Significant at 1% level

It means that if the women are married then they will spend less on reinvestment and consumption specially, on education.

Primary education is highly positively significant for education consumption. Education of the women, higher than the primary level, is positively significant for food consumption and education consumption. It means if the women are educated up-to primary level they will more likely to spend more on their children's education and if the women are educated more than primary level they will spend more on food consumption along with the education for the children. Education above primary level is statistically significant for medical consumption. Log of monthly income of the women is statistically significant for reinvestment, food consumption, education consumption but not significant for medical. It could be due to the fact not every day people get sick so monthly income does not have any impact on medical consumption.

Holding of cash asset is negatively significant for food and education consumption. It means that if the women want to hold more cash they will likely to spend less on food and education consumption. Holding of jewellery or other semi-cash asset (other asset), is not significant for any variables. Ownership of house is negatively significant for food consumption. Productive asset is positively related to reinvestment and not significant for any independent variables.

Section 4: In this section we shall discuss the influence of women's income and asset holding on bargaining power.

The regression model (Table 7) shows the probit model where the husband's treatment is the dependent variable. The above table is indicating that women's asset control and monthly income have no significant effect on husband treatment except productive asset. Productive asset means ownership of shops. It means that increasing asset ownership does not change the women's bargaining power over their husbands but only if they invest their money in ownership of shops they may exert some power. Why it is so? It is very obvious that if the women invest their money in shops that mostly their husband will run the shop and they will treat their wife well as the women are source of the capital.

Table 7
Impact of Asset Control on Husband Treatment: Probit Model Dependent Variable: HUSTREAT

Variable	*Coefficient*	*z-Statistic*
AGE	-0.057462	-1.871447*
CHIL	0.044250	0.042655
NOC	0.407153	2.186966**
LOG(AMON)	0.273228	0.463291
LOG(BMON)	-0.059602	-0.114402
ASSET	-0.453407	-0.903252
OTHERASS	-0.112912	-0.202909
OWNHOUSE	-0.092508	-0.167289
PROASSET	1.278437	2.322522**
AGRI	0.921161	1.625503*
TRADING	1.105548	2.037670**
Y1	0.299185	0.603110
C	-0.719242	-0.194311
Log likelihood	-70.05450	
Restr. Log likelihood	-83.84736	
LR statistic (12 df)	27.58572	
Probability(LR stat)	0.006358	
S.D. dependent var	0.385083	
Akaike info criterion	0.933197	
Schwarz criterion	1.65574	
Hannan-Quinn criter	1.027432	
Avg. log likelihood	-0.393565	
McFadden R-squared	0.164500	

*Significant at 10% level **Significant at 5% level

The above table is showing that age of the women is significant and it is negatively related to husband's treatment, indicating that as the women get older they receive worse treatment from their husbands. Other two significant variables are sources of income, trading and agriculture. It means that as more women are using their loan money in trading and agriculture, they are receiving better treatment from their husbands. Again it is obvious that in agriculture they are investing their money in the land where their husbands are working and for trading most probably they are investing their money where their husbands are helping them. The above table is showing that monthly income after the micro-loan is positive (AMON) but not significant and income before taking the micro-loan is negative (BMON) but not significant as well.

Summary and Findings

As the log of monthly income of the women is increasing total expenditure after taking the micro-loan, clothing expenditure, expenditure on children's education are also increasing.

Monthly income of the women does not increase food expenditure but it increases the overall food consumption, indicating higher supply of food from own land of the borrower or from farming, poultry where they are investing their loan money.

Holding cash asset is increasing expenditure after micro-loan.

Ownership of house and ownership of asset like jewellery have no effect on expenditure.

Holding of productive asset is only negatively significant with other expenditure, indicating as more women invest their loan money on ownership of shop, they will tend to spend less on their children's education as they need them for running the shop.

Holding of cash asset is negatively significant for food consumption, education consumption and for medical consumption.

Ownership of house is negatively significant for food consumption.

Holding of productive asset like a shop indicates higher proportion of reinvestment.

Asset ownership has no effect on husband's treatment except productive asset.

Older women get worse treatment from their husbands.

If the women invest their money in agriculture or trading they will receive better treatment from their husband.

CONCLUSION

This paper has demonstrated that men and women have non-identical preferences for the use of the loan. It also demonstrated that women's income is increasing the consumption expenditure as well as changing household consumption pattern. Our study fails to identify any improvement of the husband's treatment towards their wife as a result of their direct contribution in the household expenditure.

Our findings from the study can be summarised as follows, men decision-making and women decision-making is significantly different regarding reinvestment decision. If men are taking decision over the use of income from the loan they are most likely prefer reinvestment whereas women do not prefer reinvestment of their loan.

The women's monthly income from the loan uses is significantly changing the consumption expenditure as well as the consumption pattern of the household.

Haddinott and Haddad (1995) show that an increase in women's relative cash income is positively related to the expenditure shares of food and fuel and negatively related to alcohol and cigarettes. According to these authors household expenditure patterns are shaped by the relative power of different members over income. Our findings is consistent with this findings that women's income is increasing the food, clothing and educational consumption in the household.

Economic resources are the major determinant of bargain power (Quisumbing *et al.* 2000) Here we took women's command over asset as the determinant of bargaining power. Our findings is showing that holding cash asset by the women is increasing the total money expenditure after taking the micro-loan but holding any other form of asset has no effect on expenditure. In case of holding productive asset like ownership of shop or cultivable land is decreasing expenditure on children's education.

To sum up our study found out that, women's monthly income positively affects on both consumption expenditure and consumption pattern of the household. The husband and wife have different preference for reinvestment decision.

Our study has been undertaken in rural area in Bangladesh where women are highly dominated by their husbands. Our findings are certainly a positive breakthrough, which shows, that even in this strong patriarchal dominance and highly knitted Islamic culture women are still exerting their individual preference for household decision-making. Our finding about the intra-household relationship, where we try to find out the change of behaviour of the husbands towards their wife, reveals that husbands are treating their wives well, only if the wife acquire productive asset like cultivable land or ownership of shop where the husbands certainly have equal interest or if the wives are young and have more children. These findings are further conforming to the patriarchal culture of rural Bangladesh where men prefer younger wives and more children as a safeguard for smooth future. But again further research is recommended in this field due to the limitation of our data.

Finally, this study rejects the unitary household model and advocates that in household women have their own preferences for the household expenditure, which changes, as they become the direct income earner in the household. But their earning does not effect on the treatment they are getting from their husbands.

From this paper as a policy prescription we can conclude that women's income is certainly helping to increase the household expenditure for food and education but the women who have education more than primary education tend to spend more on their children's education expenditure. In respect of the consumption pattern our result is showing that, women who have education more than primary education level tend to spend more on education consumption, food consumption as well as medical consumption. Our findings are strongly advocating the necessity of the women's education those are in general more concern about the household consumption.

NOTES

1. Cited in Dwyer *et al.* (1988).
2. We could not get the same data of women individual decision making from IFPRI (1994) data.
3. Cited in Kusago *et al.* (2001).
4. Cited in Evans Alison (1991).
5. EEPs affect the relative desirability of being single and may include access to common property resources and divorce laws.
6. For details see Haddad, L., J. Hoddinott and H. Alderman (eds.) (1997), Intra-household resource allocation in developing countries: Methods, models and policy, International Food Policy Research Institute, Johns Hopkins University Press, Baltimore, Md.
7. Manser, M. and M. Brown (1980), Marriage and household decision-making: A bargaining analysis, *International Economic Review,* 21 (1): 31-44.
8. McElroy, M.B. and M.J. Horney (1981), Nash-bargained household decisions: Towards a generalization of the theory of demand, *International Economic Review,* 22 (2): 333-349.
9. For details see *The Journal of Economic Perspectives*, 10(4): 139-158.
10. Guyer, J.(1981), Household and community in Africa, *African Studies Review*, XXIV(2/3).
11. Cited in Quisumbing A.R. *et al.* (2000).
12. Cited in Kusago *et al.* (2001).
13. Lampietti *et al.* (1999), Gender and preferences for malaria prevention in Tigray, Ethiopia, Policy Research Report on Gender and Development, Working Paper Series No. 3, World Bank, Washington, DC.
14. Smith Lisa C. and Chavas Jean-Paul (1999), Supply responses of West Africa agricultural households: implications of intra-household preference heterogeneity, Food Consumption and Nutrition Division Discussion Paper 69, IFPRI, July.
15. See for details, Adato Michelle *et al.* (2000), The impact of proegresa on women's status and intra-household relations, *Final Report, IFPRI*, Washington DC, July 2000.

16. The income from micro-credit may enter into the wife's indirect utility function either as non wage come or extra-household parameter.
17. Montalto C.P. (1995), Measuring relative bargaining power using an economic model of cooperative Nash Bargaining, Department of Family Resource Management/Textiles and Clothing, Ohio State University, Ohio, Mimeo.
18. See for details Doss Cheryl R. (1996), Testing among models of Intra-household resource allocation, World *Development*, 24 (10): 1597-1609.
19. Here, due to the data restriction we limit our analysis only to the husbands other than mother-in law, father in law and their children.
20. We had another item of expenditure which we have dropped latter on as most of borrower they leave either in their husbands house or if not, pay very little amount as monthly rental.
21. Here we include the clothing expenditure only for the women.

APPENDIX

The following symbols are used throughout the paper as G =gain from cooperation; h= husband; w= wife; i=individual h or w; j=good 0, h or w; L_h =labour supply function husband; L_l=labour supply function wife; l_h=labour supply husband; l_w=labour supply wife; l_{max}=maximal individual labour supply; m=vector of wage rates (m_h, m_w); m_h=wage rates of husband; m_w=wage rates of wife; n=total household non-wage income; n_h=non-wage income of h; n_w= non-wage income of w; p=vector of the goods prices (p_0, p_h, p_w); p_h =price of the private consumption good of husband; p_w=price of the private consumption good of husband; p_0=price of the good which is a public good within the household; S=utility possibility set for husband and wife; U_i=individual utility function for I; u_h=utility value for husband; u_w=utility value for wife; v = threat point (v_h, v_w); V_i = indirect utility function for I; v_h= threat point utility for husband; v_w=threat point utility for wife; X_i=Marshallian demand function for good j; x_h=amount of the private consumption good of husband; x_w=amount of the private consumption good of wife; x_0=amount of the good which is public good within the household; Z_h=indirect utility function of husband in the Nash bargaining model; Z_w= indirect utility function of wife in the Nash bargaining model; α=vector of extra-environmental parameters (EEPs); γ=household characteristics

REFERENCES

Adato Michelle *et al.* (2000), *The Impact of Proegresa on Women's Status and Intra-Household Relations*, Final Report, IFPRI, Washington DC.

Agarwal, B. (1997), *Bargaining and Gender Relations: Within and Beyond the Household*, FCND Discussion Paper No. 27, March 1997.

Becker, G. (1965), A Theory of the Allocation of Time, *Economic Journal,* 75: 493-517.

Becker, G. (1973), A Theory of Marriage Part I, *Journal of Political Economy*, 81: 813-826.

Becker, G. (1974), A Theory of Marriage Part II, *Journal of Political Economy*, 82: 811-826.

Becker, G. (1981), *A Treatise on the Family,* Harvard University Press, Cambridge.

Carter, M., and E. Katz. (1997), Separate Spheres and the Conjugal Contract: understanding the Impact of Gender-biased Development, In: L.Haddad et al. (eds.), *Intra-Household Resource Allocation in Developing Countries: Methods, Models, and Policy*, Johns Hopkins University Press for the International Food Policy Research Institute, Baltimore, Md.

Dwyer Daisy and Judith B., (1988), *A Home Divided: Women and Income in the third World,* Stanford, California.

Doss Cheryl R. (1996), Testing among Models of Intra-Household Resource Allocation, *World Development*, 24(10): 1597-1609.

Evans Alison (1991), *IDS Bulletin*, Institute of Development Studies, Sussex, 22(1): 51-59.

Frankenberg E. and Thomas, D. (2001), *Measuring Power,* FCND Discussion Paper No.113, IFPRI, Washington DC.

Guyer, J. (1981), Household and Community in Africa, *African Studies Review*, XXIV (2/3).

Hallman Kelly (2000), *Mother-Father Resource Control, Marriage Payments, and Girl-Boy Health in Rural Bangladesh,* FCND Discussion Paper No. 93, September 2000.

Haddad, L., J. Hoddinott, and H. Alderman (eds.) (1997), *Intra-Household Resource Allocation in Developing Countries: Methods, Models, and Policy*, Johns Hopkins University Press for the International Food Policy Research Institute, Baltimore, Md.

Hoddinott, J., and L. Haddad (1995), Does Female Income Share Influence Household Expenditures? Evidence from Côte d'Ivoire, *Oxford Bulletin of Economics and Statistics,* 57: 77-96.

Kusago (2001), Preference, Heterogeneity, Power, and Intra-Household Decision-Making in Rural Malaysia, *World Development*, 29 (7): 1237-1256.

Lampietti *et al.* (1999), *Gender and Preferences for Malaria Prevention in Tigray, Ethiopia. Policy Research Report on Gender and Development*, Working Paper Series No. 3, World Bank, Washington DC.

Lundberg S.J., R.A. Pollak, (1993), Separate Spheres Bargaining and the Marriage Market, *Journal of Political Economy,* 101 (6): 988-1010.

Lundberg, S.J., R.A. Pollak, and T.J. Wales (1997), Do Husbands and Wives Pool their Resources? Evidence from the United Kingdom Child Benefit, *Journal of Human Resources,* 32 (3): 463-480.

Manser, M., and M. Brown (1980), Marriage and Household Decision-Making: A Bargaining Analysis, *International Economic Review,* 21 (1): 31-44.

McElroy, M.B. and M.J. Horney (1981), Nash-Bargained Household Decisions: Towards a Generalization of the Theory of Demand, *International Economic Review,* 22 (2).

Montalto C.P. (1995), *Measuring Relative Bargaining Power using an Economic Model of Cooperative Nash Bargaining,* Department of Family Resource Management / Textiles and Clothing, Ohio State University, Ohio, Mimeo.

Nash, J. (1953), Two-Person Bargaining Games, *Econometrica,* 21: 128-140.

Pitt. M. and Shahidur R. Khandker (1996), *Household and Intra-Household Impact of the Grameen Bank and Similar Targeted Credit Programs in Bangladesh*, World Bank Discussion Paper #320, IBRD, Washington DC.

Quisumbing, A. and Brendicte de la Brire (2000), *Women's Assets and Intra-Household Allocation in Rural Bangladesh: Testing Measures of Bargaining Power*, FCND Discussion Paper No. 86, April 2000, IFPRI, Washington DC.

Quisumbing, A. and Maluccio (2000), *Intra-Household Allocation and Gender Relations: New Empirical Evidence from Four Developing Countries,* FCND Discussion Paper 84, IFPRI, Washington DC.

Rao, V. (1997), Wife-Beating in Rural South India: A Qualitative and Econometric analysis, *Social Science and Medicine,* 44 (8): 1169-1180.

Samuelson, Paul (1956), Social Indifference Curves, *Quarterly Journal of Economics*, 70:1-22.

Smith Lisa, C. and Chavas Jean-Paul (1999), *Supply Responses of West Africa Agricultural Households: Implications of Intra-Household Preference Heterogeneity,* Food Consumption and Nutrition Division Discussion Paper 69, IFPRI, July.

Sen (1966), Labour Allocation in a Cooperative Enterprise, *Review of Economic Studies*, July; Reprinted in 1984, 33:73-89.

Sen (1966), Peasants and Dualism with or without Surplus Labour, *Journal of Political Economy*, October; Reprinted in 1984, 74: 37-72.

Thomas, D. (1990), Intra-Household Resource Allocation: An Inferential Approach, *Journal of Human Resources, 25* (4): 635-664.

Thomas, D. (1993), The Distribution of Income and Expenditure within the Household, *Annales de Economie et de Statistiques,* 29 (January-March): 109-136.

Thomas, D., D. Contreras and E. Frankenberg (1997), *Child Health and the Distribution of Household Resources at Marriage*, University of California at Los Angeles and the RAND Corporation, Santa Monica, Calif.

2

GENDER-BASED EMPLOYMENT AND PERFORMANCE ANALYSIS OF SMALL-SCALE INDUSTRIES IN THE CENTRAL REGION OF GHANA

JOHN V. MENSAH AND FATIMA L. ADAMU

INTRODUCTION

Economic growth has close ties with employment growth as more labour is needed to meet the rise in output requirement, without discounting the contributions of higher productivity to growth (Addison 2005). Absorbing the growing labour force in productive employment in most developing countries is one of the principal challenges of development. Much of this labour force is absorbed in traditional agriculture while an increasing number of people seek employment in non-farm occupations including the small-scale industry (SSI) sector. Small and medium enterprises in Asia, Africa and Latin America contribute over 70 per cent of all manufacturing employment (Elaian 1996; ILO 1972). Ghana's SSI sector provides 85 per cent of manufacturing employment, but contributes only 30 per cent of manufacturing value-added (World Bank 1983).

Expansion of the SSI sector to generate the sustained employment and income and to enhance rural industrialization, urban informal sector development; and optimal use of local human and material resources depend on its business performance. Firms with high business performance are capable of undertaking investment expansion and human resource development.

Both men and women play important role in the SSI sector but quite often women are given marginal attention. Sustainable development requires the involvement of women in all development activity (Armitage and Hyma 1997). In the last 30 years or so, women's contribution to the development process has gained much attention. For example, in the United Nations Decade for Women (1975-85), development agencies and national governments began to set aside resources specifically for women's projects and programmes. By the mid-1980s, most international donor agencies had set up Women in Development (WID) units with the aim of integrating women into the development process (Barrett 1995; Jahan 1995). The assumption is that increasing women's participation and improving their shares in resources, land, employment, and income, relative to men would lead to dramatic improvements in their living conditions (Sen and Grown 1987).

The gender and development (GAD) perspective emerged with the realisation that merely giving women what men had in terms of access to employment, technology, income and other resources would not change their subordinate position in society (Moser and Levy 1986; Moser 1989; Stamp 1989). Rather, new employment and income generation schemes and newly introduced technology could often result in the emergence of new structures of subordination (Rogers 1980; Sen and Grown 1987). GAD programmes attempt to train women so that they can strategically work towards desired changes. By recognising the underlying structures that oppress women and hinder their participation in development activities, GAD projects seek to improve women's position in society (Rogers 1980; Young 1988).

It is in recognition of the above that projects and programmes should take into account the link between women's productive and reproductive roles, the cultural and political factors in relation to women's access to and control of resources, and the legal and economic realities in relation to women's participation in these programmes. Such a view is increasingly offered by those writing on gender and SSIs.

Berger (1989) argues that the dual domestic and productive responsibilities of the female entrepreneurs may hamper growth and limit business profits, which are used to maintain household consumption. Various empirical studies conclude that women operated enterprises differ from enterprises created and managed by men. Frequently, women's businesses are part of the micro and small enterprise sector and are therefore subject to discriminations these businesses usually suffer from. Generally, however, SSIs in developing countries face problems such as inadequate finance, managerial problem, low technology, limited market, inadequate raw materials and unfavourable regulatory environment (Abaka and Mayer 1994; Mensah 1996; Staley and Morse 1965; Steel and Webster 1991).

In Ghana, successive governments, sometimes with foreign support, have established promotion institutions and schemes to address the needs of the small enterprise sector. These institutions include Ghanaian Enterprises Development Commission (GEDC), National Board for Small-Scale Industries, Ghana Regional Appropriate Technology Industrial Services (GRATIS), and Regional Technology Transfer Centres (RTTCs) (ISSER 1992; Abaka and Mayer 1994; Mensah 2002). These promotion institutions are supposed to support both men- and women- operated small-scale firms.

This paper compares the employment and business performance of the small-scale industries operated by men and women. The employment issues focuses on composition and type of labour, labour relations and conditions of work while the business performance is examined in terms of output-labour ratio, output-capital ratio, capital-labour ratio, job created, capacity utilisation, profit-capital investment ratio and price-cost margin.

The paper is organised into five sections. The next section reviews literature on gender, employment and assessment of business performance. The third focuses on the research methodology. The fourth section presents the survey results in terms of characteristics of the sampled firms and proprietors, employment capacity and business performance of the firms operated by the two genders. The last section draws the conclusions.

LITERATURE REVIEW

Gender and SSIs

Gender is different from sex. Sex deals with the biological differences between male and female while gender talks about the social relationship between male and female in which the female is often systematically subordinated. The relations between males and females are socially constructed. Male and female play different roles in society and their gender differences are shaped by ideological, historical, religious, ethnic, economic and cultural determinants (Whitehead 1979). These roles show similarities and differences between other social categories such as class, race and ethnicity (Moser 1993).

Gender refers to the social differentiation of women and men through processes, which are learned, changeable over time and vary within and between cultures. At the economic level, gender appears as a sexual division of labour in which some types of work are strongly associated with women and some types with men. The costs and benefits of the sexual division of labour are unequally shared between men and women to the disadvantage of the latter (Elson 1993).

Research in Africa and Asia show that females and males exhibit significantly different priority in production and consumption. Females contribute larger proportions of their personal income toward household expenditures than males and thus are able to retain less profit for reinvestment (Bruce and Dwyer 1988). Downing (1990) suggests that females have different business strategies and objectives than men. Women's motivation is often household survival, while men are more often business-motivated. Therefore, male business owners are more likely to reinvest profits into the business.

Effective policies and programmes to support the development of small-scale enterprises depend critically on adequate knowledge of characteristics and constraints of small-scale enterprises. Given the growth of entrepreneurship among women, it is important to understand the social and economic factors influencing the success of female-owned small business (Swiss Agency for Development and Co-operation 2001).

NGOs reaching a significant per centage of women are providing services to the poor, since women predominate at the bottom of the pyramid of micro-enterprise production (Otero and Rhyne 1994). The need to strengthen access to credit for women, small rural or urban producers, landless farmers, people with low or no income and vulnerable groups was underlined by the World Summit for Social Development held in Copenhagen in 1995 (United Nations 1995).

Essel (1996) found that men have access to rural bank credit than women. He noted that this marginalisation of women was partly due to institutional and cultural factors. The institutional factors include the rigid demands by banks (e.g. collateral) while the socio-economic factors included:

- The fear of women to take risks, as perceived by the women themselves;
- Lack of awareness leading to reduced access to credit; and
- The skewed ownership of traditional resources (which can be used as collateral) in favour of men.

Women's access to credit is vital to their ability to undertake economic ventures. Lack of credit availability may be the result of several factors (Molnar 1987, 1991; Kinnaird and Hyma 1993) including:

(a) The exclusion of women from male-dominated community credit institutions;

(b) The failure to account for women's greater transaction costs when seeking formal credit that often competes with domestic chores;

(c) Few credit packages aimed at women's traditional activities;

(d) Little collateral requirement flexibility as collateral requirement is generally based on buildings, land, or cash crops, assets women rarely control; and

(e) Little sensitivity to female-headed households that follow less diversified economic activity, a result of labour constraints.

In an effort to improve this situation, it has been suggested that female-dominated sectors be targeted. Credit will be significantly more beneficial for women under the following circumstances:

(a) Small loans are made available, allowing women with little or no collateral access to the needed credit;

(b) Women's groups take the responsibility for repaying loans. Women's organisation can more effectively work with banking institutions and management bureaucracy. When women's organisations take responsibility for the credit, there will be greater peer pressure for individual women to assume responsibility for the loan; and

(c) Collateral requirements are made less stringent and reduced.

For group activities, it has been argued that women are burdened with various time and labour constraints as they undertake several activities such as agriculture, water collection, fuel wood and fodder collection, and marketing. If a project demands excessive time and labour inputs from women, or fails to take into account the seasonal variation of women's work and labour, it may prove ineffective (Molnar 1987; Thomas-Slayter and Rocheleau 1995).

Social, political and class structures constrain women's participation in productive activities. As a result, it is important to realise:

(a) How women's roles are influenced by family and community social structures;
(b) Whether women act separately or in groups;
(c) Whether they are segregated by age; and
(d) Who the organisers are.

Understanding household gender relations and complementary uses of natural resources may be critical if a project is to be targeted at women. This is due to the fact that women often have limited access to the resources their spouses' control. Similarly, understanding political and class structures and their effects on women's participation are critical importance to proper programme design. The heterogeneous nature of many cultures can lead to significant problems during project implementation. For instance, varying educational background, age, status and economic interests within a population lead to difficulties in terms of co-operation or benefit distribution arrangements (Armitage and Hyma 1997).

Gender and SSI Promotion in Ghana

In Ghana, access to credit is, generally, difficult but even more difficult for women than for men (Ekumah and Essel 2001; Tsikata 2001). Tsikata (2001) observes that women's low level of education, lack of property to use as collateral, the small-scale nature of the businesses and lack of proper book-keeping methods, all affect their ability to secure formal banking loans. Since the early 1990s, several organisations have targeted women for credit. In principle, the establishment of rural banks guarantees access to credit for many women. In practice, however, it has had a limited impact as most of the loans and credit have tended to go to women in trade and others in organised groups such as fish mongers and women in co-operatives.

Since 1989, Freedom from Hunger, an international NGO, has worked with local partners to develop and disseminate a cost effective integrated programme called Credit with Education for Women (CREW). The goal is to improve the nutritional, financial status and food security of poor households in rural areas of Africa, Latin America and Asia. CREW has provided over 9,000 individuals small loans with a total value of about US$600,000 to poor women in rural and urban areas who have been hard to reach through the traditional banking system (Ekumah and Essel 2001). Women participating in the CREW programme at the Lower Pra Rural Bank in the Western Region of Ghana and seven other institutions had much success with about 92% repayment rate (MkNelly and Dunford 1998).

Ekumah and Essel (2001) observed that even though the proportion of women that gained access to credit was more than that of the men in two rural banks after the Financial Sector Reforms (FSR), both women and men alike continue to be marginalised in acquiring credit. The innovations have reduced the long process of acquiring credit, especially for women, who are specially the target. They have also encouraged the adoption of non-economic factors like trust and confidence as basis for accessing group loans. Both males and females in the less urban areas had more access to informal sources of credit than those in urban areas.

In the Central Region, the main SSI promotion institutions are National Council on Women and Development (NCWD), National Board for Small-Scale Industries (NBSSI), Business Advisory Centre (BAC), Central Region Development Commission (CEDECOM), Regional Technology Transfer Centre (RTTC) and Entrepreneurial Development and Training Programme (EMPRETEC). They are required to provide both financial and non-financial services to small-scale enterprises in the region. Their promotional activities, however, have covered few enterprises with marginal impact on business performance (Mensah 2002). Both SSI firms and promotion institutions have their own constraints that hinder effective business performance.

As mentioned earlier, one of the major strengths of SSIs in Africa is its role in providing employment to the population. In Ghana, the SSIs provide 85% of employment in the manufacturing sector and women are active players in the sub-sector.

Employment

Employment is the use of labour as a factor input in the production process of goods and services. The study of labour is influenced by four main schools of thought namely neo-classical, Keynesian, institutional and radical approaches (Thomas 1991).

The neo-classical perspective focuses on the rather abstract study of the demand and supply sides of labour markets at the micro level. The demand side analysis is strongly embedded in the marginal productivity approach, which reflects the behaviour of profit-maximising entrepreneurs within highly competitive market structures. The supply-side analysis is based on individual worker's preferences between work and leisure or between work and investment in human capital. In this way, one obtains a coherent analytical framework that yields seemingly precise outcomes for wage structures and employment levels.

After World War II, the Keynesian analysis complemented the micro-economic neo-classical analysis. The Keynesian perspective focused on macroeconomics and gave unemployment a central role in its analysis. It identified various types of unemployment: structural, cyclical, seasonal and frictional. The Keynesian analysis asserted that the neo-classical approach of relying on the market in the determination of wages did not hold in a world where a limited effective demand would cause involuntary unemployment.

The institutional school deals with the main actors in the labour market: trade unions, employers and the government. The central theme focuses on the in-depth analysis of bargaining processes between these actors. The outcomes are the details of payment conditions and the legalities of work contract. This school assigns an important role to the government as a mediator in conflicts and as an intervening force through its education, manpower and social policies. Ample *prima facie* evidence exists about the weak, unprotected, unorganised and low skilled nature of work with SSIs, and therefore unemployment in SSIs forms one of the sub-markets of the labour market (Thomas 1991).

The radical school is based on the Marxist hypothesis that capital owners exploit workers. This approach tends to examine the wider societal relations of power inequalities in the specific markets and their institutional underpinnings. The radical view on exploitation, discrimination and income inequalities offers a broader scope for application to the developing countries where unemployment is pervasive. It sets out primarily to reveal the underlying power structures that have an overriding impact on all markets and institutions.

The four approaches have generated different research methods in terms of the objects of analysis, the research questions and the techniques applied. The neo-classical approach tends to concentrate on demand-supply analysis for work and labour; the Keynesian approach emphasises unemployment issues; the institutional approach tends to examine the actors in the labour market and collective bargaining; and the radical approach focuses on class differences on the supply side and the control of labour in the context of national power relationships on the demand side. Even though there are some very good scientific and political reasons why these paradigms are different, the study of labour should combine the elements of different approaches (Magnum and Philips 1988; Thomas 1991).

Analysis of labour and employment in the SSI sector in many countries usually concentrates on the economic aspects such as growth potential and sectoral statistics, without in-depth studies of other economic aspects of the labour situation such as hours of work and earnings. Indeed, conditions of work and employment should form an important component of developmental policies (Thomas 1991). Employment creation through viable investment activities is an important national objective as the level of employment is a basic measure of economic well-being of a nation or an industry. Increasing unemployment is a major concern to all citizens because of its social consequences and costs to both individuals and society while improvement in the employment situation is a source for hope in the future.

Employment growth can signal good or bad news. Where the economy is prospering and buoyant aggregate demand results in an expansion of productive enterprises, employment can signal prosperity. However, when the economy is languishing or the population growth rate is high, an increase in employment may simply reflect the bad news that small enterprises are acting as a sponge, soaking up excess workers in marginal activities (Liedholm and Mead 1999).

In sub-Saharan Africa including Ghana, SSI acts as a labour sponge but contributes only 2.9-8.3 of GDP (Boateng 1996; Liedholm and Mead 1987:16; Mensah 2005a). Workers –including both employees and proprietors in small-scale industry generally receive low remuneration due to modest revenues and minimal profits (Mead 1999; Mensah 2000, 2005a). Employment is characterised by a lack of formal contracts and regular pay; non-existent social protection and codes for hiring and firing; and social relations of work based on family and moral values (see Morrisson *et al.* 1994). While some proprietors belong to business associations, the employees of SSIs have no associations to press for better working conditions.

Assessing Business Performance in Small-scale Industries

Conventional economic performance assessment can be carried out using a dynamic measure principally firm-level total factor productivity growth or a static measure such as an annual cost-benefit ratio, output-labour ratio, output-capital ratio, capital-labour ratio, job created, capacity utilisation, profit-capital investment ratio and price-cost margin. However, for small-scale industries, it is rare to see dynamic measures involving comparison between data for at least two time periods, and cost-benefit applied due to inadequate data emanating from poor record keeping of the firms. Only about 25% of the sampled firms kept records (Mensah 2000).

Accurate cost benefit calculations require a significant disaggregation of input and output e.g., a decomposition of raw materials into different items, and the economic valuation of these different components. Economic value of traded goods requires the use of world prices while that of non-traded goods is based on either willingness to pay (where the demand side of a market is affected) or marginal production cost (where the supply side is affected). Output valuation for small-scale enterprises can be particularly difficult since the bulk of sales will be of non-traded items that differ in quality significantly from goods sold on the world market. 'Willingness to pay' estimates can be problematic where actual market prices are not readily available.

Partial efficiency measures such as capital-labour, output-labour and output-capital ratios are often applied to firms (Uppal 1996). A low capital-labour ratio implies that a small amount of capital is required to employ one unit of labour and the technique may be termed as labour-intensive. Conversely, a high ratio means a capital-intensive method of production signifying a large capital investment for every unit of labour employed. Employment generation is an important performance of firms. The ability of SSIs to create additional employment is usually indicated by cost per job created (i.e. capital-labour ratio). SSIs create more additional employment per unit of investment than large industries because SSIs tend to apply more labour intensive technology (Elaian 1996; Ryan 1993).

Output-labour ratio is indicative of labour productivity. A high ratio means a large output per worker. Two main approaches used are output-labour ratio in terms of total number of workers involved in the production process; and wage productivity, which measures output-labour ratio in terms of total wage bill (Uppal 1996).

A major limitation of the first approach is its assumption that all labour is homogeneous and that a single wage-rate prevails. In reality, however, labour is heterogeneous. Usually, the 'more complex a machine, the more the skill of the operator in running it... Therefore, SSIs generally employ a skill-mix which is inferior and dominated by unskilled workers due to the simplicity of the machines used...Large factories by virtue of the superior machine technology have no option but to employ skilled workers and trained technicians to protect plant and machinery' (Uppal 1996: 58-59).

SSIs tend to employ a larger number of labourers for a lower wage-rate in comparison to large firms, which may employ a small number of unskilled workers but pay a higher wage-rate. This implies that each technology variant has its own wage-rate and a corresponding wage bill. 'Therefore, if wage bills are taken into account then a single worker in the large factory may be equal to three or four workers in the small factory. If this adjustment is done then the various ratios used in the analysis to determine plant size efficiency may well move in entirely different directions' (Uppal 1996:59). Such adjustments distinguish between skilled and unskilled labour but they often fail to distinguish between seasonal and permanent labour that exist in the SSI sector (Mensah 2000).

Output-capital ratio shows the efficiency with which the capital is being used. The higher the ratio the higher the productivity of the capital employed, implying a high efficient firm. The partial measures imply that the single input is the only scarce factor of production. The partial productivity indices are useful and easier to estimate but they fail to distinguish increase in output per worker or per capital input from increases resulting from technical efficiency. They also fail to distinguish between different qualities of the products.

Capacity utilisation is used as a proxy of efficiency measure in a sense that a production unit that improves upon its capacity utilisation in the short run could be seen to be minimising its cost of unit per output, thereby becoming more efficient. The level of capacity utilisation measures the extent to which assets is productively employed (Weiss 1988). High level of capacity under-utilisation in the midst of scarce investment funds is a significant resource misallocation (Havrylyshyn 1990; Winston 1971).

Profit enables firms to survive and grow as well as to finance capital needed for industrialisation, which in turn stimulates output and profits. It is the difference between total revenues and total expenses over a period of time (see Mensah 2000; 2002; 2005b). Several profitability measures in the literature include price-cost margin, net profit to net sales, return to net investment, net profit to net worth, and operating expenses to net sales (Bansal 1991; Little *et al.* 1987). The most relevant ones to SSI studies in a developing country like Ghana are profit-capital investment ratio and price cost margin.

Price cost margin (PCM) which is based on the Lerner Index[1] reflects the ability of the firm to raise its price above the level of competitors. In pure competition, PCM is equal to zero in the long run but it may be equal to or greater or less than zero in the short run. A proxy indicator of PCM[2] is the ratio of economic surplus to gross output at current prices (Mensah 2002; Weiss 1992). When PCM increases, profit from sales will increase. From the shareholders' point of view, the higher the PCM, the better the firm's performance.

Bansal (1991) notes that poor operational performance may lead to poor sales revenue and hence poor profits while poor profitability may be the result of inefficient control over the costs and expenses. He then highlights four profitability ratios that measure the efficiency of the firm's activities and its ability to meet its obligations. These ratios are net profit to net sales, net profit to net worth, net profit to total capital employed, and operating expenses to net sales[3].

Based on the preceding discussions, this paper compares the performance of the men and women operated small-scale firms in terms of output-labour ratio, output-capital ratio, output-wage ratio, capital-labour ratio, capacity utilisation, profit-capital investment ratio and price-cost margin.

RESEARCH METHODOLOGY

This paper is based on both primary and secondary data, which were collected using structured and unstructured interview schedules, case study, observation and library research. The fieldwork covered the proprietors or managers of 320 small-scale industries[4] and the executives of seven associations in five districts in the Central Region. The districts were Assin[5], Cape Coast, Asikuma-Odoben-Brakwa, Gomoa and Twifu-Hemang-Lower Denkyira as shown in Table 1. This study is a follow-up of a study conducted by the principal author in four districts in the region in 1998.

Table 1

Number of Selected Firms in Various Activities by District

Activities	*District*					*Total*
	Assin	*Asikuma-Odoben-Brakwa*	*Cape Coast*	*Gomoa*	*Twifu-Hemang-Lower-Denkyira*	
Dress making	11	12	15	14	12	64 (20.0)
Wood work	10	12	12	7	10	51 (15.9)
Hair dressing	10	10	12	10	8	50 (15.6)
Oil Processing	6	7	4	3	13	33 (10.3)
Bakery	6	7	8	4	5	30 (9.4)
Tailoring	5	6	6	5	4	26 (8.1)
Blacksmithing	5	4	4	3	6	22 (6.9)
Block making	2	1	4	2	1	10 (3.1)
Soap making	2	3	0	2	1	8 (2.5)
Pottery	0	3	0	5	0	8 (2.5)
Roofing Tiles	2	0	2	0	3	7 (2.2)
Kente Weaving	5	0	0	0	2	7 (2.2)
Salt Extraction	0	0	0	4	0	4 (1.3)
Total	64 (20.0)	65 (20.3)	67 (21.0)	59 (18.4)	65 (20.3)	320 (100.0)

Note: Figures in parentheses are percentages.
Source: Field Data [2003]

The selection of the study area, settlements and owners of the SSIs followed a multi-stage sampling technique involving census, stratified and random sampling. The steps involved in the sampling technique are first, purposive selection of five out of twelve districts of the Central Region to meet the resources available for the study and the characteristics of the region. The second stage involved the selection of 40 out of 251 settlements in the sampled districts with more than two firms, based on information from the SSI promotion institutions and the District Medium Term Development plans. The third stage involved purposive selection of the district capital and quota sampling of seven other settlements in each district, thereby forming a total of 40 settlements. In the fourth stage, a census covering 1562 small-scale firms was conducted in the 40 settlements with the help of chiefs, assembly members and executives of small-scale business associations in each selected settlement. The commendable support from the local authorities facilitated in locating the various firms in these settlements. The fifth stage determined a sample size of 320 firms and then allocated the firms among various activities and districts by using the proportional stratified random sampling technique.

The seven associations purposively selected, using the case study approach, are presented in Table 2. Secondary data were also gathered from the reports, brochures and records of enterprises, associations, SSI promotion institutions, and the District Assemblies[6]. The fieldwork was carried out from August to November 2003.

Table 2
Selected Business Associations

Association	*Settlement*	*District*
1. Small Scale Carpenters Association	Cape Coast	Cape Coast
2. Small Scale Block Manufacturers Association	Cape Coast	Cape Coast
3. Somuye Women's Association	Twifu-Hemang	Twifu-Hemang-Lower-Denkyira
4. Ahoto Microenterprise Association	Twifu-Mampong	Twifu-Hemang-Lower-Denkyira
5. Asikuma-Odoben-Brakwa District Association of Entrepreneurs	Bremen Asikuma	Asikuma-Odoben-Brakwa
6. Ghana National Tailors & Dressmakers Association	Apam	Gomoa
7. Ghana Hairdressers and Beauticians' Association	Assin Nsuta	Assin

Source: Field Data [2003].

Data from the survey were coded and processed using the Statistical Package for the Social Sciences (SPSS). Statistical measures of central tendency and dispersion such as the mean, standard deviation and coefficient of variation as well as chi-square and F-Statistic were used to analyse the data.

SURVEY RESULTS

Characteristics of the Firms and Proprietors

Most enterprises operated in temporary housing structures, with only 5.8% of the sampled 320 operating in what could be termed 'factory' conditions. Dressmakers, tailors and hairdressers mainly occupied kiosks and residential buildings, while the majority of oil processors, blacksmiths and woodworkers operated either in open spaces or in wooden or iron sheds.

About 69.6% of the firms were established within the last ten years, with an average age of 9 years. Even though the male enterprises were slightly older than the female counterparts, the difference was statistically insignificant as indicated by the F-ratio of 0.35 at 59.7% significance level. The vast majority of enterprises (90%) were owner-run as sole proprietorships, with 6% established by proprietor's parents. The virtual absence of business partnerships in the SSI sector could be attributed to the limited trust among Ghanaian enterprises (Sowa *et al.* 1992:23).

The majority of firms (65%) were in the micro category (1-5 workers), which is consistent with other surveys[7]. The majority (58%) of entrepreneurs were female although these were concentrated in particular activities dressmaking, baking, oil processing and hairdressing with all other activities dominated by males. Only a quarter (i.e. 31% and 20% of male and female respectively) of the entrepreneurs reported that they kept records, implying that careful questioning was required to elicit information on operations. Record keeping tends to increase with firm size. Only 0.9% of the entrepreneurs had tertiary education but 62.2% had primary education. Nearly 48% of the proprietors had other work in addition to the enterprise surveyed and this proportion tended to be higher in rural areas. Hence, for most rural proprietors, the SSIs offered part-time work with agriculture providing the main alternative activity.

Nearly 43.7% of the entrepreneurs belonged to business associations (see Table 3). Major findings from Table 3 include:

- Associations existed for the majority of the activities.
- Business association membership varied significantly in terms of activity, firm size, urban-rural location, district and gender as indicated by the corresponding chi-square. The percentage of entrepreneurs belonging to associations in dressmaking, block making, hairdressing, pottery, tailoring and salt making was relatively higher than in other activities. The larger the firm size, the more likely that the entrepreneurs would belong to an association.
- More urban firms (57%) than the rural firms (33%) belonged to associations. One of the reasons for this phenomenon was that there were more SSI associations in the urban areas than in the rural areas, which was consistent with Mathuva (1996) cited by Haan 1999: 157) that informal sector associations in Ghana and Kenya seemed to be mainly urban phenomena. Haan (1999) noted that rural MSEs faced more handicaps to form associations because they were more spread out. This implied that geographic proximity (cluster) was an important factor in SSI association formation.
- The female entrepreneurs were more likely to belong to associations than the males, which is consistent with the findings of Edusah (1999) and Mensah (2000).

Most of these differentiations could be related to the activities of the promotion institutions in the region especially the female-targeted organisations as well as the general conception that association members were more likely to obtain institutional support. The benefits derived from associations by 81% of the members included experience sharing at association meetings and informal contacts; and training. The benefits could help to increase the employment, productivity and income of their member firms.

Generally, the firms had low capital investment as reflected by their housing structure and working capital. Very few enterprises had a sizeable capital investment. The mean capital investment of female-owned businesses was half that of the male-owned businesses.

However, inadequate finance continued to be a major constraint to both gender enterprises alike. The proprietors largely depended on income from family members, friends and personal sources as well as supplier's credit to finance their business operations and expansion (see Acheampong 1991; Mensah 1996; Steel and Webster 1991). Many small entrepreneurs began with very small amounts of capital from personal savings and steadily built up their enterprises by reinvesting profits (Aryeetey *et al.* 1994).

Many proprietors faced critical shortage of funds, but could not borrow from the credit market because of various structural rigidities and imperfections. More than three-quarters of the enterprises had no access to various credit schemes launched in their districts and Ghana. Wrong targeting, inadequate funds, irregular disbursement procedures and inconvenient repayment arrangements featured most of the schemes. Some of the proprietors were also uncomfortable to borrow funds due to low demand for their commodities, which would restrain their repayment capabilities.

Only 10% of the surveyed firms received credit from the banks, promotion institutions and District Assemblies. About two-thirds of the proprietors who had received credits considered them as 'not useful' because the credits were meagre, received very late and very expensive in terms of time expended and the transport and other associated costs. However, the District Assembly Poverty Alleviation faced low loan recovery of less than 25% despite its low interest rate.

Table 3
Business Association Membership by Activity Type, Firm Size, Location, District, Gender and Educational Level

Item	*Responses*		*Total*	*Per cent*	*Chi-square (Pearson's)*	*DF*	*Sig. Level*
	Yes	*No*					
Activity							
Dressmaking	41	23	64	20.0	*56.07	12	0.000
Woodwork	10	41	51	15.9			
Hairdressing	34	16	50	15.6			
Oil Processing	9	24	33	10.3			
Bakery	11	19	30	9.4			
Tailoring	13	13	26	8.1			
Blacksmithing	3	19	22	6.9			
Block making	7	3	10	3.1			
Soap making	0	8	8	2.5			
Pottery	5	3	8	2.5			
Roofing Tiles	2	5	7	2.2			
Kent Weaving	1	6	7	2.2			
Salt Extraction	4	0	4	1.3			
Firm Size					*21.52	2	0.000
Micro	75	133	208	65.0			
Very Small	39	33	72	22.5			
Small	26	14	40	12.5			
Location					*25.33	1	0.001
Urban	82	63	145	45.3			
Rural	58	117	175	54.7			

Contd....

Item	*Responses*		*Total*	*Per cent*	*Chi-square (Pearson's)*	*DF*	*Sig. Level*
	Yes	*No*					
District					*26.14	4	0.006
Assin	24	40	64	20.0			
AOB	26	39	65	20.3			
Cape Coast	37	30	67	21.0			
Gomoa	26	33	59	18.4			
THELDA	27	38	65	20.3			
Gender					*18.52	1	0.000
Male	38	97	135	42.2			
Female	102	83	185	57.8			
Educational Level					8.06	4	0.32
No education	19	42	61	19.1			
Primary	93	106	199	62.2			
Secondary	21	28	49	15.3			
Post Secondary	6	2	8	2.5			
Tertiary	1	2	3	0.9			
Total Sample	140	180	320	100.0			
Per cent	43.7	56.3	100.0				

Note: *Significant difference at 5% level; DF = Degree of freedom.
Source: Survey Data [2003]

Employment Capacity of Firms

Generally, the SSI sector's employment in the Central Region is characterised by no formal contracts, no regular pay and no social protection (Mensah 2000; 2005a). The work force in the SSI sector consists of the entrepreneurs[8], apprentices, family helpers and hired labour. Based on gender roles, the male entrepreneurs dominated blacksmithing, salt extraction, tailoring and woodwork while their female counterparts dominated dressmaking, hairdressing, bakery and oil processing. The implication is that any policy and promotional scheme should recognise gender differentiation in the SSI sector.

The mean firm size was 4.2 workers. The majority (72%) of the total workforce of 1344 of the sampled firms were apprentices. Many firms (except those in salt making and block making, which used entirely hired labour) used apprentices extensively because they were the cheapest. Most (75%) apprentices were Middle School or Junior Secondary School leavers while the rest had primary or no education. Apprentices were predominant in dressmaking, tailoring, blacksmithing, woodworking and hairdressing. Most entrepreneurs recruited their apprentices on the recommendations of parents, friends or neighbours.

The survey revealed that apprentices in some hairdressing and dressmaking firms paid monthly fees ranging from US$0.20[9] to US$1.20 to the entrepreneurs. However, entrepreneurs in male- dominated activities such as woodwork, blacksmithing and tailoring paid daily subsistence allowance ranging from US$0.05 to US$0.25 to their apprentices. The amount an apprentice received depended on his seniority as well as the firm's sales or work available. Some entrepreneurs allowed the apprentices to use the tools and equipment in the firms to do their private 'jobs' during the break period rather than paying the daily subsistence allowance. During busy periods, some female entrepreneurs occasionally gave 'tips' to their apprentices. Due to the low daily subsistence allowances, parents, guardians and relatives often supported their wards and spouses who worked as apprentices.

Family labour included the spouses, children or close relatives of the proprietor. It was very common in micro-firms and female dominated activities such as pottery, bakery and oil processing. Such workers were not paid but were either completely or partially catered for by the entrepreneur in areas of payment of school fees, food and clothing.

The few wageworkers received more than the daily minimum wage of US$1.3 but the majority operated on casual basis. The remuneration paid depended on the nature of work, time spent on the work and the bargaining power of the proprietor and the employee rather than the gender. The proprietors attributed their inability to engage permanent wageworkers to low profits, low capacity utilization, poor market, seasonality of activities and; rising wage bills and inadequate capital investment. Only 24.9% of the firms had their proprietors receiving more than the minimum wage per annum, suggesting the SSI sector was acting as a sponge for the owners, as they search for activities to sustain themselves (Mensah 2005a).

Normally, the sampled firms worked for 8 hours per day. However, the male-operated firms worked slightly longer than their female counterparts because the workers of the latter had to attend to domestic chores as well.

The majority (70%) of the proprietors who used different types of workers, irrespective of sex, preferred apprentices because apprentices were cheaper to maintain and train, loyal, obedient and more reliable to work with. About 20% of the respondents held the view that all types of workers were important because they were useful depending on the work available. Salt makers and block-makers preferred male hired labour because the work was manual and very tedious.

Business Performance

Even though the male operated enterprises had higher values for various performance indicators than the female-operated enterprises, most differences were statistically insignificant as indicated by the corresponding F-ratios (Table 4). The significant differences were recorder in area of Output-Wage Ratio, Profit-capital Investment Ratio, Profit-capital Investment Ratio# and Price-Cost Margin#.

Table 4
Performance Measures of Firms with and without Association Membership

Performance Measure	*Mean*	*Coefficient of Variation*	*No. of Cases*	*F-Statistic*	*Sig. Level*
Output-capital Ratio				0.2445	0.3346
Men operated firms	1.42	1.74	122		
Women operated firms	1.37	1.09	127		
Output-labour Ratio				1.2154	0.4463
Men operated firms	$579.47	2.36	124		
Women operated firms	$485.21	1.58	127		
Output-Wage Ratio				*5.06	0.0382
Men operated firms	1.67	5.25	121		
Women operated firms	0.83	1.42	123		
Capital-Labour Ratio				0.3362	0.4322
Men operated firms	$589.50	2.49	130		
Women operated firms	$524.62	1.45	136		
Capacity Utilisation				0.8211	0.4381
Men operated firms	35.42%	1.58	128		
Women operated firms	33.01%	0.96	130		
Profit-capital Investment Ratio				*6.6201	0.0402
Men operated firms	2.58	1.88	121		
Women operated firms	1.44	1.51	122		
Profit-capital Investment Ratio#				**3.1200	0.0716
Men operated firms	-1.61	-2.75	121		
Women operated firms	-2.99	-2.85	123		
Price-Cost Margin				1.6928	0.4415
Men operated firms	0.67	0.63	123		
Women operated firms	0.59	0.54	129		
Price-Cost Margin#				*6.8328	0.0391
Men operated firms	-0.78	-2.01	120		
Women operated firms	-2.72	-2.48	123		

Note: Total number of cases less than 320 due to missing cases.
* Significant difference at 5% level; Exchange rate: US$1= Ë 8,500
#Ratio takes into account proprietor's labour cost.

Source: Field Data [2003]

The Output-Wage Ratio of the surveyed enterprises ranged from 0.01 to 20.54 but the mean was 1.67 with the standard deviation 3.26. About 70% of the firms had a ratio of less than 1, implying low wage productivity for most firms. The significant difference in wage productivity shows the female operated firms had lower value added in relation to wage bill than their male counterparts.

Generally, the male-operated firms had slightly higher gross annual profit and capital investment than their female counterparts (see also Mensah 2000, 2004). The difference could be attributed to the fact female proprietors tend to concentrate on a few specific activities, produce a narrow range of products and services, thereby competing for a limited market. Their mean capital investment is less than a half of that of the male counterparts. They also had dual domestic and productive responsibilities (Berger 1989).

Despite the gender differences, the performance of the sampled firms was still poor. For example, the capacity utilisation was less than 35%, just slightly above 33.6% by the 1998 survey (Mensah 2000). Without accounting for proprietor's labour cost, all the sampled firms were able to cover the raw material cost and employees' labour cost but the majority of the firms had marginal profits. The consequences were the positive mean values of profit-capital investment ratios and price cost margins. By accounting for proprietor's labour cost, only 24.9% run at profit compared to 26% in 1998. The resulting effects were negative mean values of corresponding profit-capital investment ratios and price cost margin.

Another striking result from Table 4 is that within any particular set of firms (i.e. male and female operated firms); there were substantial variations in the various performance measures as indicated by the corresponding coefficient of variation. The implication is that SSIs are not homogeneous and therefore gender considerations should be incorporated in policy and intervention to improve their performance.

CONCLUSION

The evidence from this survey shows that the SSI sector consisted of gender-based activities as some were male-dominated while others were female-dominated. The female entrepreneurs were more likely to belong to associations than the males. Each firm employed an average of four people and employment was characterised by no formal contract, low remuneration and temporary wage engagements. Most of the firms, irrespective of gender, were apprentice dominated.

The majority of the enterprises hardly kept consistent data, and had low capital investment, marginal profit and low business performance. There were no significant differences in business performance between male and female operated firms in terms of output-capital ratio, output-labour ratio, capital-labour ratio, capacity utilization, profit-capital investment ratio and price cost margin (i.e., when profit measures exclude labour cost). The implication is both gender-operated firms had similar or common constraints to their performance and therefore gender differentiation may not necessary.

However, the gender differentiation becomes paramount when assessing business performance in terms of output-wage ratio, profit-capital investment ratio, profit-capital investment ratio and price-cost margin (i.e., when profit measures include labour cost). Therefore, policy measures and interventions aimed at improving SSI performance must take into account gender differences as well as individual proprietors. It is important to note that these results are inconclusive because conditions may change and there are other important factors such as types of activities, firm size, location and educational background of the proprietors that must also be considered when formulating and implementing interventions.

Policy interventions and actions should focus on management training, record keeping, micro-credit, product finishing and packaging, marketing, group formation and lending, strengthening promotion institutions and business associations, industrial visits, and provision of basic infrastructure and services. Action is needed by all stakeholders in the SSI sector.

NOTES

1. The Lerner Index [i.e. PCM = (P—MC) /P] indicates the monopoly profit where maximising profit depends largely on the excess of price (P) over marginal cost (MC) of the product as proportion of price (Ornstein 1975; Devine *et al*. (1985).
2. PCM = (V—W)/Q where V = value-added (output minus material inputs excluding capital charges), W = total wages, Q = output at current market prices.
3. For details, see Bansal (1991:158-164), Dunning (1968:22-34) and Little *et al*. (1987:22).
4. This paper adopts the commonest definition used in Ghana which states that SSIs include those production and service units, which generally employ up to 30 people (see e.g. Thomi and Yankson 1985; Osei *et al*. 1993 and Steel and Webster 1991). Most of the firms sampled could be described as 'simple manufacturing' but hairdressing was included in order to obtain a broader coverage of female-owned enterprises.
5. The Assin District was divided into two parts namely Assin North and Assin South in 2004.
6. District Assemblies are the highest political and administrative bodies at the district level responsible for overall development.
7. Sowa et al. (1992: 24) and Mensah (2000: 64) found that 91% and 67% of the surveyed firms in Ghana were in this category.
8. The word 'entrepreneur' is used interchangeably with the 'owner' or 'proprietor' of the small-scale firm.
9. Exchange rate at the time of survey in 2003 was US$1 = ¢ 8,500.

REFERENCES

Abaka, E.K. and Mayer, P. (eds.) (1994), *Promotion of Small Enterprises in Ghana*, National Board for Small-Scale Industries and Friedrich Ebert Stiftung, Accra.

Acheampong, I.K. (1991), *Production Technologies in Small-Scale Soap Manufacturing,* Research Report Series No. 24, Centre for Development Studies, University of Cape Coast, Cape Coast.

Addison, E. (2006), Job Market Records High Turnout, *Daily Graphic,* 334:13.

Armitage, D.R. and Hyma, B. (1997), Sustainable Community-based Forestry Development: A Policy and Programme Framework to Enhance Women's Participation, *Singapore Journal of Tropical Geography*, 18 (1): 1-19.

Aryeetey, E, Baah-Nuakoh, A., Duggleby, T., Hettige, H., and Steel, W. F. (1994), *Supply and Demand for Finance of Small Enterprises in Ghana,* Discussion Paper No. 251, Technical Department, Africa Region, World Bank, Washington, DC.

Bansal, S.K. (1991), *Financial Problems of Small Scale Industries,* Anmol Publications, New Delhi.

Barrett, H. (1995), Women in Africa: The Neglected Dimension in Development, *Geography*, 80(3): 215-224.

Berger M. (1989), Giving Women Credit: The Strengths and Limitations of Credit as a Tool for Alleviating Poverty, *World Development,* 17 (7): 1017-1032.

Boateng, K. (1996), Employment, Unemployment and Underemployment, In Ghana. Friedrich Naumann Stiftung (ed.), *Agenda 196: Preparing Ghana for the 21st Century; Some Economic and Social Issues*, Anansesem Publications Limited, Accra.

Bruce, J. and Dwyer, D. (eds.) (1988), *A Home Divided: Women and Income in the Third World,* Stanford University Press, Stanford.

Downing, J. (1990), Gender and the Growth and Dynamics of Micro Enterprises, *GEMINI* Working Paper No. 5, GEMINI, USAID, Washington DC.

Edusah, S.E. (1999), *The Socio-Economic Significance of Rural Small-Scale Industries in Ghana*, Unpublished PhD Thesis, Development and Project Planning Centre, University of Bradford.

Ekumah, E.K. and Essel, T.T. (2001), *Gender Access to Credit under Ghana's Financial Sector Reform: A Case Study of Two Rural Banks in the Central Region of Ghana*, IFLIP Research Paper, ILO, Geneva.

Elaian, K. (1996), Employment Implications of Small-scale Industries in Developing Countries: Some Evidence from Jordan, *Science Technology and Development*, 14(1): 80-101.

Elson, D. (1993), Gender-aware Analysis and Development Economics, *Journal of International Development*, 5(2): 237-247.

Essel, T.T. (1996), *The Impact of Rural Banks' Lending Operations on Rural Development: A Case Study of Kakum Rural Bank*, Unpublished M.Phil Thesis, University of Cape Coast, Cape Coast.

Haan, H.C. (1999), MSE Association and Enterprise Promotion in Africa, In K. King and S. McGrath (eds.), *Enterprise in Africa: Between Poverty and Growth*. Intermediate Technology Publications, London.

Havyrylyshyn, O. (1990), Trade Policy and Productivity Gains in Developing Countries: A survey of the Literature, *The World Bank Research Observer*, 5 (1): 1-24.

International Labour Organisation (ILO) (1972), *Employment, Incomes and Equality: A Strategy for Increasing Productive Employment in Kenya,* ILO Report, Geneva.

Institute of Statistical, Social and Economic Research (ISSER) (1992), *The State of the Ghanaian Economy in 1991*, ISSER, University of Ghana, Legon.

Jahan, R. (1995), *The Elusive Agenda: Mainstreaming Women in Development*, Zed Books, London.

Kinnaird, V. and Hyma, B. (1993), In Search of Working Models of Gender Sensitive Participatory Research, *Environments*, 21(1): 9-20.

Liedholm, C. and Mead, D.C. (1987), *Small-scale Industries in Developing Countries: Empirical Evidence and Policy Implications,* International Development Paper, No.9, Michigan State University, Michigan.

Liedholm, C. and Mead, D.C. (1999), *Small Enterprises and Economic Development: The Dynamics of Micro and Small Enterprises,* Routledge, London.

Little, I.M.D., Muzumdar, D. and Page, J.M. Jr. (1987), *Small Manufacturing Enterprises: A Comparative Study of India and Other Economies*, Oxford University Press.

Magnum, G. and Philips, P. (eds.) (1988), *Three Worlds of Labour Economics,* M.E. Sharpe, New York.

Mead, D.C. (1999), MSEs Tackle both Poverty and Growth but in Different Proportions, In K. King and S. McGrath (eds.),

Enterprise in Africa: Between Poverty and Growth. Intermediate Technology Publications Ltd., London.

Mensah, J.V. (1996), *Promotion of Small-Scale Industries in the Central Region of Ghana,* Discussion Paper Series 4, Centre for Development Studies, University of Cape Coast, Cape Coast.

Mensah, J.V. (2000), *Small-Scale Industries in Ghana's Economic Development: Comparative Economic Efficiency of Rural and Urban Small-Scale Industries in the Central Region,* Unpublished PhD Thesis, Development and Project Planning Centre, University of Bradford.

Mensah, J.V. (2002), Promotion Institutions and Business Performance of Small-scale Industries: Evidence from the Central Region, *The Indian Journal of Economics*, LXXXII (327): 465-482.

Mensah, J.V. (2004), The Profits of Urban and Rural Small-Scale Industries in Ghana: Evidence from the Central Region, *The Global Journal of Finance and Economics*, 1(2): 227-248.

Mensah, J.V. (2005a), Small-Scale Industry as a Sponge? Empirical Survey in the Central Region, Ghana, *Singapore Journal of Tropical Geography,* 26(2): 212-226.

Mensah, J. V. (2005b), Business Associations and Performance of Small-Scale Industries in Ghana Evidence from the Central Region. *Indian Development Review*, 3(1): 51-71.

MkNelly, B. and Dunford, C. (1998), *Evaluation of the Lower Pra Rural Bank in Shama*, Western Region, Ghana, Mimeo.

Molnar, A. (1987), Forest Conservation in Nepal: Encouraging Women's Participation', In A. Leonard (ed.), *Seeds*, 10:1-20.

Molnar, A. (1991), Women and International Forestry Development, *Society and Natural Resources*, 4:81-90.

Morrisson, C., Lecomte, H.S., and Oudin, X. (1994), *Micro-Enterprises and the Institutional Framework in Developing Countries*, Development Centre of the Organisation for Economic Co-operation and Development, Paris.

Moser, C. and Levy, C. (1986), *A Theory and Methodology of Gender Planning: Meeting Women's Practical and Strategic Needs,* Development Planning Unit, Barlett School of Architecture and Planning, University College London.

Moser, C. (1989), Gender Planning in the Third Word: Meeting Practical and Strategic Gender Needs, *World Development*, 17(11): 1799-1825.

Moser, C. (1993), *Gender Planning and Development: Theory, Practice and Training,* Routledge, London and New York.

Ornstein, O.I. (1975), Empirical Uses of Price-cost Margin, *Journal of Industrial Economics*, XXII (2) (December).

Osei, B., Baah-Nuakoh, A., Tutu, K. and Sowa, N.K. (1993), Impact of Structural Adjustment on Small-scale Enterprises in Ghana, In A.H.J. Helmsing and Th. Kolstee (eds.), *Small Enterprises and Changing Policies,* Intermediate Technology Publications, London.

Otero, M. and Rhyne, E. (eds.) (1994), *The New World of Microenterprise Finance: Building Healthy Financial Institutions for the Poor,* Intermediate Technology Publications, London.

Rogers, B. (1980), *The Domestication of Women: Discrimination in Developing Societies,* Routledge, London.

Ryan, P. (1993), *An Evaluation of Small Enterprise Lending: Evidence from Malawi,* Research Monograph 5, April, DPPC, University of Bradford.

Sen, G. and Grown, K. (1987), *Development Crisis and Alternative Visions: Third World Women's Perspective*, Monthly Review Press, New York.

Sowa, N.K., Baah-Nuakoh, A., Tutu, K. and Osei, B. (1992), *Small Enterprises and Adjustment: The Impact of Ghana's Economic Recovery Programme on Small-Scale Industrial Enterprises,* Overseas Development Institute and University of Ghana, London and Accra.

Staley, E. and Morse, R. (1965), *Modern Small Industry for Developing Countries*, McGraw-Hill, New York.

Stamp, P. (1989), *Technology, Gender and Power in Africa: A Reader,* Earthscan Publications, London.

Steel, W.F. and Webster, L.M. (1991), How Small Enterprises in Ghana Have Responded to Adjustment, *The World Bank Economic Review*, 6(3): 423-438.

Swiss Agency for Development and Co-operation (2001), *Analysis of Swiss Contact's Experience in the Promotion of Women Entrepreneurs in Micro, Small and Medium Sized Enterprises,* SED-Issue Paper 6, March 2001.

Thomas, H. (1991), Labour and Work in Small-scale Enterprises, In H. Thomas, F. Uribe-Echevarria and H. Romijn (eds.), *Small-Scale Production: Strategies for Industrial Restructuring*, IT Publications, London.

Thomas-Slayter, B. and Rocheleau, D. (1995), *Gender, Environment, and Development in Kenya: A Grassroots Perspective*, Lynne Rienner Publishers, Colorado.

Thomi, W.H. and Yankson, P.W.K. (1985), *Small Scale Industries and Decentralisation in Ghana,* University of Ghana and Goethe Universität.

Tsikata, D. (ed.). (2001), *Gender Training in Ghana: Politics, Issues and Tools,* Woeli Publishing Services, Accra.

United Nations (1995), *World Summit for Social Development*, Copenhagen Conference Proceedings, New York.

Uppal, Y. (1996), *Economics and Management of Small Enterprises: Development and Viability towards 21st Century,* Deep and Deep Publications, New Delhi.

Weiss, J. (1988), *Industry in Developing Countries: Theory, Policy and Evidence*, Routledge, London and New York.

Weiss, J. (1992), *Industrial Policy in Mozambique in the* 1980s, Development and Project Planning Centre, University of Bradford, Bradford.

Whitehead, A. (1979), Some Preliminary Notes on the Subordination of Women, *Institute of Development Studies Bulletin*, 10(3).

Winston, G.C. (1971), Capital Utilization in Economic Development, *The Economic Journal*, 81(321): 37- 60.

World Bank (1983), *The Industrial Sector of Ghana,* World Bank, Washington DC.

Young, K. (1988), *Women and Economic Development,* Burg/ UNESCO, New York.

3

MICRO-FINANCING AND GENDER-BASED POVERTY: THE CASE OF WOMEN'S GROUP IN NAIROBI

TABITHA W. KIRITI-NGANGA

INTRODUCTION

Poverty can be viewed in absolute and relative terms. Absolute poverty refers to subsistence below the minimum and socially acceptable living conditions. On the other hand, relative poverty compares the lowest bracket of a population with the upper bracket. UNDP's definition of poverty notes definition of poverty incorporates the view that poverty is 'not merely in the impoverished state in which the person actually lives, but also in the lack of real opportunity due to social constraints as well as personal circumstances to lead valuable and valued lives' (UNDP 1997:15).

Since independence, the Kenya government has had a stated goal of fighting illiteracy, poverty and disease in order to achieve sustainable national development. However, in the last one and a half decades, the educational attainment, health and poverty status of Kenyans have shown declining trends. Poverty has worsened from an estimated 43.8% in 1994 to an estimated 60 per cent in 2005 (Republic of Kenya, Economic Survey 1994, 2003 and 2005). Between 1994 and

2000, rural poverty in Kenya increased by 12.85 percentage points, from 46.75 per cent to 59.6 per cent. Although the incidence of poverty in rural areas is higher than in urban areas, it does not follow that urban poverty in Kenya is not a matter of concern. Urban poverty in Kenya has risen rapidly in recent years not only because of growth in urban population but also as a result of worsening of the unemployment situation. In 1994, urban poverty stood at 45.49 per cent.

POVERTY AND GENDER INEQUALITY

According to UNDP (1995), poverty has a woman's face with over 70 per cent of the poorest people in the world being women. It is also asserted that poverty among women is rising faster than poverty among men. In Africa, women comprise the largest single segment of the poorest in most countries. The vast majority of Africa's women find their total livelihood within agriculture and in the informal sector in urban areas. Most women in informal sector employment are concentrated in low-semi-skilled and non-skilled jobs.

Although they are the majority in Kenya, women are the hardest hit by poverty, and female-headed households have the highest poverty rates. For example, in 2000, 63.13 per cent of female-headed households in Kenya were living in absolute poverty compared to 54.47 per cent of male-headed households (Mwabu *et al.* 2005). Female heads constitute a higher proportion of the rural poor (54.1 per cent) compared with 52.5 per cent for male heads.

Steady jobs and income elude the very poor especially women. To get by, they create and run their own tiny businesses 'micro-enterprises' in the unregulated, 'informal' sector. They might sell produce at the unregulated market, weave mats, or make *mandazi* (a form of cake), repair clothes, operate tea kiosks, sell second hand clothes, shoes or groceries or even sell their own bodies and so on. Micro-enterprises may be small, but their cumulative impact is expected to be huge.

These activities performed by women contribute to economic development in various ways and despite them being the majority in Kenya they remain the most vulnerable people in the society. Therefore, the strategic thrust for poverty alleviation should help redirect the overall pattern of development and the macroeconomic strategies of growth. In particular, in order for economic growth to be sustainable, poverty alleviation programmes should lead to capital accumulation especially for the poor and vulnerable groups such as women. Poverty alleviation should be based on a pro-poor perspective where the poor can contribute to growth and human development. One growth strategy is to increase the marginal lending to the poor and this can be done by mobilizing lending to the poor and helping them to invest the money in economic activities. Mobilizing lending for the poor is complex because they lack the basic requirements necessary in the formal financial institutions. Hence, they become the target of micro-finance institutions (MFIs).

OVERVIEW OF KENYA'S FINANCIAL SECTOR

Kenya's financial sector has been growing steadily from the 1990s due to government adopting a relaxed regulatory framework so as to encourage the growth of locally owned financial institutions. The number of commercial banks increased significantly in the 1980s from 16 in 1981 to 26 in 1990, 50 in 1996 and 55 in 1998 before declining gradually to 50 in 2000, 48 in 2001, 44 in 2002, and 43 in 2003. The number of Non Banking Financial Institutions (NFBI) also increased due to the lower entry requirements, which also faced no interest rate restrictions (Atieno 2001). The NFBI more than doubled from 23 in 1981 to 54 in 1988. However, there was a decline from 51 in 1993 to 43 in 1994, 24 in 1997, 16 in 1998, 7 in 2000 and 2002 and 2 in 2003 and 2004. The decline in the number of NBFI was as a result of harmonisation of capital requirements and interest rate regulation for both banks and NBFI leading to a number of NBFI converting to commercial banks.

The financial market in Kenya is divided into two, formal and non-formal. The formal segment has been dominated by a few commercial banks. These meet the major financial demands for large clients and they have no track record of lending to small enterprises (Kimuyu and Omiti 2002). The informal sector micro-finance institutions fill this gap.

The Kenya banking sector is dominated by a few large firms that mainly focus on short-term lending. The largest 4 banks (Barclays Bank, Standard Chartered Bank, Kenya Commercial Bank and the National Bank of Kenya) control over 75 per cent of the deposits. Their short term lending and selective lending to corporate clients have implied indifference to small savers and borrowers (Atieno 2001) thus locking out a huge number of potential borrowers and investors from their services. The bank charges for services rendered also make the costs of banking prohibitive to the majority of the population especially women. The requirement for collateral denies women credit as most women do not have access to property such as land as this is traditionally owned by men. Economies rely upon the financial intermediary function to transfer resources from savers to investors. In market economies, this function is performed by commercial banks and the capital markets. However, in many developing countries, capital markets are still at a rudimentary stage, and commercial banks are reluctant to lend to the poor largely because of the lack of collateral and high transactions costs. The poor would borrow relatively small amounts, and the processing and supervision of lending to them would consume administrative costs that would be disproportionate to the credit. Also, complicated loan procedures and paperwork, combined with a lack of accounting experience, limit poor people's access to formal sources of credit.

MICRO FINANCING AND POVERTY

In July 1997, the UN office of the Special Coordinator for Africa and the Least Developed Countries together with the governments of Japan and Thailand and UNDP, organized the Asia-Africa Forum on the Economic Empowerment of Women, which was held in Bangkok. The Forum adopted a framework for action, which includes a recommendation for the promotion of women's economic empowerment through the promotion of micro-financing schemes including group financing without collateral, and savings and credit facilities.

Micro-credit programs extend small loans to very poor people for self-employment projects that generate income, allowing them to care for themselves and their families. Micro-credit, also called 'microfinance' and 'micro-lending' means providing small working capital loans to the self-employed poor. Even small amounts of capital typically Ksh.1000 to Ksh.30000 can make the difference between absolute poverty and a thriving little business generating enough income to feed the family, send kids to school, and build decent housing. These micro-finance institutions are non-profit organizations dedicated to reaching the poor with small loans that enable borrowers to work their way out of poverty. Today there are several large micro-credit agencies, including the Grameen Bank, which lends to 2 million poor women in Bangladesh.

Micro-credit is a concept that has gained widespread acceptance by international development agencies and major donors. It is viewed as a way to correct both governmental and market failure in Sub-Saharan Africa. Many view micro-credit as a method for linking the formal and informal sectors of African economies to increase the reach of the formal sector. Extending the reach of the formal economy through micro-credit is possible, and desirable, depending on macroeconomic reforms, respect for traditional financing relationships, and local control of institutions. However, very little has been done to determine the extent to which micro-credit programs actually increase economic well-being. The model program, Grameen Bank of Bangladesh, has been studied and evaluated, but replications may not be inherently successful. The literature accepts that micro-credit will increase economic well-being, if programs are correctly designed. Program design issues cannot be resolved, however, until economic well-being is measured and associated with specific designs (Snow and Buss 2001).

In Kenya, failure by formal financial institutions to meet the credit needs of the small-scale enterprises and to the poor has led to an expansion of the informal financial sector, which has acted as an important source of finance to the poor and small-scale entrepreneurs in Kenya (Dondo 1994). This sector includes small and medium scale credit and savings facilities established by Non-governmental Organizations (NGOs) to provide micro-credit services as alternative sources of finance. There are currently 19 major micro-finance institutions, which include Kenya Rural Enterprise Programme (K-REP) Group Ltd, K-REP Bank Ltd, Kenya Women Finance Trust (KWFT), Faulu Kenya, Kenya Ecumenical Church Loan Fund (KECLOF), Small and Micro Enterprises Programme (MSEP) and so on. The Kenya Rural Enterprise Programme (K-REP) has been cited as a good example of an informal institution dealing with micro-finance. However, it is important to note that K-REP has now converted to a fully-fledged commercial bank shutting out many small-scale borrowers.

Most of these micro-finance institutions are mainly found in urban areas where there is good infrastructure. They are said to discriminate against the very poor and small-scale enterprises, and have high cost of borrowing, though ostensibly they are supposed to be helping the poor. All these make access to credit by the majority of the poor in both rural and urban areas very difficult. The other sources of credit include friends and relatives, shylocks, Rotating Savings and Credit Associations (ROSCAS) but these provide very little credit to the members due to limited resources.

Micro financing has long been praised as a stepping-stone out of poverty (Crossette 2005). Provision of credit has increasingly been regarded as an important tool for raising incomes of the poor as it is expected to generate self-employment in farm and non-farm activities through provision of working and investment capital. Evidence exists to show that poor people are capable of moving out of poverty if financial services are available to them in the form of credit (Dondo 1994).

Microfinance is said to be so successful in reducing poverty that even the World Bank and other major international institutions have increased their commitment to micro lending, and there are new organizations engaging in micro-lending every day.

Johnson and Rogaly (1997) contend that availability of credit for Small and Micro Enterprises has positive effects on businesses as credit provision can enable household's income to rise. It also enables clients to be self-employed, improve their income and empower them.

The potential benefits of a reliable and stable savings and investment facility for poor communities and households are many. Credit acts as a form of insurance during lean periods caused by drought, illness and unemployment. Thus, it cushions the effects of a fall in income or rise in costs. Credit can promote enterprise growth and bring long term benefits to the poor and may be needed to purchase assets or as working capital, for health expenditure, customs and rituals, pay school fees, or repay previous debts.

As mentioned earlier, over 50% of Kenya's population is poor (Republic of Kenya, Economic Survey 2005). With modest employment opportunities created in the formal sector and majority in the informal sector, it implies that the potential increase in employment and incomes that are necessary for poverty reduction lie in the informal sector majority of who are women. Improving availability of credit to the poor and the small and micro enterprises is one of the incentives that have been proposed for stimulating growth ad improving the wellbeing of the poor (Republic of Kenya, Economic Survey 1994; World Bank 2000). The formal financial and Non-Governmental Financial Institutions (NGFI) have lending terms that lock out the poor especially women from accessing credit. Action-Aid Kenya (1992) observed that the demand for financial services in rural areas and among the poorest of the poor remain unmet due to huge investment in terms of capital outlay required and that the adaptation of the Grameen Bank model in Kenya by the many micro-finance institutions is not poverty friendly and favours persons with growing need for business finance. This leaves the poor at the mercy of the exploitative moneylenders.

Nevertheless, there are still those poor people who go for credit from the informal financial sector to meet some of their basic needs and expand their small businesses. Some of these informal financial institutions are out to make profits and may impose some requirements for one to qualify for a loan to ensure that the credit is repaid. They may even impose a penalty for non-repayment. Most micro-finance schemes charge close to the market rates of interest though paid on weekly or daily basis. Such high rates are unaffordable to the poor women and though they may still go for this credit, they may find themselves having repayment difficulties since there is no grace period.

Informal and small-scale lending arrangements provide the rural/urban population with access to savings·within the local area and with a certain cushion against economic fluctuations, and they encourage a cooperative and community feeling. The groups formed provide joint collateral and serve as instruments for spreading valuable information that is useful for economic and social progress.

These schemes are characterized by relatively small loans of less than Ksh. 50000. The repayment period is relatively short (one year) and this is paid on a weekly basis. In many developing countries, overall interest rates are relatively high to begin with so that rates charged by micro-lending schemes are quite high when the risk premium is added. Many of these micro-institutions claim a high rate of repayment. This is attributable to the informal participatory structures, which create an atmosphere in which debtors respect their obligations. While this may be true, it is important to ask whether the repayment of the loans usually comes from the profits generated from expansion of business or that the debtors result to borrowing from friends and relatives or even selling some their household properties to offset the loan. Who are the main beneficiaries of these loans? Are they the very poor or the well to do? Kikula *et al.* (2005) found that in Tanzania, the very poor had a better chance of accessing credit from formal and quasi-formal financial institutions. Is this the case in Kenya?

The question is whether use of credit can be used as an instrument for poverty eradication especially due to difficulties in identifying the poor and targeting credit to reach the poorest of the poor. Added to this is the fact that many people, especially the poorest of the poor, are usually not in a position to undertake an economic activity especially because they lack business skills and even motivation for business. And so they are tempted to use the credit for consumption purposes.

In situations where group lending is used, other members of the group may exclude the very poor because they are seen as a bad credit risk, jeopardising the position of the group as a whole. The staff of the micro-credit scheme can also avoid the poor again on the grounds of repayment risk. This study set out to answer the following questions. What determines that a woman will receive credit from a micro-finance institution? Are the better-off women in a better position to receive credit than the very poor women? Is micro-financing a panacea for gender-based poverty?

LITERATURE REVIEW ON MICRO-FINANCING AND POVERTY

The condition of poverty has been interpreted conventionally as lack of access by poor households to the assets necessary for a higher standard of income or welfare (World Bank 2000). Micro-credit programmes target one of the most vulnerable groups in society women who live in households that own little or no assets. It is expected that these credits would significantly increase women's security, autonomy, self-confidence and status within the household.

Lack of assets is readily understandable in terms of the absence of collateral that the poor, especially women can offer conventional financial institutions, in addition to the various complexities and high costs involved in dealing with large numbers of small, often illiterate borrowers. The poor and mainly women thus have to rely on loans from either shylocks at high interest rates, or friends and family, whose supply of funds is mainly limited (Kiriti 2003).

FAO (1984); Otero and Downing (1989) agree that women are discriminated against in the formal financial markets. They attribute this to women's lack of control over economic resources and that the nature of their economic activities restricts their access to formal credit than men's. Institutional requirements, cultural and social norms also act as constraints to women's access to credit. Micro-finance institutions try to overcome some of these barriers through innovative measures such as group lending as well as the establishment of close links between poor clients and staff of the institutions concerned.

House (1978); Adam *et al.* (1984); Boomgard (1989); and Mutua (1996) contend that limited availability of credit services has undermined rural micro-enterprise activities due to lack of capital for investment and has prevented farmers from adopting improved farming practices because of their inability to purchase the necessary inputs required for production. Adam *et al.* (1984) attribute the rapid development reached in Europe and Asia to availability of credit. This implies that availability of credit would go along way in poverty alleviation.

The theoretical analysis of MFIs in Kenya shows that majority of people especially women do not have access to credit. A baseline survey done in 1999 revealed that only a very small proportion of people borrow especially those in micro and small enterprises (MSE). Majority of the poor in Kenya, for both initial and additional capital for any business use own funds or funds from family sources (Kimuyu and Omiti 2000).

Kimuyu and Omiti (2000) stressed the need to empower women through education, formation of women groups and strengthen and expand micro-finance programmes so that larger women enterprises, that is disadvantaged than their male counterparts can borrow.

The importance of empowering all people by increasing their access to all people by increasing their access to all the factors of production including credit is one of the factors that have increased the interest in micro-credit. The UN

Secretary General contends that with micro-credit, the latent capacity of the poor for entrepreneurship would be encouraged. This would allow them to be self-reliant, create employment opportunities and engage women in economically productive activities. Currently there are estimated to be about 3000 micro-finance institutions in developing countries. However there have been allegations that in fact the very poor are so weak as not to benefit from micro lending, and that it is the better off that benefit (Kimuyu and Omiti 2000).

The way micro-credit is organized is that the women's group borrows from the micro-finance institution at full cost interest rates without collateral that are repayable on a weekly basis. The group then lends to the members but with collateral (furniture, cookers, fridge, beds, televisions, radios and so on) such that tin the event that such a member is unable to pay, the group can liquidate the collateral to repay the loan to the institution on behalf of the whole group. The women's group meets on a weekly basis (attendance is compulsory) for repayment of loan installments and the collection of savings.

STUDY SITE AND DATA COLLECTION

The study was conducted in urban informal sector among women groups. Nairobi is the capital city of Kenya with good infrastructure for MFIs. The poverty headcount in 2003 was 44% but this varies by division from a low of 32% in Westlands division to a high of 58.5% in Makadara Division as shown in Table 1.

It is clear from Table 1 that 75% of the poor are concentrated in 5 divisions each of which contribute over one hundred thousand poor people. The poor in Westlands are on average 11.4% below from the poverty line compared to 24% in Makadara.

Data collection was through interviews. This was through key informants of various women's micro-enterprises. This was accompanied by a structured questionnaire, which was administered, on the women to identify the factors that determine access to micro-credit. Data was collected from those who have received credit and those who have not. A pre-survey was done to determine the number of women's group's small and micro-enterprises in both Nairobi. This information was obtained from the Provincial Headquarters where these Small and Micro-Enterprises (SMEs) are registered. The SMEs gave dates and meeting venues to these offices and so we arranged to interview them either during their, before or after their meetings.

Table 1
Poverty in Nairobi by Division in 2003

Division	*Population Below Poverty Line (%)*	*Total Population*	*Number of Poor People*
Central	44.6	205,225	91,530
Makadara	58.5	184,541	107,958
Kasarani	47.6	320,739	152,672
Embakasi	41.6	408,921	170,111
Pumwani	46.4	183,468	85,129
Westlands	32.2	188,107	60,570
Dagoretti	46.2	229,612	106,081
Kibera	40.7	271,111	110,342
Nairobi	44.3	1,991,724	884,126

Source: Republic of Kenya, Economic Survey [2003]

DATA ANALYSIS

The variables assumed to influence access to credit (RECEIVE) are age (AGE), number of years of education (EDU), income level (EXPEND, number of household assets such as Television sets, fridges, sofa sets, cookers and so on. to be used as collateral (ASSESTNO), value of assets (ASSETS), number of children that a women has (CHILD) occupation (OCCUP), ownership of land (OWNLAND, marital status (MASTATUS) and a woman whose idea it is to borrow credit and not that of her husband or a brother (OWNIDEA).

The age of the women interviewed ranged from 30 to 68 years with an average of 46.6 years. From the sample of respondents, 58.1% of them were married while 41.9% were unmarried (divorced, separated or widowed). Their education levels ranged from 2 years to 16 years of education. Out of these, 60.5% had 8 years or less of education meaning that they were primary school dropouts. Thirty point two (30.2%) per cent of the women had between 8 and 12 years of education implying that they were form four-drop outs while 9.3% had between 12 and 16 years of education showing that they had some form of tertiary education. Only 16.3% of the women were in the formal sector in terms of occupation while the rest, 83.7% were in the informal sector doing petty business.

The number of children among the respondent ranged between 0 and 14 and the average number of children per women was 6.4 children, which is way ahead of the national average of 4.8 children. In terms of assets, 27.9% of the respondents did not have any assets at all; 44.2% had between 1 and 3 assets while 27.9% had between 4 and 8 assets. The most common assets were a radio; a cooking stove using charcoal or a simple television. However, there were some who reported having bought modern coloured televisions, gas cookers, video decks, sofa sets and gas cylinders using loans borrowed from the micro-finance institution through their women groups. The value of assets ranged from 0 to Ksh. 9.7 million with an average of Ksh.260210. The correlation coefficient between value of assets and number of assets was 0.315 and the two variables were retained in the regression analysis.

The income of the respondents, using expenditure as a proxy ranged between Ksh.4150 and Ksh.75000 with an average income per annum of Ksh. 30815 which translated to Ksh84.4 per day, which translates to a dollar per day at Ksh.73 per dollar. Considering that these are women who may be heads of households and with children, this shows that they belong to the poor segment of the urban residents. Out of the total number of women interviewed, 30.2% said that their husbands or male relatives had talked them into applying for a loan from the micro-finance institutions while 69.8% said that it was their idea of applying for a loan. Out of those respondents who had applied for a loan, 46.5% had received it while 53.5% who had applied did not receive the loan.

We can estimate a log-linear multiple regression model for determining the factors influencing access to micro-finance using Ordinary Least Squares (OLS). However, some women may report having not received any credit from the micro-finance institutions and in that case we shall have the dependent variable taking on the value of zero in some instances. In that case OLS will produce biased estimates of the coefficients. We can overcome this problem by using a Tobit or a Binary Logit model for our analysis (Amemiya 1984; Gujarati 1995; Khandker 2003; Kiriti 2003; Wilson and Tisdell 2002). The Tobit model can be described as follows:

$$Y_i = \alpha_0 + \beta^i X_i + u_i \qquad if\ RHS \geq 0$$

$$Y_i = 0\ otherwise$$

Where

Y_i is the dependent variable

α_0 is a constant

X_i is a K*1 vector of known variables

β^I is a K*1 vector of unknown parameters.

υ_I are the residuals with $E(\upsilon_i) = 0$ and a common variance, σ^2. We also assume $\upsilon \sim N(0, \sigma^2)$.

THE DETERMINANTS OF ACCESS TO CREDIT FROM MICRO-FINANCE INSTITUTIONS

A Tobit regression analysis was conducted to ascertain the factors that influence significantly to accessibility to credit among women in Nairobi. The dependent variable was access to credit (whether a women accessed credit or not). This was regressed on level of income (using expenditure as a proxy), years of formal education, (EDU), value of assets (ASSETS), number of assets (ASSETNO), occupation of the woman, whether in formal or informal, (OCCUP, ownership of land (OWNLAND), whether the idea to borrow credit was the woman's or the husband, or even someone else's (OWNIDEA), age of the woman (AGE) and marital status of the woman, whether married or unmarried (MASTATUS). Among these factors, income level, value of assets, number of assets, years of education and ownidea, were found to significantly influence and woman's chances of accessing credit from the micro-finance institutions. The results of the Tobit regression analysis are shown in Table 2.

Table 2
Determinants for Access to Microfinance

RECEIVED	*B*	*Standard Error*	*Significant*
.00 Intercept	4.434	1.994	0.209
EXPEND	.113**	0.040	.005
ASSETS	3.63E-02*	.021	.091
ASSETSNO	1.319*	.607	.030
CHILD	-3.92E-02	.027	.146
EDU	.838*	.461	.069
AGE	4.405E-02	.079	.577
[OWNIDEA=.00]	0a	0	
[OWNIDEA=1.00]	1.130*	.682	.097
[OWNLAND=.00]	0a	0	
[OWNLAND=1.00]	.460	.543	.398
[OCCUP=.00]	0a	0	
[OCCUP=1.00]	3.817E-02	.087	.660
[MASTATUS=.00]	0a	0	
[MASTATUS=1.00]	9.65E-03	.007	.183
Log likelihood	808.245		
Chi-Square	120.378		.000
N	172		

Source: Author's Fieldwork [2006].
Note: *Significance at 5%, **Significance at 1%

As initially hypothesized, a woman's level of income is a major determinant for access to credit. The relationship between income levels and access to credit is significant with a positive coefficient implying that those with high levels of income had better chances to access credit from micro-finance institutions. This contradicts Kikula *et al.* (2005) who found that in Tanzania, the income variable had a negative and significant coefficient implying that those with low income had better chances to access credit from formal and quasi-formal financial institutions.

Value of assets, was also found to positively and significantly influence access to credit for a woman. This means that those who have more valuable assets have a higher chance of accessing credit than those who have less valuable assets. Number of assets was also found to positively and significantly influence the possibility for a woman accessing credit from a micro-finance institution.

It is believed that access to credit from both formal and informal financial institutions improves with increase in levels of education. This was proved true in this study in that the years of education variable was found to positively and significantly influence access to credit in the micro-finance institutions. This is unlike Kikula *et al.* (2005) who found that years of formal education negatively and significantly determined ones chances to access formal and quasi-formal credit.

There are some women who in most cases may be talked into borrowing credit by their husbands. It seems that women groups have their own ways of assessing those women who may have been influenced by their husbands to do so and their chances of acquiring a loan are minimized while those whose idea it is to borrow a loan increase their chances of accessing credit.

Occupation was expected to be significant but this turned out not to be. It does not matter whether a woman's activities are in the formal or informal sector for them to access a loan. This result concurs with that of Kikula *et al.* (2005) who also found that occupational activity or the type of investment requirement did not significantly influence access to credit in Tanzania.

The number of children that a woman has negatively influences her chances of accessing a loan. This means that in their assessment on who qualifies to get a loan, the micro-finance institutions might be linking more children to be a risk in repayment of the loan since the recipient might be tempted to se the loan for consumption purposes.

CONCLUSION

This study has found that apart from being discriminated against by the formal financial institutions, the very poor women continue to be marginalized by the micro-finance institutions. Years of formal education were found to significantly influence the chances of accessing a loan from the micro-finance institutions. The very poor whose incomes are so low, less than a dollar a day, who have very few or no assets, whose assets are almost valueless, whose levels of education are so low cannot benefit from credit from the micro-finance institutions. It seems that just like the formal fiancé institutions find them a risky group to lend to, the microfinance institutions also o find them a risky and hazardous group to lend to. This means that these poor women are condemned to poverty since the only way out for them is blocked.

This study recommends an evaluation and revision on the terms and conditions of micro-finance if it has to succeed as a poverty alleviation strategy. It also recommends that the government should come up with a method of targeting these very poor women by giving them some kind of transfers that are not tied to profit generating to lift them from these poverty stricken circumstances.

REFERENCES

Action Aid-Kenya (1992), *Kariobangi Savings and Credit Programme*, Kenya.

Adams, D.W., Douglas, H.G., and J.D. Von Pischke (eds.) (1984), *Undermining Rural Development with Cheap Credit*, Westview Press, Boulder.

Amemiya, T. (1984), Tobit Models: a Survey, *Journal of Econometrics*, 24(1 & 2): 3-61.

Atieno, R. (2001), *Formal and Informal Financial Institutions: Lending Policies and Access to Credit by Small-Scale Entrepreneurs in Kenya: An Empirical Assessment,* African Economic Research Consortium (AERC), Research Paper No. 11, Nairobi.

Boomgard, J.J. (1989), *Taking Stock of A.I.D Micro-Enterprise Portfolio: Synthesis Report*, Development Alternatives, Inc. and Robert R. Nathan Associates, Inc., Washington DC.

Crossette, B. (2005), Reproductive Health and the Millennium Development Goals: The Missing Link, *Studies in Family Planning*, 36(2): 132-134.

Dondo, A. (1994), *Credit to the Informal Sector Approaches and Models Experienced in Kenya,* K-REP Occassional Paper No. 27, Nairobi.

FAO (1984), *Promotion of Women's Activities in Marketing and Credit: An Analysis, Case Studies and Suggested Actions*.

Gujarati, D.N. (1995), *Basic Econometrics, Third Edition,* McGraw-Hill Inc., New York.

House, W.J. (1978), *Nairobi's Informal Sector: A Reservoir of Dynamic Entrepreneurs or a Residual of Surplus Labour*, IDS Working Paper No. 347, University of Nairobi.

Johnson, S. and Rogally, B. (1997), *Micro-Finance and Poverty Reduction*, Oxfam Publication, UK.

Khandker, S. (2003), *Micro-Finance and Poverty: Evidence Using Panel Data from Bangladesh*, World Bank Policy Research Paper No. 2945, World Bank, Washington DC.

Kikula, I., Kipolola, J. Shivji, I., Semboja, J., and Tarimo, B. (2005), Access to Formal and Quasi-Formal Credit by Smallholder Farmers and Artesian Fishermen: A Case of Zanzibar, In *Researching Poverty in Tanzania: Problems, Policies and Perspectives*, Mkuki na Nyota Publishers, REPOA Dar es Salaam.

Kimuyu and Omiti (2000), *Institutional Impediments of Access to Credit by Micro and Small Scale Enterprises in Kenya,* IPAR, Discussion Paper No. 026, Nairobi.

Kiriti T. (2003), *Gender Inequality in Agricultural Households in Kenya: An Economic Analysis*, Unpublished PhD Thesis, University of Queensland, Australia.

Mutua, A.K. (1996), *Regulatory and legal Issues: A Practitioner's Perspective, West Africa High Level Policy Forum on Micro-Finance*, Bamako, Mali.

Mwabu, G., Mwangi, K., Kimalu, P., Nafula, N. and Manda, D. (2005), Predicting Rural Household Poverty: Methodological

Issues and the PRSP Process in Kenya, In Frank Ellis and H. Ade Freeman (eds.), *Rural Livelihoods and Poverty Reduction Policies,* Routledge, London and New York.

Otero, M. and Downing, J. (1989), *Meeting Women's Financial Needs: Lessons from Formal Financial Institutions*, Paper presented at the Seminar on Informal Financial Markets in Development for the Ohio State University, USAID and the World Bank, Washington DC.

Republic of Kenya (1994, 2003 and 2005), *Economic Survey*, CBS and Ministry of Finance and Planning, Government Printer, Nairobi.

Snow, D.R. and Buss, T.F. (2001), Development and the Role of Micro Credit, *Policy Studies Journal*, 29 (2): 296-307.

UNDP (1997), *Human Development Report,* Oxford, New York.

Wilson, C. and Tisdell, C. (2002), *OLS and Tobit Estimates: When is Substitution Defensible Operationally?* Economic Theory, Applications and Issues, Working Paper No. 15, University of Queensland, Australia.

World Bank (2000), *World Development Report 2000/01: Attacking Poverty*, World Bank, Washington DC.

4

INJECTABLE CONTRACEPTIVE CONTINUATION RATES AND DIFFERENTIALS IN PAKISTAN

MOHAMMAD PERVEZ WASIM

INTRODUCTION

Population planning has been a high priority project of the Government of Pakistan with ups and down for the last five decades. Family planning activities though initiated in 1950, a full-fledged national family planning programme was launched in 1965. Since then various strategies have been implemented to increase the level of acceptance of contraceptives. A variety of contraceptives viz., oral pill, IUDs, injectables, Condom, and female sterilization were made available to the population. But since 1965, contraceptive use rate has been slowly increasing in Pakistan.

The first National Impact Survey (NIS) 1968 69 indicated that ever users were 12.1 per cent and current users were 5.5 per cent (Population planning Council, Government of Pakistan 1968). Findings from the Pakistan Fertility survey (PFS) of 1975 showed that nearly 75 per cent of the married woman in reproductive age group knew at least one method of family planning but only 5.2 per cent of sample women were current users. Pakistan Lactation and Fertility Survey (PLFS) 1983 revealed that 14.3 per cent were ever user, and

11.3 per cent, were current users (Table 1 and Figure 1). Pakistan contraceptive Prevalence Survey (PCPS) 1984 85 indicated that contraceptive awareness were 61.5 per cent, ever use 11.8 per cent and current use 9.1 per cent. The Pakistan Demographic Survey (PDS) 1990 91 indicated that 77.9 per cent of the currently married women had knowledge of family planning method and 20.7 per cent ever used any contraceptive method while 11.8 per cent were then using any method and only 9 per cent a modern method. The 1996 97 Pakistan Fertility and Family Planning Survey, the latest nationally represented survey undertaken under National Population Studies (NPS), indicated that 21.2 per cent were current user of any method. Current use rates though increased in 1990 91 and 1996 97, but not as expected.

Table 1
Current Use of Contraception and the Method Used

Contraceptive Methods	*Ever Use*				*Current Use*			
	PLFS 1983	*PCPS 1984-85*	*PDHS 1990-91*	*PFFPS 1996-97*	*PLFS 1983*	*PCPS 1984-85*	*PDHS 1990-91*	*PFFPS 1996-97*
All Methods	14.3	11.8	20.7	-	11.3	9.1	11.8	21.2
Oral Pill	1.9	4.6	4.5	-	1.2	1.4	0.7	1.6
IUD	1.9	1.6	3.3	-	1.3	0.8	1.3	3.4
Injections	1.4	0.5	3.3	-	1.4	0.6	0.8	1.4
Condom	5.2	4.0	7.2	-	4.1	2.1	2.7	4.2
Female Sterilization	2.7	2.2	3.6	-	2.6	2.6	3.5	6.0
Other	1.2	2.8	8.9	-	1.0	1.6	2.8	4.6
Proportion of Injectable Users to all Users	9.7	4.2	15.9	-	6.0	6.6	6.8	6.6

Source: (a) Pakistan Lactation and Fertility Survey (PLFS) 1983 84, National Research Institute of Fertility Control, Government of Pakistan
(b) Pakistan Contraceptive Prevalence Survey (PCPS) 1984 85, Ministry of Population Welfare, Government of Pakistan
(c) Pakistan Demographic and Health Survey (PDHS) 1990 91, National Institute of Population Studies
(d) Pakistan Fertility and Family Planning Survey (PFFPS) 1996 97, National Institute of Population Studies, Government of Pakistan

Pakistan Population Welfare Programme adopted many strategies to increase the use rate of contraceptive methods but although knowledge of contraceptive methods increased its use rate remain low. One of the major reasons was inadequate coverage of service delivery.

Figure 1: Current Use of Contraception and the Method Used 1983 1996

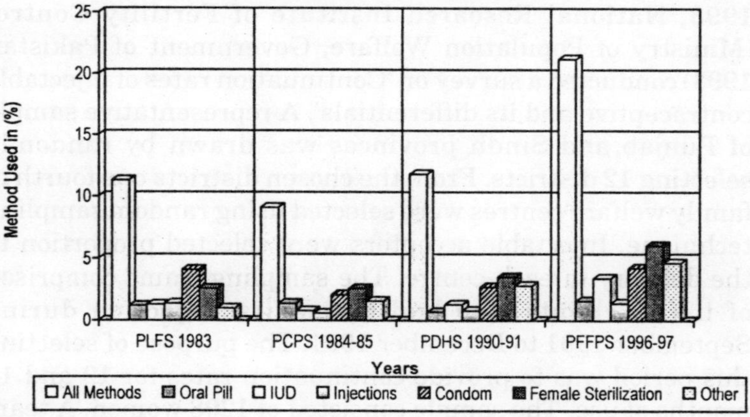

The share of injectable contraceptives in the National Population Programme was very small. Only 6.6 per cent of the contraceptive current users were on injectables according to Pakistan Fertility and Family Planning Survey 1996 97. The service statistics reveal that the annual delivery of injectable has been rising sharply. In 1983 it was 96035 that increased to 1111088 in 1996 97 (Population Welfare, Government of Pakistan 1983 1997 Mimeograph). In Pakistan, Contraceptive use level among currently married couples was 21.2 per cent as per PFFPS 1996 97 whereas injectable current users were 1.4 per cent.

OBJECTIVES AND DATA SOURCE

The major objectives of the study are:

(a) To assess the continuation rates of injectable contraceptive.

(b) To study differentials in continuity rate by geographic, social and demographic characteristics.

(c) To identify the reasons for discontinuation and to suggest measures for improving the continuation rates.

The issue of continuation rates of injectable contraceptive and its differentials is very important, both for increasing injectable continuation rates and for reducing dropouts. In 1993, National Research Institute of Fertility Control (Ministry of Population Welfare, Government of Pakistan 1993) conducted a survey on 'Continuation rates of injectable contraceptive and its differentials'. A representative sample of Punjab and Sindh provinces was drawn by randomly selecting 12 districts. From the chosen districts one fourth of family welfare centres were selected using random sampling technique. Injectable acceptors were selected proportion to the delivery in each centre. The sampling frame comprised of list of clients who had taken first injection during September 1991 to December 1991. The purpose of selecting this period was to provide continuation rates for 12 and 18 months of use. The sample consisted of 1298 women. A team of qualified and experienced female interviewers was imparted intensive training before sending in the field.

Only 59.0 per cent women were contacted from the sample list. Nearly 20 per cent could not be located, 10 per cent had shifted, 10 per cent were not present at the time of visit. Only 1 per cent refused interview. The present study discusses the results of that survey; based on 766 respondents using injectable, and analysis the injectable continuation rates and its differentials. A female's choice of injectable contraceptive use is influenced by the factors as district, age, urban-rural, province, occupation, education and family size.

INJECTABLE CONTINUATION RATES

In Pakistan the use level of contraceptive method is not only low but the discontinuation rate is very high. Studies on international level have revealed that 60 per cent or more of injectable users continue with the method for one year; in Indonesia it was 83.2 per cent, in Bangladesh 62.7 per cent, in India 64.3 per cent and in multi-centred comparative trials it was 63.2 per cent. On the contrary, studies conducted in Pakistan have shown 25 to 40 per cent of continuation rates that are close to Mexico, 43 per cent. These studies were carried out on small scale and at initial stages. No study on national level in Pakistan has so far been undertaken after introduction of injectables. The present study is an attempt to obtain results of that study in terms of injectable continuation rates and its differentials.

Current Injectable Status

Of the 766 respondents in this study 32.0 per cent were using injectable at the time of survey (Table 2).

Table 2
Proportion Currently Using Injectable by Province by Interval between First Injection Date and Interview Date

Interval	*Punjab*	*Sindh*	*All*	*N*
7-12	41.8	45.6	42.1	279
13-18	25.7	25.0	25.6	266
19-24	25.7	36.9	27.5	221
All	31.1	37.0	32.0	766

The proportion of continued users was higher in Sindh as compared to Punjab. Being 37.0 and 31.1 per cent respectively. Table 2 shows further break down of respondents according to period of injection taken. Majority of the respondents (73.6 per cent) had taken first injection more than a year before the interview. Among those who had taken first injection less than a year before interview 42.1 per cent were currently using injectables. In this cohort proportion of continuing users Sindh was better (45.6 per cent) as compared to Punjab (41.8 per cent).

Looking at urban-rural differentials in continuation rates, contrary to expectation, it is observed that in rural areas the proportion of current users was higher than urban (Table 3).

The respective proportions were 34.4 per cent and 30.9 per cent respectively. The differential was particularly high for those who had their first injection over 18 months previously.

Table 3
Proportion Currently Using Injectables by Location by Interval between First Injection Date and Interview Date

Interval	*Urban*	*Rural*
< 12	41.0	44.3
13-18	27.0	23.3
19 +	22.8	35.3
All	30.9	34.4

The discontinuation was highest in the middle age group (Table 4).

Table 4
Proportion Currently Using Injectables by Age by Interval between First Injection Date and Interview Date

Age	< 12	13-18	19 +	All
15-24	46.2	17.9	7.7	30.0
25- 29	45.7	32.2	30.6	37.4
30-34	29.0	24.3	22.0	25.1
35-39	48.0	21.5	32.8	33.0
40-44	43.0	25.0	30.4	33.0

There does not appear any trend in the age related continuation. Except in age group 35 and over, there seems to be declining continuation as the interval increases between first injection and the time of interview. There is no reasonable explanation for this discrepancy.

Mean Duration of Use

On an average the injectable acceptors continued use for about 9 months. The duration of use increased with increasing age as well as duration of marital life. Table 5 depicts the pattern of use.

The young couples started injectable use for spacing for short period. The older women and those with longer duration of marriage used injectable for longer period. This could be due to their decision not to have any more children.

Table 5
Injectable Acceptors by Duration of Marriage by Age by Mean Duration of Use

Age	*Duration of Marriage*						
	0-5	*6-10*	*11-15*	*16-20*	*21 +*	*All*	*N*
15-24	5.1	6.8	8.5	-	-	5.9	80
25-29	5.2	8.1	10.4	-	-	8.1	52
30-34	6.5[a]	8.8	9.2	7.6	-	8.6	191
35-39	12.0[a]	6.4	13.4	11.2	12.3	11.3	179
40-49	-	1.0[a]	19.5[a]	11.3	12.1	11.9	62
All Ages	5.6	7.9	10.6	10.3	11.8	9.1	766

Note: [a]Less than 10 cases

Life Table Continuation Rates

Continuation rates using a life-table method have been calculated at the end of 6 months, 12 months, 18 months and 24 months using survey information. The rates have been computed to yield differentials by province by district, by age of acceptor, by parity, by urban-rural location of clinic, by educational level, by occupation, by cost of injections, by complaints, by distance of clinic from residence and by reasons of discontinuation.

Continuation Rates by Province

The overall continuation rates at the end of 12 months and 24 months were 42.0 per cent and 22.0 per cent (Table 6 and Figure 2).

Table 6
Cumulative Life Table Continuation Rates of Injectables by Province

Months	*Punjab*	*Sindh*	*All*
2	0.859	0.892	0.867
6	0.657	0.734	0.674
12	0.401	0.504	0.423
18	0.277	0.406	0.313
24	0.195	0.301	0.220

In Sindh, the continuation rates were higher than in Punjab. At the end of one year the continuation rates were

50.4 per cent and 40.1 per cent in Sindh and Punjab respectively. At the end of two years 19.5 per cent in Punjab and 30.1 per cent in Sindh continued use of injectable.

Figure 2: Cumulative Life Table Continuation Rates of Injectables by Province

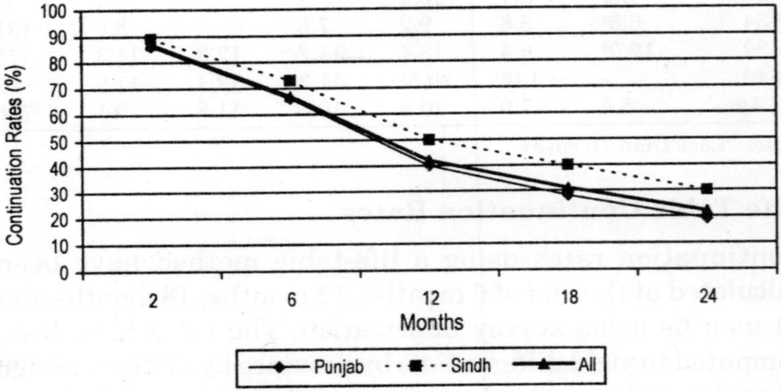

Table 7
Cumulative Life Table Continuation Rates of Injectables by District

Districts	*Duration in Months*				
	2	*6*	*12*	*18*	*24*
Bahawalpur	81.4	57.3	31.4	18.9	-
Faisalabad	85.4	60.2	27.8	16.2	-
Kasur	75.0	59.1	31.0	25.8	-
Lahore	80.3	58.1	28.4	21.6	15.9
Multan	94.6	65.4	44.4	36.3	23.2
Rawalpindi	68.7	59.9	27.5	-	-
Sahiwal	91.4	71.0	57.3	24.4	8.6
Sargodha	90.0	79.6	45.0	34.1	-
Sialkot	87.8	73.5	40.9	19.8	6.6
Karachi	88.0	74.2	49.9	47.3	27.4
Hyderabad	87.6	68.1	36.9	13.3	12.3
Tharparkar	97.7	87.9	-	-	-

Continuation Rates by District

There is considerable difference between district variations in continuation rates. The continuation rates at the end of

12 months was highest in Sahiwal 57.3 per cent, followed by Karachi 49.9 per cent, Sargodha 45.0 per cent, Multan 44.4 per cent, Sialkot 40.9 per cent (Table 7 and Figure 3). Rawalpindi and Faisalabad were among poor continuation rates, 27.5 and 27.8 per cent respectively.

Figure 3: Cumulative Life Table Continuation Rates of Injectables by District

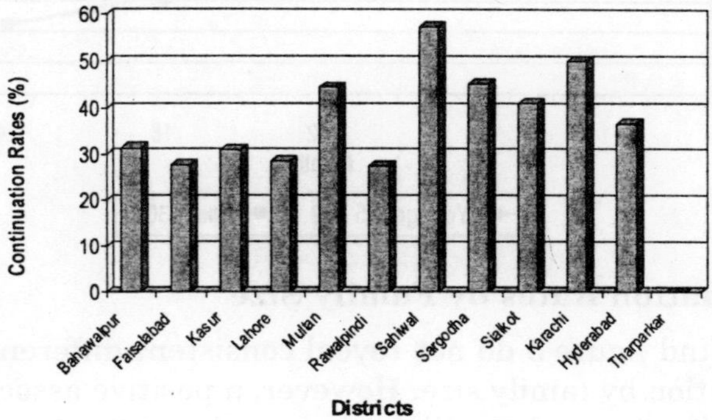

Continuation Rates by Age

Continuation rates at 12 months were 40.7 per 100 women among young women less than 30 years age group and 43.5 per 100 women among 30 years and above (Table 8 and Figure 4).

Table 8
Cumulative Life Table Continuation Rates of Injectables by Age

Months	15–29	30 +
2	0.856	0.874
6	0.655	0.690
12	0.406	0.435
18	0.294	0.324
24	0.226	0.222

Thus women under age 30 were less likely to continue than women aged 30 and over. However, the differences at various intervals were very small.

Figure 4
Cumulative Life Table Continuation Rates of Injectables by Age

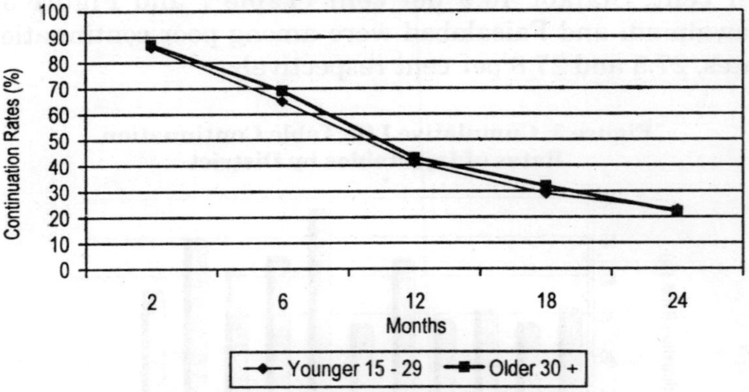

Continuation Rates by Family Size

Table 9 and figure 5 do not reveal consistent differences in continuation by family size. However, a positive association exists between number of living sons and continuation rates.

Table 9
Cumulative Life Table Continuation Rates of Injectables by Family Size

Months	*1 – 3*	*4 +*
2	0.836	0.887
6	0.684	0.671
12	0.403	0.432
18	0.324	0.310
24	0.218	0.221

Those having 3 or more sons continued 10 points ore than their counterparts with less than 3 sons. Number of daughters did not affect continuation rates. The findings clearly indicate sex preference and need for contraceptive use after having two sons. As such they continued longer.

Continuation Rates by Urban-Rural Location

The accepters were not asked about their residence. However, location of the clinic was known. It was observed that majority

Figure 5: Cumulative Life Table Continuation Rates of Injectables by Family Size

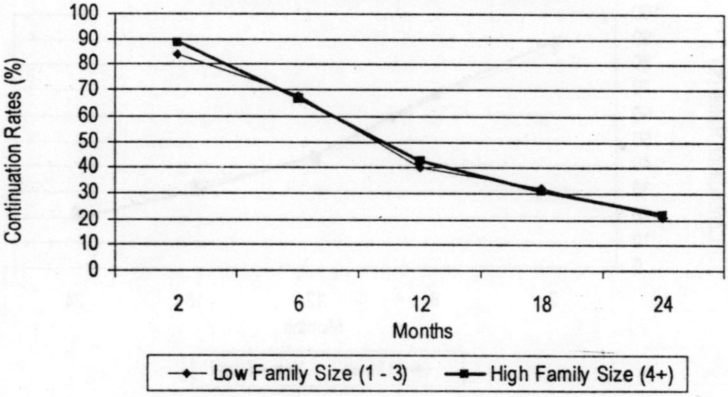

of the clients received supply from the nearest clinic. The analysis is done accordingly. Looking at continuation rates in Table 10 and figure 6 below, the variations by location of the clinic were not very distinct and consistent. The continuation rates were higher in rural clinics at the end of one year while opposite trend was observed at 18 months and 24 months of use.

Table 10
Cumulative Life Table Continuation Rates of Injectables by Rural-Urban Location

Months	*Urban*	*Rural*
2	0.852	0.890
6	0.670	0.682
12	0.411	0.444
18	0.329	0.296
24	0.234	0.201

Continuation Rates by Education

It is believed that use of contraception is influenced by education. Educated women are supposed to continue longer. On the other hand they are more sensitive to after effects. Although it was expected that continuation among educated

Figure 6: Cumulative Life Table Continuation Rates of Injectables by Rural-Urban Location

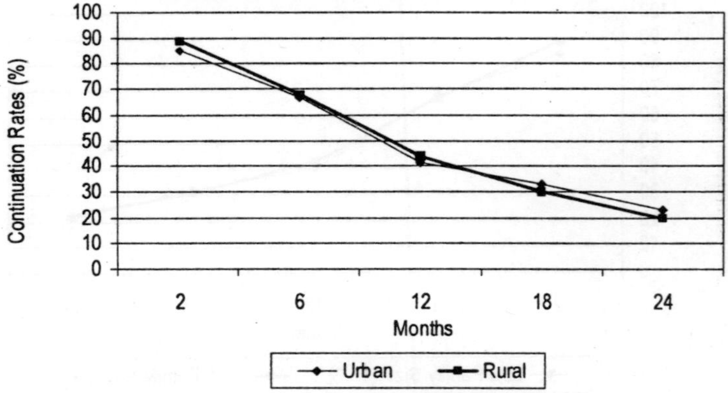

group would be much higher, but this study does not show any significant difference (Table 11 and Figure 7).

Table 11
Cumulative Life Table Continuation Rates of Injectables by Education

Months	*Uneducated*	*Educated*
2	0.809	0.803
6	0.565	0.590
12	0.332	0.340
18	0.243	0.252
24	0.179	0.138

Continuation Rates by Occupation

A very small proportion of the sample consisted of workingwomen hence the results in table 12 and figure 8, cannot be generalized. The table indicates a little higher continuation rate among housewives that is contrary to expectation. In my opinion since housewives mostly remain in house therefore they always has a risk to become pregnant more frequently as compared to working women. They give birth to more babies as compared to workingwomen. So in order to avoid pregnancy more frequently they utilize a little higher injectable continuation rates.

Figure 7: Cumulative Life Table Continuation Rates of Injectables by Education

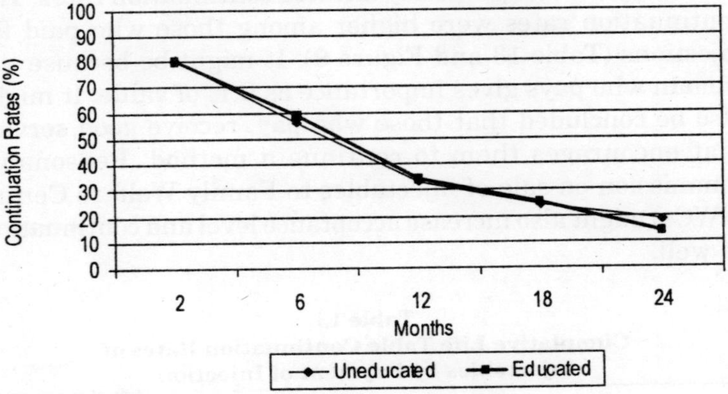

Table 12
Cumulative Life Table Continuation Rates of Injectables by Occupation

Months	*Working*	*Housewives*
2	0.830	0.803
6	0.532	0.583
12	0.326	0.338
18	0.228	0.251
24	0.128	0.180

Figure 8: Cumulative Life Table Continuation Rates of Injectables by Occupation

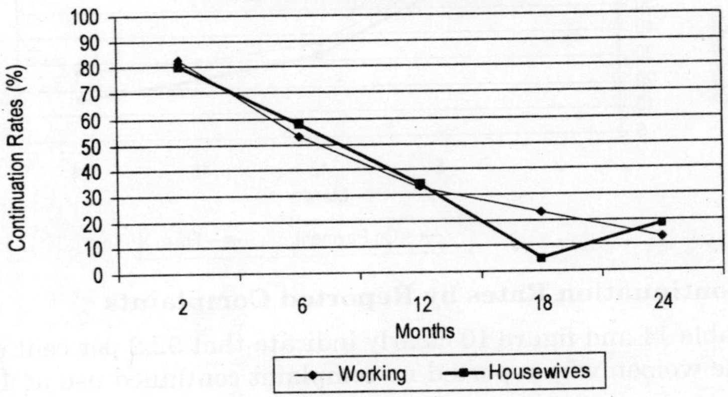

Continuation Rates by Cost of Injection

Cost of injectables positively affected continuation rates. The continuation rates were higher among those who paid for injections (Table 13 and Figure 9). It might be because the woman who pays gives importance as it is of value. It might also be concluded that those who pay, receive good service that encourages them to continue a method. Reasonable commission on sale of injectables to Family Welfare Centre (FWCs) might also increase acceptance level and continuation as well.

Table 13
Cumulative Life Table Continuation Rates of Injectables by Payment of Injection

Months	*On Payment*	*Free*
2	0.826	0.798
6	0.604	0.565
12	0.368	0.324
18	0.299	0.227
24	0.260	0.160

Figure 9: Cumulative Life Table Continuation Rates of Injectables by Payment of Injection

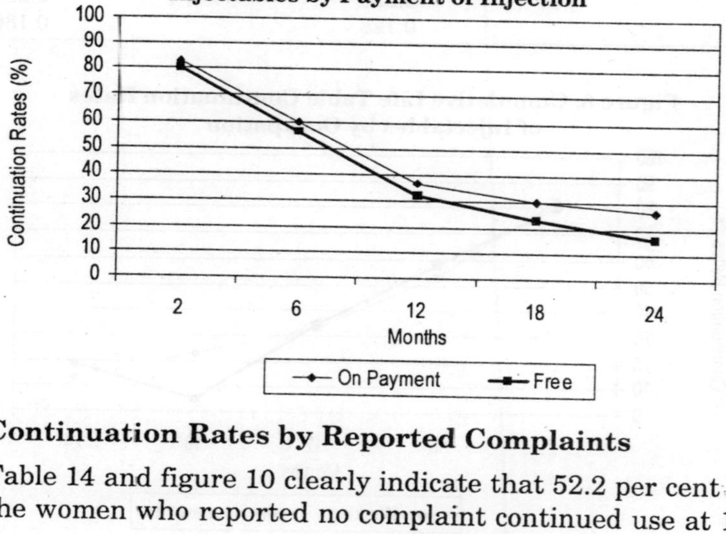

Continuation Rates by Reported Complaints

Table 14 and figure 10 clearly indicate that 52.2 per cent of the women who reported no complaint continued use at 12 months as against those reporting menstrual complaints (27.0 per cent). Only 20.1 per cent of the women with bleeding problems continued injectable use after one year. At 18 months, 88 per cent discontinued injectables due to bleeding while the discontinuation rate was 55 per cent only when they mentioned no complains.

Table 14
Cumulative Life Table Continuation Rates of Injectables by Type of Complaints

Months	*No Complaints*	*Bleeding*	*Other*
2	0.930	0.724	0.712
6	0.731	0.463	0.579
12	0.522	0.201	0.271
18	0.450	0.110	0.117
24	0.308	0.075	0.117

Figure 10: Cumulative Life Table Continuation Rates of Injectables by Type of Complaints

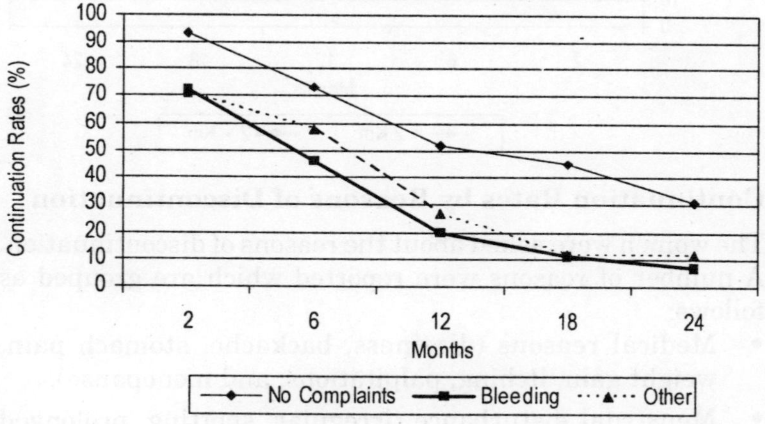

Continuation Rates by Distance

It was expected that those who lived nearer to clinic would continue the use longer (Table 15 and Figure 11). In this sample the continuation rates were just a few points higher when the clinic was nearer to residence.

Table 15
Cumulative Life Table Continuation Rates of Injectables by Distance between Residence and Clinic

Months	*< 2 Km.*	*2 + Km.*
2	0.798	0.819
6	0.580	0.572
12	0.341	0.329
18	0.260	0.231
24	0.178	0.168

Figure 11: Cumulative Life Table Continuation Rates of Injectables by Distance between Residence and Clinic

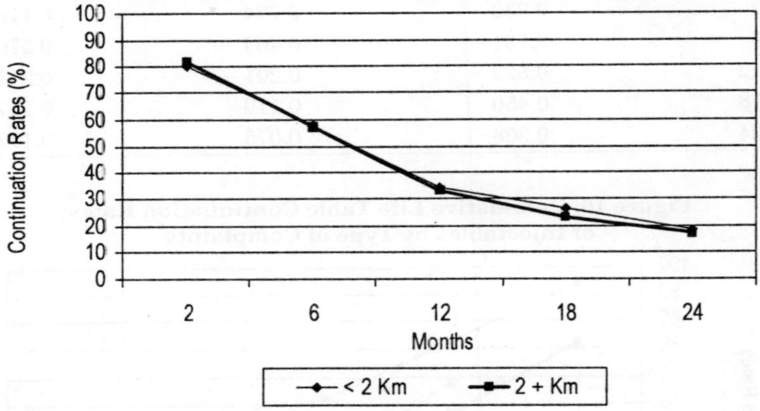

Continuation Rates by Reasons of Discontinuation

The women were asked about the reasons of discontinuation. A number of reasons were reported which are grouped as follows:

- Medical reasons (dizziness, backache, stomach pain, weight gain, itching, palpitations, and menopause).
- Menstrual disturbance (irregular, spotting, prolonged bleeding, and amenorrhea).
- Method related (cost, short supply, clinic distance, dissatisfaction with clinic staff, pregnant, switch over to other method).
- Personal reason (husband's objection, date missed, husband out of station, and desire for children).

Table 16 and figure 12 revealed that most prevalent reason for low continuation rate was the menstrual disturbance. At 12 months, 57 per cent discontinued for menstrual problems, 29.2 per cent for personal reasons, 26.9 per cent for method related reasons, and 22.5 per cent for other medical reasons. At 24 months discontinuation rate due to menstrual disturbance was 67 per cent, followed by method related factors, 46 per cent and lowest due to personal reasons 36 per cent.

Table 16
Cumulative Life Table Continuation Rates of Injectables by Reasons of Discontinuation

Months	*Menstrual Complaints*	*Medical*	*Method Related*	*Personal*
2	0.813	0.923	0.975	0.939
6	0.627	0.865	0.879	0.821
12	0.430	0.774	0.731	0.707
18	0.373	0.699	0.632	0.689
24	0.330	0.607	0.544	0.642

Figure 12: Cumulative Life Table Continuation Rates of Injectables by Reasons of Discontinuation

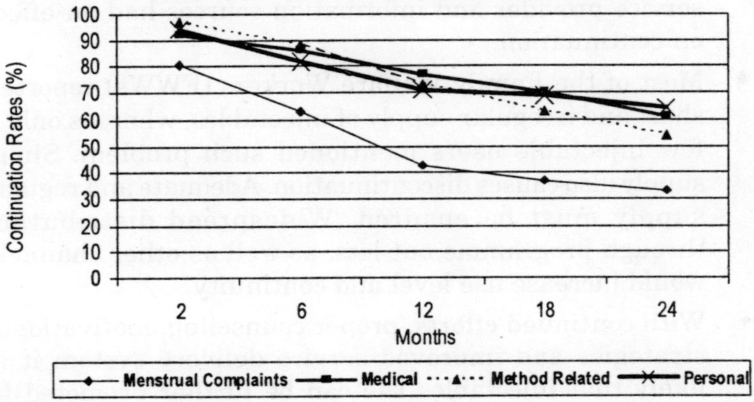

MEASURES FOR IMPROVING THE CONTINUATION RATES

- It is quite evident that continuation rates may be increased significantly by minimizing bleeding disturbances. Proper care and treatment could be an effective measure. Adequate counseling and information in advance could prepare a client psychologically to tolerate probable side effect and thus enhance continuity.

- The injectables are free of cost but a sizeable number of respondents reported that fee was charged. Fee was found to be associated with higher continuation rate than no fee at all. It is recommended that a moderate amount should be charged for injectables. Out of this a reasonable commission could be given to the provider (FWW). It would have multiple advantages: (1) the acceptor would gain a sense that the method is of value (2) it would be an incentive for providers, they will try their best to increase sale and re-supply (3) false reporting can be minimized.
- The follow-up visits are very rare that should be facilitated by providing transport or giving transport charges to FWWs. The continuation can be improved by reminding users of the next injection date, further more the complaints could be treated during home visits. The research suggests that acceptor's personal contact with service provider and information sources had an effect on continuation.
- Most of the Family Welfare Workers (FWWs) reported short and irregular supply of injectables, whereas only a few injectable users mentioned such problem. Short supply also causes discontinuation. Adequate and regular supply must be ensured. Widespread distribution through programme out-lets, as well as other channels would increase use level and continuity.
- With continued efforts, proper counseling, motivational strategies and improved service delivery system it is likely that injectables use can be further promoted to the desired level in the next five year plan.
- Record keeping is an essential element as it serves multiple functions: it keeps track of clients, monitors continuation and side effects and provides a supervisory

tool. Contrary to this, the record keeping in most of the centers was found extremely poor. The clinic staff either is not aware of its importance or deliberately avoids writing addresses for certain reasons. Incomplete addresses of clients make follow-up impossible. There is a need to explain the importance of record keeping and collecting basic information that is pre-requisite for monitoring and research. Thus conscientious record keeping must be assured.

CONCLUSION

Long-acting progestogen injections provide users with one of the most effective reversible method of fertility regulation available today. Norethisterone Enanthate (Nei-En) has been included in the Pakistan's Population Programme as a mainstream contraceptive option, since about twenty years. The Pakistan Fertility and Family Planning Survey (1996 97) indicated that 7 per cent of the contraceptive current users were on injectables. The popularity of injectable is increasing tremendously but still the performance is less than 50 per cent of the annual target fixed by Ministry of Population Welfare.

The injections are mainly provided by 1250 Family Welfare Centres, which on an average deliver 1.3 injections per day an extremely low performance. This needs to be promoted through worker's dedication, adequate counseling of Clients, and wide publicity. Printed material in Urdu and local languages stating full explanation of the method, mode of action, probable side effects and advantages of the method should be provided at clinics.

This study has attempted to investigate social and demographic characteristics of injectable acceptors and their experience with the method and sources. It aimed at identifying the reasons for discontinuation of the method after a given period. The results of the study are promising. The injectables appeared to be the most preferred method that is acceptable to a substantial proportion (67 per cent) of the study population who chose to use it when decided to practice family planning. The injectables have been found very effective and safe. Only nine pregnancies were reported as the cause of discontinuation during two years. About 42 per cent of the injectable acceptors continued the method at 12 months of use and 27.5 per cent at 24 months. Similarly, the life table cumulative continuation rates were 42.3 per 100 women at 12 months and 22.0 per 100 women at 24 months. The status of users at 24 months should be viewed with caution, as the number of cases was small in this group.

Comparing with international studies the continuation rates were close to Mexico (43 per cent), but much lower as compared to India (64.3 per cent), Bangladesh (62.7 per cent), and Indonesia (63.2 per cent) (Ministry of Population Welfare, Government of Pakistan 1993).

There were marked differences in continuation rates in the two provinces as well as districts, indicating needs for further research on clinics influence on acceptance and continuation. Certain socio-economic, demographic and method related variables also affected continuation rates, whereas urban rural location, education, and parity did not appear to influence much. Women, who were older, already had several children continued use a little longer. Cost of injectable was positively associated with continuity. The most prominent factor found responsible for discontinuation was menstrual complaints and other side effects. About 80 per cent of the women reporting bleeding complaints discontinued injectable use at 12 months. In contrast only 48 per cent having no complaints discontinued the method at 12 months. While life table continuation rates by reasons of discontinuation, were 43.0 and 37.4 per 100 women at 12 months and 18 months respectively for menstrual disturbance while with other complaints the continuation rate was as high as 70 per cent.

REFERENCES

Government of Pakistan (1968), *National Impact Survey Report*, Population Planning Council.

Government of Pakistan (1983-1997), *Performance of Contraceptive Delivery Service by Category of Service Outlets* (Mimeograph).

Government of Pakistan (1983-84), *Pakistan Lactation and Fertility Survey*, National Research Institute of Fertility Control, Karachi.

Government of Pakistan (1984-85), *Pakistan Contraceptive Prevalence Survey*, Ministry of Population Welfare and Population Council, Islamabad.

Government of Pakistan (1990-91), *Pakistan Demographic and Health Survey*, National Institute of Population Studies, Islamabad.

Government of Pakistan (1993), *Injectable Contraceptive Study*, National Institute of Fertility Control, Ministry of Population Welfare.

Government of Pakistan (1996-97), *Pakistan Fertility and Family Planning Survey,* National Institute of Population Studies, Islamabad.

5

GENDER RESPONSIVE NATIONAL BUDGET INITIATIVES IN BOTSWANA

DONATILLA KOKWANGUHA KAINO AND MALEBOGO BAKWENA

INTRODUCTION

Traditional macroeconomic frameworks are modelled on an 'economic man', who is unaffected by historical context, gender, social class, sexual orientation, race, geographic location, or any other determining factor. In reality, this abstract person does not exist. Gender relations have a clear effect on the distribution of wealth, access to services and resources, and the opportunities needed to fully develop human potential. In turn, national budgets, prepared annually, are the main expression of macroeconomic policy at the national and sub-national levels. They have largely inherited this failure to acknowledge the different circumstances women and men face, and their differentiated needs. While budgets have been instrumental in transmitting and reproducing gender biases, they also offer the possibility for transforming existing gender inequalities.

The Beijing Platform for Action specifically calls for gender sensitive budgets under the heading 'Financial Arrangements'. This does not aim at producing a separate budget for women but it involves the integration of a gender perspective in budgetary decisions on policies and programmes, as well as the adequate financing of specific programmes for securing equality between women and men. It requires the governments to systematically review how females and males benefit from public sector expenditures; adjust budgets to ensure equality of access to public sector expenditures. However, for this to be achieved there is a need of developing a gender–sensitive conceptual frameworks and national economic statistics that can reveal linkages and feedbacks between gender relations and macroeconomic outcomes (Cagatary *et al.*1995). In Pakistan for example, although the budget for education may have no intention of favouring boys, it was found that public expenditure per male student was 56 Rupees compared to 26 Rupees per female student (World Bank 1995). Therefore with a gender-blind Budget, it is difficulty for the government to attain gender equality and meaningful positive impacts on economic growth and development.

South Africa is an example where the analysis by the Women's Budget Initiative revealed that the 1997-98 budget allocation of resources to the Commission on Gender Equality (which is under the department of justice), in its first year of operation, was not even sufficient to cover the remuneration of commissioners, and provided nothing to pay executive staff and office costs. It was also far less than that allocated to the Human Rights Commission and the Youth Commission. The Parliamentary Joint Committee on the Improvement of the quality of Life and Status of Women highlighted this fact, and the government subsequently increased the Commission's budget allocation substantially (Budlender 1998).

Gender Responsive Budget Initiatives (GRBIs) are mechanisms by which governments, in collaboration with lawmakers, civil society groups, donor and other development agencies, can integrate a gender analysis into fiscal policies and budgets. A GRBI is not a separate budget for women but an attempt to disaggregate expenditure and revenue according to their different impacts on women and men. The objectives of GRBIs are: To strengthen the capacity of governments to incorporate a gender analysis in the planning and evaluation of revenue-raising measures and expenditure allocations at all levels; To support strategies for women participation in economic decision-making through their engagement in the budget process; to improve the mechanisms used by countries to account for action taken on international communities to gender and development, including the Convention on the Elimination of All Forms of Discrimination Against Women (CEDAW); and to contribute to the achievement of the International Development Targets (IDTs'). GRBIs can include different components that usually vary across countries and regions depending on the specific social, political contexts and the institutions that carry out the implementation. In some cases other categories (together with gender) such as class, age, ethnicity, etc are used to disaggregate GRB. For example, in order to determine the impacts of government expenditure on white men and women in comparison with their counterparts in other racial groups, the South African 'women's budget' exercise combined a race analysis with a gender analysis (Hewitt *et al.* 2001)

STATEMENT OF THE PROBLEM

The government of Botswana signed the Beijing Platform for Action to express its commitment to gender equality objectives and to gender mainstreaming as well as its commitment to greater transparency and accountability. A major step towards this commitment was to formulate the National Gender Programme Framework (NGPF), which is in line with the country's 'Vision 2016'. The first of six main areas of concern discussed in the Framework is 'Women and Poverty' including 'Economic Empowerment of Women'. It was noted that women and female-headed households are limited to income and economic opportunities mainly because of high dependency ratio, low labour productivity, and limited access to and control of productive resources and development programmes. The availability of women for full time income-generating activities is limited by their multiple roles in their homes. It was further noted that there is an increasing incidence of deprivation among elderly, mostly female, when they can no longer participate in productive activity, but do not have viable family support. Other factors identified to have aggravated poverty among women included are retrenchment, unemployment and under-employment (Government of Botswana 2000). To help women get out of these situation different strategies, actions, public policies and programmes have been set. Among the set public policies are: the integration of gender into development planning, policy formulation and programme review; review of collateral requirement to include the poor women; develop incentives and policies to promote the adoption of deliberate measures to appoint women to top decision-making level in the corporate and public sectors and to promote gender sensitivity in the acquisition and transfer of technology and skills. It is important therefore to analyse the national annual budgets and see its implication on women and poverty including economic empowerment of women.

SELECTED LITERATURE REVIEW

Economic Costs of Gender Inequality

Elson points out that the gender inequality is not only costly to women but to society as a whole. If this problem is solved women will have more control over resources and there will be gains for society as a whole. Research has shown that gender inequality reduces agricultural production in Africa. For example, the study in Kenya by Saito and Spurling (1992) found that women farmers, when given the same level of agricultural inputs and education as men farmers, could increase their yields by more than 20%. Gender inequality also reduces the productivity gains in the future. The evidence from World Bank Report (1995) is that increasing women's well-being increases productivity of the next generation. The probability of children being enrolled in school increases with their mother's educational level, and extra income going to mothers has more positive impact on household investment in nutrition, health and education of children than extra income going to fathers. Also gross national product (GNP) declines if there is no investment in female education. Hill and King (1995) argue that if everything else remains constant, countries with the ratio of female-to male enrolment in primary or secondary education less than 0.75 can expect their levels of GNP to be roughly 25% lower than countries with less gender disparity in education. Women's income and national income increase as a result of elimination of gender discrimination across occupations and salaries benefits (Tzannatos 1991).

Research also shows that gender inequality hampers a positive supply response to structural adjustment measures. A good example is given by Brown (1995), that when crop prices rise, the expectation is that farmers will produce more. But if the payments go mainly into the hands of male farmers, women farmers will not have a direct incentive to produce more. The small amount that goes to women farmers may not be used to produce more for the market because they have to produce for their families, collect water and fuel and look after children.

ECONOMIC GAINS FROM GENDER RESPONSIVENESS

Potential benefits to the society which can be gained if macroeconomic policy was designed in ways that reduce or eliminate gender inequality include greater output of goods and services, more leisure, increased capability to live a satisfying life and better conservation of the environment. This could occur directly or indirectly (Elson 1991). Example of direct effect that can lead to higher productivity is an increase in public expenditure on schooling, extension services and credit to women. Indirect positive effect on productivity may also occur if for instance macroeconomic policy promotes increases in family income, which leads to families educating their daughters to the same extent as their sons. A study by Tibaijuka (1994) shows that the benefits from reducing gender-based constraint in a community of smallholder coffee and banana growers in Tanzania increased household cash incomes by 10%, labour productivity by 15% and capital productivity by 44%.

There is an increasing recognition that 'trickle down' effect of macroeconomic aggregates (and national economic prosperity) is not automatic; rather, governments need explicitly consider human development objectives (e.g., concerns of poverty and inequality, including gender inequality) when formulating macroeconomic policy. Among the three key forms of macroeconomic policy (i.e., exchange rate, monetary and fiscal), fiscal policy is considered to be the most promising entry point for integrating a gender analysis and its instruments can be grouped under revenue and expenditure (Budlender *et al.* 2002). Normally these two groups are brought together in a national budget, which is prepared annually and sets out revenue and expenditure plans for the coming year. However, the budget appears to be gender–neutral policy instrument. It is presented in terms of aggregates like totals, and sub-totals of expenditure and revenue, and the resulting budget surplus or deficit. This kind of budget is more accurately described as 'gender blind' because it fails to take into account that men and women have different roles, responsibilities and resources in society, it overlooks the different impacts that policies have on men and women in the country. Waring (1989); Elson (1991); Cagatay, Elson and Crown (1995), argue that gender blindness which exist in the conceptual frameworks and statistics used to prepare national budgets fail to recognize that: (a) There is an underestimation of women contribution to the macro-economy because of biased markets and missing and incomplete statistics; (b) Women provide unpaid vital services for the paid economy (e.g., caring for and maintaining the labour force and social framework or capital); (c) The parameters of aggregate production, savings, investment, imports and exports in the paid economy may be sensitive to different patterns of gender relations and gender distribution of resources. Therefore, gender responsive budgeting can make such policy design more effective as it contributes to the reduction in gender inequality, and hence reduces gender constraints to successful macroeconomic outcomes. Consequently, there is an improvement in economic growth and human development performance in ways that also empower women (Budlender *et al.* 2002).

Gender responsive budget initiatives (GRBIs) are mechanisms for mainstreaming gender into public expenditure and public revenue decision-making, which can lead to more effective policy design and outcomes. However, political support is crucial, particularly from finance ministries and officials in key sectoral ministries. Ministers responsible for women's affairs are important advocates but often lack political influence to mobilize support and lack the capacity to address macroeconomic issues. Hence in order to have consistency between social commitments and economic goals, Budlender *et al.* (2002) recommend that a broad-based coalitions, sex-disaggregated indicators, the development of tools for revenue analysis, and more work at the sub-national level are needed.

When considering the effectiveness of public expenditure, which is judged in terms of achieving the intended results at the lowest possible cost, a gender perspective introduces the questions of 'results for whom?' and 'costs to whom?' Some ways of addressing these questions which are suggested by Elson include: The assessment of needs and beneficiaries; analysis of quality of service indicators, for instance, enrolment rates in schools, bed occupancy rates in hospitals; assessment of `invisible' costs, for example, discharging patients more rapidly from hospitals with intention of reducing cost, transfers costs of care from paid hospital to unpaid women in families and communities, therefore there is no cost saving as intended; and assessment of benefits of equal opportunities in service delivery for instance education and employment. In order to understand the effect of government expenditure on both men and women the analysis need to be disaggregated by gender in all these cases (Budlender *et al.* 2002).

CONCEPTUAL FRAMEWORK OF GENDER RESPONSIVE BUDGET INITIATIVES

A gender responsive budget initiative aims to analyse any form of public expenditure, or the method of raising public money, from a gender perspective, identifying the implications and impacts for women and girls as compared to men and boys. Mainly it tries to find the impact this fiscal measure has on gender equality i.e., if it reduces or increases gender equality; or if leaves it unchanged. However, there is no single way of doing this. There are a number of analytical tools that can be used.

Most of Gender Budget Initiatives (GBIs) around the world begin with the three categories developed by the Australian initiative, using some sort of country-specific adaptation. Some of them introduce subcategories for women-targeted expenditures, with various ways of distinguishing what is gender-focused. The Australian Women's Budget as also proposed by Rhoda Sharp, requires the breakdown of each agency's expenditure into the following three main categories:

Gender-specific Expenditures: These consist of monies allocated for programmes and policies that are specifically targeted on gender lines. These expenditures come closest to the way in which people usually first interpret the words "Women's Budget" in that they are separate and relatively easily distinguishable amounts.

Expenditures which promote gender equity within the public service: These consist of monies allocated to affirmative action and other programmes, which promote equal opportunity initiatives in the public sector. Equity here would mean not only equal numbers of women and men employed, but also equal representation within management and decision-making posts, equal representation across different occupations, and equitable pay and conditions of service.

Mainstream expenditures: These consist of the remaining expenditures not covered by the first two categories. In the much better resourced Australian context, each of the first two categories accounted for at best 1% of total expenditure. So, unless this third category is addressed, a gender budget analysis will be dealing with what are essentially peripheral issues.

The identification and analysis of women specific expenditures in the budget, however has been the work of GBIs, mainly because the tracking of targeted expenditures is much easier than analyzing the mainstream expenditures from the gender perspective. Though this highlights the scarcity of resources allocated to women, it restricts gender equality concerns to isolated issues and hence it may underestimate the impact of the budget allocations on gender inequality. In order to solve this problem it was felt that it is important the gendered implications of mainstream budget allocations be unpacked. A number of methodological tools, which have been designed to serve the purpose, have also been used with different degrees of country-specific adaptations. The tools as presented in the BRIDGE Gender and Budgets Cutting Edge Pack include:

Gender-aware policy appraisal tool is designed to analyse policies and programmes from a gender perspective, and identify the ways in which these policies and resources allocated to them are likely to reduce or increase existing gender inequality. Another tool *'Gender disaggregated beneficiary assessment'* is used to evaluate the extent to which programmes for services are meeting the need of actual or potential beneficiaries, as identified and expressed by them.

The evaluation of distribution of budget resources among women and men, girls and boys by estimating the unit costs of a certain service and calculating the extent to which this service is being used by each of the groups is done by using the tool known as *'Gender-disaggregated public expenditure benefit incidence analysis'*. A tool designed to establish a link between budget allocations, the services provided through them and the way in which different members within household spend their time is known as *'Gender-disaggregated analysis of impact of the budget on time use'*. The incorporation of a gender perspective into the medium-term frameworks of policy development, planning and budgetary allocations, such as by disaggregating variables by gender, combining highlighting and challenging the gender blind underlying assumptions about how the economy works, is done using a tool called *'Gender-aware medium-term economic policy framework'*.

The other two tools *'Gender-aware budget statement'* and *'Disaggregated tax-incidence analysis'* respectively, refers to reports generated by government agencies on the implications of their expenditure on gender and equity objectives and assesses the differential impacts of taxation on women and men, as well as evaluates the level of revenue raised in relation to the needs and demands for public expenditure.

This paper utilizes the last two tools mentioned above to analyse the Botswana government budget of 2004-05. Basically it examines the implications that the expenditures budgeted for some ministries have on objectives under 'women and poverty including women empowerment' and assesses the differential impacts of taxation on women. This gender budget analysis is based on an understanding that budgets should follow policy and not the other way round. Policy, in turn, should reflect the situation in the society. Basically the analysis of 2004-5 budgets is done to show the extent to which the budget reflects the appropriate gender-sensitive policies described above. This reflects the central argument of the paper that budget is central in determining effective government policy. Basically authors assert that, without gender responsive budget, gender-sensitive policies will be ineffective, no matter how sensitive they are.

ANALYSIS OF BOTSWANA'S 2004-05 BUDGET

Government Revenue

The Botswana's 2004/05 budget shows that the major sources of government revenue include: Minerals revenue, custom and excise revenue, non mineral Income Tax, and Value Added Tax (VAT) each accounts for 44%, 18%, 14% and 11% of total revenue respectively. The budget states that the VAT law will be fully enforced with enhanced auditing capabilities as the Government expects the taxpayers to have understood the tax system. Furthermore, the tax on housing benefits will be at full market value and the factor for calculating the benefits from rated properties will increase from 6% to 10% and that of non-rated properties from 5% to 8%. However, all sources of revenue are not disaggregated by gender.

From a gender perspective the revenue side of the budget seems not to recognize the contribution of unpaid labour to the economy and therefore is excluded from the sources of revenue. Also it does not recognize the negative impact of VAT on the poor and especially women. The focus on unpaid labour is in line with the work of Elson (1997) and others on the 'care economy'. It challenges the idea that the firms and government are two producing sectors in the economy, and household is a consuming sector. It argues that each of the three sectors both consumes and produces. Economists, however, overlook the production by household, the bulk of which is done by women, because it is unpaid and thus has no economic value. Elson shows the ways in which ignoring the effort and time spent on this unpaid work and the value of the goods and services produced, results in misallocation of resources and of budgets in particular.

Since unpaid and informal sector work is largely unaccounted in labour force or national accounts they remain statistically invisible, ignored in national human resource and economic policies and hence budgetary allocations. For women who are the majority in this sector, the time spent on this unpaid work constrains them from availing themselves the training and education opportunities and from participating in the formal paid labour economy which is cushioned by wages, health and safety regulations. This situation can therefore affect the health and well being of women.

The Value added Tax (VAT), which replaced the general sales tax (GST), is a highly regressive tax as it has greater impact on low-income earners. A higher proportion of their income is spent on taxes on basic consumption goods (e.g.

food, clothing, footwear energy etc) than higher income earners. One of the main differences between GST and VAT is that GST is not applicable to all goods and services. For example, raw materials purchased for manufacturing goods in Botswana are not subject to tax, nor are many food items and most building materials. Similarly, some services are excluded from the scope of the tax-construction services and bar/restaurant services, for example. VAT applies to virtually all goods and services. Therefore, the net effect of the change from Sales Tax to VAT is a significant increase in the taxpayer base.

The implication of VAT is different for men and women, in so far as women have major responsibilities for managing day-to-day household expenditure. VAT puts up costs for poor population in which women account for the larger share. It is not guaranteed that the proportion of household income available to women for meeting household needs rises commensurably. Consequently they need to spend a lot of time searching for alternative cheaper goods and services for the family.

The move by the Government to tax housing benefits at full market value and an increase in the factor for calculating the benefits from rated properties (from 6% to 10%) and non-rated properties (from 5% to 8%) will have negative effect on the disposable incomes of the households at all income levels, however the poor and women in particular will suffer more because this reduces the household disposable income.

Government Expenditure

It has been proposed that total expenditure will increase by 6% compared to the revised 2003-04 expenditures. This increase will be accounted for by the recurrent expenditure as the development expenditure is expected to decrease by P390 million. Much of increase in recurrent expenditure will be accounted for by the cost of implementing the recommendations; as amended, by the Presidential Commission on the Review of the Public Service Pay Structures for the Public Service, the Local Authorities and the Botswana Defence Force. The budget does not provide any growth in the total manpower establishment of the Public Service. The government expenditure is also not disaggregated by gender hence it is not easy to know how much of the budget is for women and how much is for men.

The proposed expenditure has many gender implications as follows:

1. An average increase of 15% in salaries proposed may favour men more than women because the number of women employed is smaller than that of men, and the majority of high posts and good jobs are occupied by men. Like in other developing countries, the majority of women are in female jobs characterized by irregular status, insecurity, low pay, and often serious occupational safety and health hazards; and women still shoulder the bulk of family responsibilities. Unless the wives have equal access to household income, increase in their husband's salaries may not necessarily improve the living standard of other family members. This may not also save the wives' time spent on unpaid labour.
2. The government also proposed to increase the allowances for old Age Pension Scheme by 10%. An important concern for pension policy, however, is the unequal distribution of benefits. Workers with coverage tend to be economically advantaged in many ways. Covered workers generally are well educated, and earn high wages. Differences in pension wealth are especially pronounced between men and women. Elderly women are less likely to receive pension income than elderly men as many were not employed. In addition, women with pensions generally receive much less pension income than men because were employed in less rewarding jobs.

   Increase in salaries and allowances are more likely to lead to higher prices and therefore higher cost of living, which affect more the poor, and women in particular. Women have to spend more time shopping for cheaper items, and food preparation will take longer time, as they have to purchase less processed foods.

3. Failure to provide more employment opportunities in the public sector may have greater negative impact on women than men. Statistics show that female-headed households in Botswana are poorer and have higher unemployment rate than male-headed households. Given the population growth rate of 3%, failure to increase public sector employment could result in higher unemployment rate than before and hence a bigger burden falling on women than on male. The designed government policy framework to provide stable business environment, where private sector is free to pursue profitable business opportunities, though is good, it is more likely to benefit more men than women because of the following factors: (a) Women are poorer than men hence lack the necessary capital or easy access to credit to establish profitable micro enterprises. Banks, by the very nature of their business, are resistant to the high-risk loans which many women small businesses represent; the would be potential women entrepreneurs may lack collateral and the business savvy to articulate what they need in business terminology; and such inexperienced business persons may also fail to present a well-thought out long-range alternative plan to cover emergencies and other contingencies. Factors such as these all contribute to the decision of a would-be financing source not to commit money to women business (b) Lack of technology and skill upgrading are factors for most women to be engaged in less processed or unprocessed traditional items by using backward technologies, denying them an opportunity to generate additional income with more processed goods. Moreover, lack of knowledge and skill has forced women to concentrate on few and similar activities with the effect of stiff competition and earn meager income. (c) Lack of marketing infrastructure is also another major problem for women engaged in small-scale income-generating activities. Many of the women engaged in income-generating activities lack adequate market information and hence are unable to speculate the market in the right

direction. In sum, they lack appropriate marketing strategy and creativity.

4. Reduction in budget deficits, which result from, cuts in public expenditures and privatization results in the great reliance on women's unpaid work to substitute for the public services. More time is likely to be allocated to survival strategies such as the participation in income generating activities even if these are not sustainable. As a result less time may be spent on reproductive work (child care and cleaning). The effect of this could be to throw this burden on to the girl child whose time spent at home in the household could be increased resulting in less time for training and education and hence poor results.

Elson *et al.* (1997) argue that cutting back public expenditure may appear to be 'sound finance' and lead to sustainable budget deficits. But it may trigger off negative feedbacks, which undermine the sustainability of the budget deficit. If cuts transfer too great a burden to the unpaid economy, there is a risk of undermining the ability of women to contribute to productive activities which generate tax revenue; and to maintain activities which promote social cohesion (e.g., time to attend effectively to the social needs of children and community). A reduction in social cohesion frequently results in greater public expenditure on social work, security, policing and health services and discourages private investment. To put it another way, the problem is that a fall in the budget deficit may result in a rise in the reproduction tax to unsustainable levels. A rise in the reproduction tax can 'crowd-out' women's investment in social capital. This can result in 'false economies', arising from the fact that women unpaid provision of complementary or substitute services is not factored into public finances.

Apart from reducing the opportunities of creating new jobs for young generation, the cut in development expenditure also has affected the development in some sectors like water and electricity. From the 2004/05 budget speech the government planned to continue with on-going water projects which are: Maun Water Supply and Sanitation design, Kanye/Molepolole Emergency Water Supply, the construction of a booster pump station for Ramotswa water supply, the construction of Ntimbale dam, the design of a detailed Thune dam, and the review of the National Water Master Plan. The development and recurrent budget specifically for water development activities could not be determined because the budget for water is combined with that of electricity at national level, and at district level is combined with other activities under the Ministry of Local Government. However, the share of water and electricity development budget on the total development budget has been decreasing over the past three financial years. It was 14.7%, in 2002/03, 14% in 2003/4, and it is 12.9% in 2004-5.

Water supply and other services are better in urban areas than in rural areas. Very few people in rural areas have access to tap water. They fetch water from wells during the rainy season and depend on local government to supply them water under emergency water supply projects, during the dry season. Therefore women spend a lot of time fetching water from wells or waiting for local government tracks to supply them with water. The reduction in government development budget for water indicates that it will take long time for rural women to have access to tap water.

The economic value of water to women can be measured directly when women use water for domestic purposes. However, this method does not value the time that women and other members of the household spend either fetching water or waiting for local government tracks supplying water. The indirect way of measuring the value of water to women is the valuation of time released by reducing time for fetching or waiting for water to be supplied. Therefore the longer the time that is released the higher the value because this time can be utilized more efficiently doing other more productive activities.

5. In some cases the reprioritisation required is not in terms of the amount allocated, but rather in terms of whom this amount reaches. A good example is the Ministry of Works and Transport, which account for 10% of total expenditure in the 2004/05 budgets. Most of activities in programmes under this ministry, apart from being labour intensive they provide short or medium-term employment primarily for people with limited or no formal skills. However, they require relatively heavy physical labour. The data on employment from CSO shows that the construction and transport and communication industries employ respectively around 11.4% and 4.5% of total number of paid employees in the country. Women who are mainly employed on menial jobs account for only 12.06% and 17.77% of employment respectively. When considering the number of employed people (both temporary and permanent) the construction industry accounts for 7.6% while transport and communication accounts for 2.4% of total national employment. Women in these two industries account for only 11.42% and 21.6% of the employment respectively. This indicates that women benefit less from government budget toward these industries.

A national evaluation of the community-based public works programme in South Africa found that over 40% of those employed were women. However, women tended to be employed on the more menial jobs. Further, while 37% of the employed men received training, only 32% of the women did. The Department of Water Affairs and Forestry estimated that in 1997 about 14% of those employed and 16% of those who received training on the water and sanitation projects were women. Meanwhile the same Department has ensured that from the beginning over half of all workers on the

Working for Water Programme have been women. Gender-sensitive reprioritisation of these expenditure allocations would involve ensuring that the first two programmes adopt the methods employed by Working for Water to ensure that they, likewise, provide both immediate income-earning opportunities in the form of jobs and future income-enhancing opportunities in the form of training to those who need them most (Budlender 1998).

The second example is the ministry of education, which deals with the development of human resources in the country. A good job has been done in terms of expansion of the education system to make sure that all Botswana children of school going age access 10 year of basic education and about 51% of junior secondary school leavers access into senior secondary schools. The decision by the government to run all community Junior Secondary Schools (with effect from the 1st January, 2004) in order to guarantee uniformity in the standard of education at this level across the country, is much welcome. The support is also to the idea of expanding tertiary education and training opportunities locally in order to reduce the number of students sent to other countries to study at great cost.

When the situation at different levels of education in 2001 is reviewed the following can be noted. In terms of enrolment, female students account for 50%, 52%, 57.2% and 38.4% of total student enrolment at the first level, second level of education, Teacher Training Colleges and Vocational and Technical Training Colleges respectively. Female dropouts accounted for 40.4% and 69.1% of total dropouts at first and second levels of education respectively; and female repeaters accounted for 38.4% and 70.1% of total repeaters at the two levels respectively. When considering the practical subjects that students take at the second level, female students are concentrated in agriculture (44.5%) and home economics (30%), while male students are concentrated in agriculture (38.6), design and technology (28.5%) and art (20.8%). Female teachers account for 80% and 47.2% of total teachers in the first level and second level of education respectively.

In the 2001-02 academic year the Botswana College of Agriculture had 126, 451, and 266 students enrolled for certificate, diploma and degree courses respectively. Female enrolment respectively accounted for 31.8%, 29% and 14.3%. In the Colleges of Education female students accounted for 54% of 1495 candidates enrolled. In the University of Botswana 1802, 819, 2255, and 2147 students enrolled in the faculties of Social Sciences, Business, Education and Humanities, whereby respectively, female students accounted for 51%, 49%, 56% and 59%. Out of 1272, and 1384 students enrolled in the Faculties of Engineering and Technology and Science, only 10% and 26% were female respectively. The Center for Continuing Education had 2036 students enrolled of which 67% were female. Though, the data on unit cost for education at different levels is not disaggregated by subject and gender, it indicates that the cost for tertiary education is 21, 9, 8, and 2 times that for primary, junior secondary and senior secondary teacher education respectively.

As indicated above, the rate of dropout and repetition is higher among female students in the second level than in the first level of education. The reason behind this could be because of pregnancy and girls at this level are old enough to help their mothers in the care economy. At home girls do not have enough time to study like boys as they are required to help their mothers in cooking, fetching water and other house work, also looking after the sick family members when their mothers are engaged in other activities. The subjects mostly studied by female could also indicate the multi-activities they are engaged in. The decision by the government to provide grants instead of loans to students who are interested and qualify for Engineering and Technology and Science courses at the university therefore increases benefits toward male students. The implication of this is that female students will continue graduating in areas whose job opportunities are less paying.

The third example is the ministry of State President, which was allocated 27% of the total development budget. Of this amount the Botswana Defence Force and Police Facilities was expected to account for 40% and 12.28% respectively.

This allocation first shows that there is a mismatch between the situation in the country and in the SADC region, the policy statements and available resources. Since the security situation in the country is good while that in the SADC is improving, and the resources available are not enough to cater for all the country's needs, one would expect the amount allocated to the Defence Force to be reasonably small. The government should be reallocating resources from maintenance of an aggressive force towards sectors, which attack the poverty and inequality. Secondly, the benefits from the funds allocated to the Defence Force normally go more to men than women because by its nature this sector employs more men than women.

CONCLUSION AND RECOMMENDATION

From analysis made above it can be concluded that the 2004-5 Government Budget is gender-blind i.e. it is not disaggregated according to gender as a result it is not easy to make a clear follow-up and see how the policies set to meet the objectives stated under the 'Women and Poverty' including 'Women Economic Empowerment', the first area of concern in the Botswana's National Gender Programme Framework, are taken care off. However, some sources of revenue and some Government expenditures imply that the gap between men and women could either remain the same or increase and hence the above objectives could not be attained.

The revenue part of the budget does not include the contribution made by unpaid labour, which is mainly accounted for by women. Apart from understating the contribution of this labour to the economy, this omission could make the government fail to allocate it resources it deserves. The use of VAT and amendments made on housing benefits, tax and factor for calculating the benefits from rated and non-rated properties could affect the poor and mainly women negatively. While the increase in Government recurrent expenditure is more likely to benefit men more than women since the sectors targeted employ more men than women, the possible negative consequences that could arise from this increase (e.g. rise in prices) are more likely to fall on women than men. The negative effects of reducing Government development expenditure could also fall more on women than on men because of their multiple activities they perform in the society. As Elson argues, the multiplicity of production, reproduction and community management roles result in high demands for a woman's time. This demand is further heightened during the period of rising prices, falling real wages, high levels of unemployment, and underemployment and during periods when there are reductions in government provision of social services. The size of expenditure on education also indicates how it benefits men more than women. Female students are enrolled more in non-science subjects whose unit cost is lower and their related job opportunities are less paying.

Based on the analysis of the budget and the summary in the previous section of the paper, the following can be adopted to help the government achieve the goal of reducing poverty among women and empowering them:

- The creation of mechanisms that allow women to participate in budget formulation and implementation processes in order to safeguard their interests and thereby secure gender equality.
- Disaggregate the annual budgets according to gender for monitoring purposes
- Highest priority should be given to promote women's education and technical skills that will help them to improve their economic situation. Most specifically, women should be trained in businesses to enable them benefit from the programmes such as Citizen Entrepreneurial Development Agency (CEDA) in Botswana.

REFERENCES

Budlender, D., Elson, D., Hewitt, G. and Mukhopadhyay, T. (eds.) (2002), *Gender Budgets Make Cents: Understanding Gender Responsive Budgets,* Commonwealth Secretariat, London.

Budlender, D. (1998), *The South African Women's Budget Initiative,* A Background Paper No. 2, Presented at the UNDP Meeting on Women and Political Participation: 21st Century Challenges, 24-26 March 1999, New Delhi, India.

Brown, L. (1995), *Gender and the Implementation of Structural Adjustment in Africa: Examining the Micro-Meso-Macro Linkages*, International Food Policy Research Institute, Washington DC.

Cagatay, N., Elson, D. and Grown, C. (1995), Introduction to Gender, Adjustment and Macroeconomics, *World Development*, 23 (11): 1827-1836.

Elson, D. (ed.) (1991), *Male Bias in the Development Process*, Manchester University Press, Manchester.

Elson, D., B. Evers and J. Gideon (1997), *Gender Aware Country Economic Reports: Concepts and Sources*, Working Paper No. 1, GENECON Unit, Graduate School of Social Sciences, University of Manchester, UK.

Government of Botswana (2000), *Botswana's National Gender Programme Framework*, Ministry of Labour and Home Affairs, Women's Affairs Department, Botswana.

Hewitt, G. and Mukhopadyay, T. (2001), Promoting Gender Equality through Public Expenditure: A Challenge for Governments, In *Gender Budgets Make Cents: Understanding Gender-Responsive Budgets,* Commonwealth Secretariat, London.

Hill, A. and E. King (1995), Women's Education and Economic Well-Being', *Feminist Economics*, 11(2): 21-46.

Saito, K. and D. Spurling (1992), *Developing Agricultural Extension for Women Farmers,* World Bank Discussion Paper 156, Washington DC.

Tibaijuka, A. (1994), The Cost of Differential Gender Roles in African Agriculture: A Case Study of Smallholder Banana-Coffee Farms in the Kagera Region, Tanzania, *Journal of Agricultural Economics,* 45(1): 69-81.

Tzannatos, Z. (1991), Potential Gains from the Elimination of Gender Differentials in the Labour Market, In G. Psacharopoulos and Tzannatos (eds.), *Women's Employment and Pay in Latin America,* Report No 10,Latin America Caribbean Technical Department, World Bank, Washington DC.

Waring, M. (1988), *If Women Counted: A New Feminist Economics*, Harper and Row, New York.

World Bank (1995), *Toward Gender Equality: The Role of Public Policy,* World Bank, Washington DC.

6

VALUES AND WITHIN NATION INEQUALITY

William R. DiPietro

INTRODUCTION

Ever since Margaret Meade, cultural anthropologists have placed great emphasis on cultural differences as a major determinant of differences in human behavior. Despite the findings of evolutionary psychology on the similarity of human beings across cultures, there is still more than sufficient room for variation in behavior due to cultural factors. Now, different cultures are likely to produce different sets of values. They are also likely to generate different attitudes and tolerance toward inequality. The primary purpose of this paper is to use cross country regression analysis to test to see whether four important values; namely, the value of family, the value of leisure, the value of religion, and value of work, are associated with income inequality.

If an association between values and inequality exists, a secondary objective is to assess the signs of the association. The signs are important with regard to policy and with respect to appraising the desirability of a country's institutions. In general, one would like to have a negative association between desirable values and inequality. If there is a positive association between a desired value and inequality, then, within a given institutional setting, efforts to reduce inequality will lead to a reduction in the desired value. This is not a very a good situation. Indeed, positive associations between desired values and inequality might be one of the underlying sources of trade-offs on the macro scene between such things as economic growth and equality. Positive associations between desired values and inequality can be considered red flags. They point to the need for institutional adjustments, modifications, and changes to make equality and desirable values more compatible.

This paper is divided into five small sections. The first section discusses the weight of income inequality and heuristically explains why it is likely to be associated with values. The second section outlines the data sources for inequality and value that are subsequently employed in the regression analysis of the third section. The next section, the third section, is the central part of the paper. It presents the results of cross-country regressions of inequality on four different values. The fourth section renders a bit of follow up to the third section. It conjectures on possible reasons for the observed signs of the coefficients of the value coefficients in the regression equations. The last, the fifth and final section concludes.

THE GRAVITY OF INEQUALTIY:ITS POTENTIAL ASSOCIATION WITH VALUES

The amount of inequality within nations is very important. On strictly humanitarian grounds, reducing inequality within nations can lead to greater welfare for less advantaged individuals situated on society's lower rungs. On stability grounds, lower levels of inequality inside nations may lead to reduced discontent, to lessened social unrest, and, in general, to a diminished likelihood of social and political upheaval. With regard to the political organization, greater inequality within nations, because of the imbedded asymmetry in power between rich and poor that inequality intrinsically entails, is likely to be at odds with the operation and proper functioning of true democracy.

During the last couple of decades, within country inequality has become a greater and greater factor relative to between countries inequalities in contributing to total worldwide inequality. This reverses the trend since the industrial revolution. It is, therefore, an auspicious time to focus on within country inequality. Trying to uncover some of the sources for differences in within country inequality is a most worthwhile endeavor.

Why might inequality and values be interrelated? From a simple common sense point of view, it seems natural that a possible reason for differences in within country inequality between nations is differences in values. Different countries have different cultures. These alternative cultures foster, inculcate, and internalize different sets of values in individuals that lead to different societal outcomes. In its turn, differences in income inequality could lead to different values. For instance, it may be that a highly unequal hierarchical society would tend to place a higher value on obedience.

From a strict economic viewpoint, there is also reason for expecting a possible relationship to exist between values and inequality.

Bowles, Gintis, and Osborne (2001) suggest that in disequilibrium labour markets nontraditional traits not directly related to the production process may be responsible for capturing quasi rents leading to dispersion of wages across individuals with similar productive skills in the very same occupation.

A potential test for the validity of this theory is to look at the divergence of within country inequality across countries to see whether or not these nonproductive traits are statistically important in deterring differences in within country wage inequality across nations. If this behavioral theory is true then at least part of the differences in the observed within country inequality of earnings across countries should be attributable to differences in these traits. In addition, while we will not test this proposition here, if behavioral theory is true, then one would expect the strength of the relationship between traits and earnings to be stronger (weaker the higher the level of development) the lower the level of economic development. If nonproductive traits are important for explaining divergence in earnings in the efficient markets of developed countries, then they will be even more responsible for explaining earnings divergence in the poorly functioning markets of developing countries that are far more prone to disequilibrium operation.

DATA SOURCE

In order to run cross-country regressions of country inequality on country values, a data set consisting of measures of values and inequality needs to be constructed.

Measures of the value placed on family, leisure, religion and work are based on questions taken from the 1990-93 World Value Survey of the University of Michigan (Inglehart *et al.* 1998). The survey provides representative samples for over forty societies. In response to each of the four questions, how important is family in your life? How important is leisure in your life? How important is religion in your life? And how important is work in your life, there are four possible responses. They are very important, fairly important, not very important, and not at all important. For each of the four values, the measure of value used is the percentage of respondents answering very important to the appropriate question.

The measure of within country inequality comes from the University of Texas inequality project. Based on earnings data from manufacturing, they compute a Theil index of inequality across industries for a whole host of countries on an annual basis from 1963 through 1997. Here, for each country, the average Theil index for the entire 1963-97 period is used as the measure of inequality.

CROSS COUNTRY REGRESSIONS OF INEQUALITY ON VALUES

Table 1 shows the results of cross country regressions of within country inequality as measured by the average Theil index from 1964-97 on the value of family, the value of leisure, the value of religion and the value of work from the 1990-93 World Value Survey.

The first column of table 1 list the names of the independent variables (the values) while the second and third column show the outcomes of a regression run. Each cell in the center of the table contains the estimated coefficient as the uppermost value with the individual t-statistic underneath in parenthesis. If a variable is significant at the one per cent level of significance or better in an equation then it is given one asterisk. If it is significant at the five per cent level of significance or better then it is given two asterisks. Finally, if it is significant at the ten per cent level of significance or better then it is given three asterisks. The second to last row show the r-squared value for an equation and the last row the number of observations (countries) entering an equation.

Table 1
Cross Country Regressions of within Country Inequality on Country Values

	(1)	(2)
Constant	.0911(1.756)***	.0979(1.790)***
Family	-.0022(-2.784)**	-.0018(-2.259)**
Leisure	.0013(2.783)**	.0012(2.539)**
Religion	.0011(3.435)*	.0014(4.821)*
Work	.0008(1.698)	
RSQ	.692	.633
N	20	20

The first equation runs each of the four values on the measure of within country inequality, the average Theil index across manufacturing industries from 1963-97. The second equation is the same as the first except that it leaves out the least significant variable in the first equation, the importance of work. Looking at the first equation, with the exception of work, all the values used as variables are significant at the five per cent level or better. Work itself is nearly significant at the ten per cent level of significance. Taken together, all four values explain nearly seventy per cent of the variation in within country inequality across countries. Leisure, religion, and work are found to be positively associated with within country inequality while family is found to be negatively associated with within country inequality. That is to say, according to the results, countries that place a higher value on leisure, religion or work tend to experience greater within country inequality, while courtiers that attribute greater importance to family tend to have lower levels of within country inequality.

Similar results are obtained when work is excluded as a variable in second equation. Once again, the values of leisure and religion are positively associated with inequality while the value of family is negatively associated with inequality.

While the number of observations is small, overall, the results tend to confirm the hypothesis of the existence of an association between inequality and values. When all four values are included, together they account for almost seventy per cent of the variation in inequality across countries.

POSSIBLE REASONS FOR THE TYPE OF RELATIONSHIPS BETWEEN THE VARIOUS VALUES AND INEQUALTIY

What sense can be made of the signs between inequality and the value variables? First, in each case it is not clear weather the causation runs from differences in values to differences in inequality or from differences in inequality to differences in values or some combination of the two. Second, it should be noted that since most countries have achieved at least a minimum threshold level of inequality so that the highest income groups represents a very small portion of the total population of a country, that the answers to the value questions are likely to be more representative of the other (the poorer) income groups. Keeping this in mind, what stories can be made up to explain the association between the inequality and the different values? Individually, let's consider each of the four values.

Why might it be that societies that place a greater value on leisure have greater inequality, or, if one considers the causation going in the reverse direction, that greater inequality tends to generate societies that value leisure? First, if the causation happens to run from values to inequality, then it may be that the more poorer working classes values leisure the less effort they are willing to put forth into finding work and, once they are gainfully employed, reduced effort on the job proper. On the other hand, looking at the causation running from greater inequality to higher value of leisure, from the perspective of poorer citizens it may be that higher inequality is coupled with (if not partially caused by) greater involuntary unemployment, so that they simply make a virtue out of a condition in which they are subject but have no control. In addition, from the perspective of the richer citizens, increased inequality may make leisure more valuable, either as a conspicuous consumption good or simply because it is a superior good that complements other goods Greater inequality may also conceivably lead the poor to greater idolization or desired emulation of the rich with the internalization of some of their values such as the high valuation of leisure.

What about the positive association between inequality and religious value? From the perspective of the poorer population, and with the causation going from greater inequality to higher value of religion, higher inequality makes the condition of this world more and more unfavorable and the chances of success in material terms less and less likely. As hope never dies, the bleakness of life in the present world is endured with the hope of a better life in the next. On the other hand, it may be that the high religious value, that places high value on the next world and smaller value on the present one, results in diminished desire, effort, and energy by the mass of people for improving material conditions of the present passing world.

Turning to the value of work, the results show a positive association between inequality and work value. They indicate that greater inequality is associated with higher value of work. Looking at the causation going from work value to inequality, some might maintain that the positive sign is hard to rationalize. They might argue that increased value on work would naturally lead to greater work effort, greater worker discipline, and higher productivity, resulting in greater growth and reduced, not increased, inequality. However, a more plausible interpretation may be that the increased worker discipline caused by higher value placed on work simply allows workers to be more easily and readily exploited causing a shift in the distribution of income from labour to capital with a consequent increase in inequality. The positive sign between inequality and work value can also be explained if the causation goes from inequality to work value. Lower wages, greater inequality, and difficulty finding employment are likely to lead to a higher premium on work by individuals subject to these conditions. In passing, it might be noted that the positive sign on work and on leisure are not necessarily inconsistent. One could at the same time value the leisure you have and value the job you do not have.

The last sign to consider, the negative sign on inequality and value of family, is rather baffling. Considering the causation to go from inequality to family value, it would be easy to reconcile a *positive* sign. One might argue that people who are denied material goods might reorient ate their value system to value people over goods. But the association between inequality and family value is found to be negative not positive. This could be the case if placing a high value on family is an indication of greater time preference. This might lead to greater savings and accumulation of capital for the poor leading to lessened inequality for future generations. On the other hand, if the causation runs from inequality to family, then it may simply be that for the poor the pressures of inequality of income places a powerful disintegrating effect on family cohesion.

CONCLUSION

The evidence from cross-country regression analysis indicates that there is an association between a country's inequality and its values. Within country inequality is found to be positively associated with the value placed by its citizens on leisure, religion, and work, and negatively associated with the value they place on family. Speculation was made as to the reason for the type of the relationship (positive or negative) between each of the four values considered and inequality. This was carried out both under the assumption that causation runs from inequality to value formation and under the assumption that causation goes in the reverse direction from values to inequality.

The existence of an association, the type of association, and direction of the association certainly matter with regard to social justice, the functioning of society, and public policy. In general, if the causation runs from values to inequality, then one would like there to be a negative relationship between a desirable value and inequality. That is to say, one would like to see a state of affairs for which higher levels of a desirable value lead to reduced inequality and not to increased inequality. If the causation runs from values to inequality, then a positive relationship between a value and inequality is a potential indictment on the institutional and policy setting. For instance, if a higher value on work, which is likely to lead to a greater work effort, causes greater inequality, then it would most definitely seem that something is not right and needs to be rectified in the structure of the social environment.

REFERENCES

Bowles, S., Gintis, H. and Osborne, M. (2001), The Determinants of Earnings: A Behavioral Approach, *Journal of Economic Literature*, 39(4): 1137-1176.

Inglehart, R., Basanez, M. and Moreno, A. (1998), *Human Values and Beliefs: A Cross-Cultural Sourcebook: Political, Religious, Sexual, and Economic Norms in 43 Societies: Findings from 1990-93 World Value Survey*, University of Michigan Press, Ann Arbor.

7

DYNAMIC AND CONSEQUENCES OF POPULATION AGEING: A COMPARATIVE INTER-REGIONAL PERSPECTIVE OF ASIAN ECONOMICS

K. Muraleedharan

INTRODUCTION

The greatest twin victory of humanity over health issues has delivered one of the greatest challenges to man: population ageing. Often described as 'Fluidization of the World', population ageing is the outcome of man's victory over death and deceases as well as unwanted child bearing (Peterson 2001). Population ageing-the process by which older individuals become proportionally larger share of the total population- is, in fact, one of the most distinctive demographic challenges the world ever has faced in 20th century and will remain in focus in 21st century as well. Initially experienced by the more developed countries, the process has recently become apparent in much of the developing world. According to the U.N. Reports on Population and Ageing released in 2003, for the near future, virtually all countries will encounter problems arising from population ageing, at varying levels of intensity and in different time frames.

An inevitable consequence of demographic transition and shift to lower fertility and mortality has been the evolution in the age structure of the world population towards higher ages. Most of the societies, especially in the more developed regions, have already attained older population age structures than have ever seen in the past, as observed by Mirking, Beth and Weinberger (2001). The consequences of the process of population ageing are diverse in different settings, particularly with respect to pattern and timing. Population ageing that evolves silently over the long term, producing consequences that are difficult to anticipate, is also a process unknown and new so far, as there are no previous historical experiences.

Though initially the developed economies are to face the challenges of population ageing, in the coming decades, as it occurs in less developed regions, they have to encounter the acute problems associated with it. Asia will have to host more than 60 per cent of the aged population in the next half a century. Population ageing, as a demographic phenomenon, is not merely a question of excessive growth and concentration of old aged population. The shift in age structure associated with population ageing has a profound impact on a broad range of economic, political and social conditions (United Nations 2002). It has wider and deeper consequences with policy implications. Public policy in the developing economies has to be geared to address and accommodate the problems of the aged population. A fair understanding of the dynamics, determinants and consequences population ageing is an essential constraint for policy formation. This paper is an attempt in this regard from a comparative perspective of Asian Region. The paper is organized in five parts. The first part has introduced the problem, explained the methodology and database and examined the global scenario of population ageing while the second part has looked in to the dynamics and determinants of it. The third part has focused the problem of population ageing in the Asian sub-continent from a comparative inter-regional perspective and the fourth part on the consequences and policy implications of the issue while the last part has concluded the discussion.

The study has drawn enormously from the various issues of U.N. Reports of Population and reports of ILO and World Bank .The study has used data related to 50 years from 1950 on various aspects of Population and U.N. Projections on various aspects of population and ageing from 2000 to 2050. Asian sub-continent is divided in to four regions such as Eastern Asia, South Central Asia, South Eastern Asia and Western Asia following the classification of U.N Reports on population periodically published.

THE GLOBAL SCENARIO

The global scenario emerging from the UN Reports on Population Ageing presents a dismal picture for the less developed economies, particularly for the Asian economies, during the coming decades. The number of persons aged 60 years or above in the world is estimated to be 605 million in 2000, which is expected to grow to nearly 2 billion by 2050, by when it will be as large as the population of children (0-14 years). Persons aged 60 or more comprised 10 per cent of the world population in 2000. The proportion of old aged is much higher in the more developed regions (20 per cent) than in less developed regions (8 per cent), which are in the earlier stages of demographic transition. It is estimated that by 2050, the older aged persons will make up a projected 22 per cent of the world population. Out of which 33 per cent will be in the more developed regions, 21 per cent in the less developed regions and 12 per cent in the least developed regions. The region wise picture of the old age population shows that the majority of the world's aged population resides in Asia (53 per cent), followed by Europe (24 per cent). It is predicted that Asia's relative share of the older population will show an increase to 63 per cent, while that of Europe will decrease to 11 per cent by 2050. In other words, while the developed economies are slowly getting relieved from the grip of ageing, the developing economies will be moving to the stronghold of it.

A clearer picture of global scenario will be emerging from the account of relative shares of the population aged above

60 in these regions. The major trends in the process of ageing are that the less developed regions will have to share more than 80 per cent of the population above 60 years of age, while the developed and least developed regions will have much a minor share. Aged population is to increase in the less developed regions, least developed regions, Asia, Africa, Latin America and the Caribbean and Northern America. Asia, as the single continent, will have the largest share of population above 60 years i.e., more than 60 per cent.

THE DYNAMICS

The pattern, the timing and intensity of population ageing vary regionally. An analysis of its dynamics, trends and determinants will be useful for capturing a clear insight of the phenomenon under study. The dynamics of population ageing is analyzed, in this study, using:

(a) Growth of population aged above 60 years
(b) Rate of growth population aged above 60 compared to that of total population.
(c) Rate of growth of old aged population in more developed and less developed regions.

The general trend surfacing from the global population data and projects can be summarized as follows.

- Firs, the number of older persons has tripled over the last 50 years and will be more than triple over the next 50 years.
- Secondly, there is the faster growth rate of older population as a group compared to that of total population.
- The regional variations will exhibit a different pattern by the mid century.

THE ASIAN PERSPECTIVE

As mentioned earlier, around 63 per cent of the aged above 60 will be residing in Asia by 2050. This fact alone warrants a detailed analysis of the process of ageing from the perspective of Asia. The dynamics of population ageing is analyzed in terms of regions such as Eastern Asia, South Central Asia, South Eastern Asia and Western Asia, as permitted by the available data on various aspects of the process of Population ageing. The percentage of population above 60, in Asia and in all the regions, has been below the global level, during the1950s. Eastern and Central Asia have shown the above average percentage of aged population even at that period. By 2050 Eastern Asia, comprising

Table 1
Percentage of Population above 60 Years in Asian Regions 1950-2050

Region	*1950*	*1975*	*2000*	*2025*	*2050*
World	8.2	8.6	10	15	21.1
Asia	6.8	6.6	8.8	14.7	22.6
Eastern Asia	7.4	7.4	11.3	20.5	30.7
South Central Asia	6.1	6.1	7.1	11.1	18.7
South Eastern Asia	6	5.7	7.1	12.7	22
Western Asia	7.1	6.5	7.1	10.4	15.6

Source: World Population Ageing 1950-2050, DESA, United Nations [2002].

China and Japan will have the highest percentage of Population above 60 or older. (30.7). The South Central Asian region will have the third place with 22 per cent of population above 60 or older in 2050 (See Table 1 and Figure 1). A detailed analysis of region wise share of population above 60, out of the total population, during these periods will make the picture clearer. Eastern Asia comprising China, Korea, Japan, Mongolia and Republic of Korea had the largest share of aged population since the 1950s. Simultaneously, the share of South Central Asia and South Eastern Asia has been increasing since 1950s. According to the projections, the current trends of the process of ageing shows that the Eastern Asia will have four to five older persons out of every 10 in Asia and South Central Asia will have more than three, by the year 2050 (See Table 2 and Figure 2). It is clear that the Eastern Asia will be the major area contributing more towards aged population in the coming decades.

Figure 1: Percentage of Population above 60 years in Asian Region 1950-2050

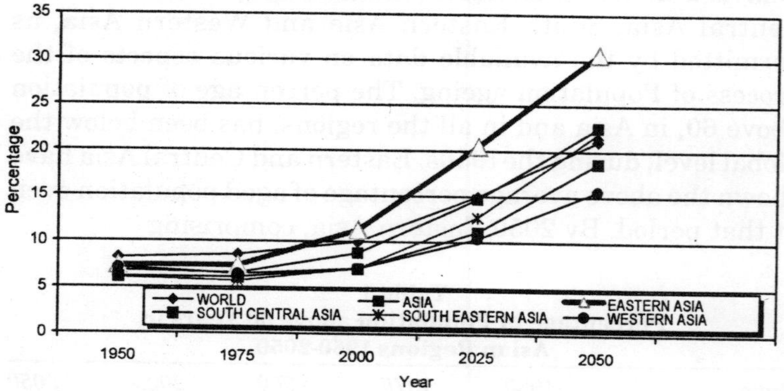

Table 2
Percentage Share of Asian Regions in Total Population above 60 during 1950-2050

Regions	*1950*	*1975*	*2000*	*2025*	*2050*
Eastern Asia	52.66	50.86	51.78	49.92	42.06
South Central Asia	32.20	33.63	32.61	33.12	38.02
South Eastern Asia	11.32	11.48	11.47	12.52	14.49
Western Asia	3.78	4.02	4.14	4.44	5.44
Total	100.00	100.00	100.00	100.00	100.00

Source: Compiled from World Population Ageing 1950-2050, DESA, United Nations [2002].

Figure 2: Percentage Share of Population above 60 in Asian Regions 1950-2050

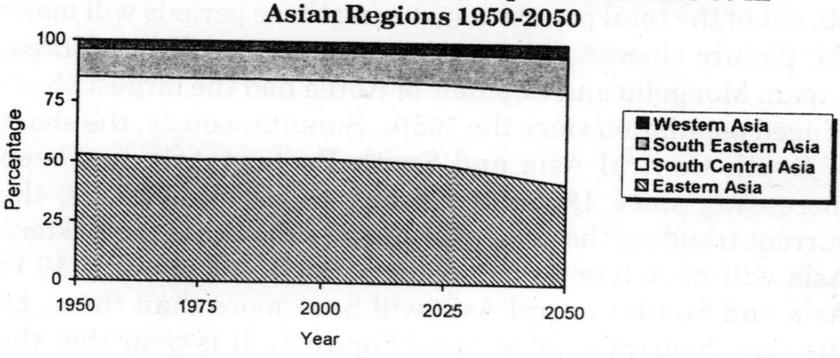

As far as the global phenomenon of population ageing is concerned, one of the major trends is the high growth rate of population above 60 years or more compared to that of total population. In the Asian context also this is true. Since 1950s onwards, the growth rate of the population above 60 years is greater than that of the total population and is projected to be so till 2050. The regional perspective of these trends is provided in the Table 3. As it can be seen from Table 3 and Figure 3 to 7, the regions present heterogeneous trends in the relation between rate of growth of above 60 populations and total population. While the regions such as Eastern Asia, South Central Asia and South Eastern Asia present common trends of higher growth rate of older population during the period from 1950 to 2050 throughout, the South Eastern Asia and Western Asia exhibit a different trend. In the case of South Eastern Asia and Western Asia rate of growth of old aged population began to exceed that of total population by 1975 and 2000 respectively. What is striking is that the projected growth rates of the population above 60 for the period 2025 and 2050 will be much higher than, even 5 times, that of total population. In the case of Eastern Asia, with the largest share of old aged population, the growth rate of population above 60 is more than twice that of total population. The difference is highest in the case of South Eastern Asia, which has a growth rate of older population five times greater than that of total population.

Table 3
Growth Rate of Population above 60 and Total Population during 1950-2050

Regions	*1950*		*1975*		*2000*		*2025*		*2050*	
	Total	*60 +*	*Total*	*60+*	*Total*	*60+*	*Total*	*60+*	*Total*	*60+*
Asia	1.9	1.8	1.9	2.6	1.3	2.4	0.7	3.3	0.3	1.7
Eastern Asia	1.8	2.1	1.4	2.8	0.7	2.3	0.2	3.3	0.3	0.7
South Central Asia	2.0	1.5	2.2	2.6	1.7	2.6	1.0	3.2	0.6	2.6
South Eastern Asia	2.1	1.0	2.2	2.4	1.4	2.7	0.8	3.7	0.4	2.0
Western Asia	2.6	1.7	2.7	1.5	2.1	2.5	1.6	3.2	1.1	2.4

Source: Compiled from World Population Ageing 1950-2050, DESA, United Nations [2002].

Figure 3: Growth Rate of Total Population and Population above 60 in Asia

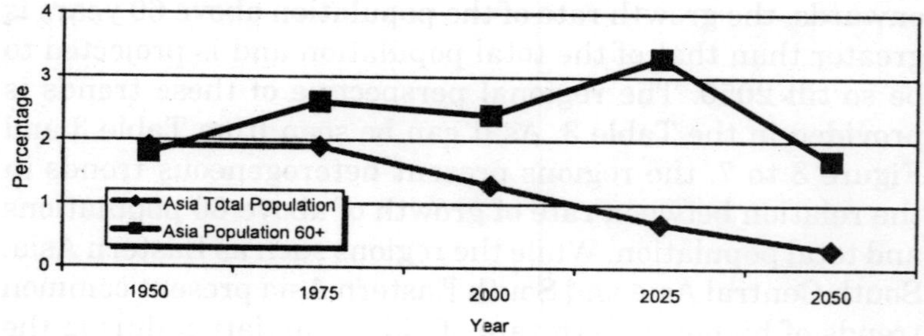

Figure 4: Growth Rate Total Population and Population above 60 in East Asia

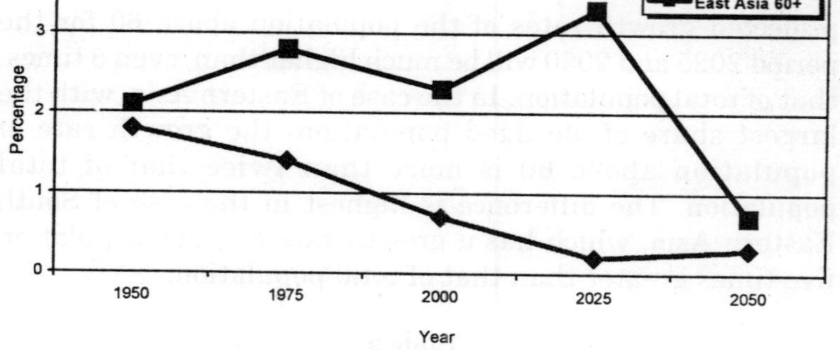

Figure 5: Growth Rate of Total Population and Population above 60 in South Central Asia

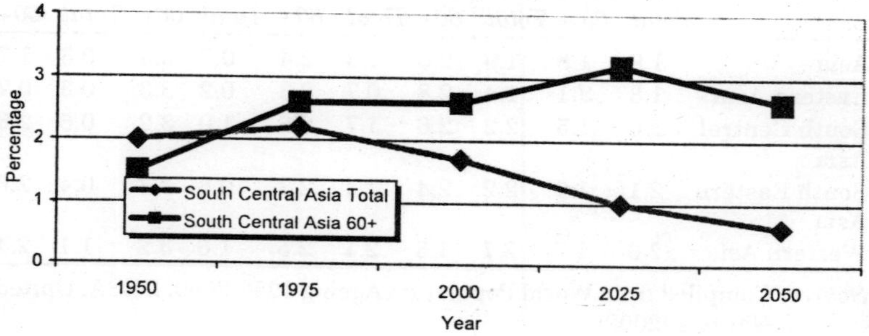

Figure 6: Growth Rate of Total Population and Population above 60 in South Eastern Asia

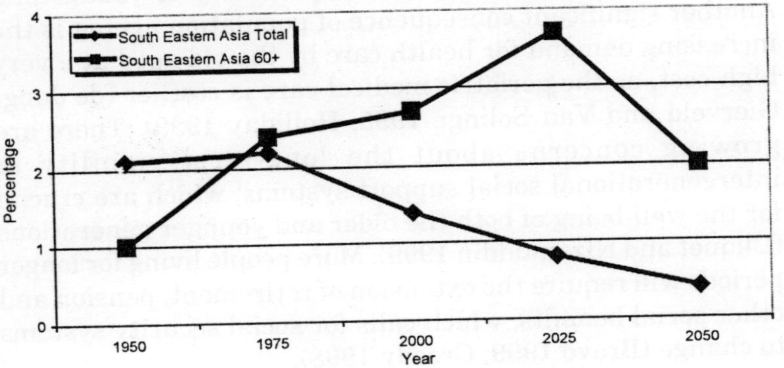

Figure 7: Growth Rate of Total Population and Population above 60 in Western Asia

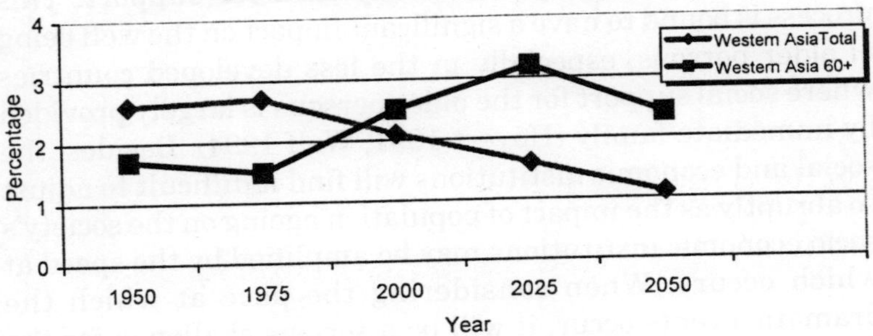

CONSEQUENCE AND POLICY IMPLICATION

Population ageing, provokes academic interest due to the consequences and wide impact, it has on the family, economy and society. The shift in age structure associated with population ageing is about to create a profound impact on a broad range of economic, political and social conditions. First, and foremost it will disturb the balance between various age groups in an economy. Reduction in birth rates and consequent decrease in the strength of healthy younger generation will result in the shortage of labour force that contributes towards national output. Population ageing will reduce the number of younger generations who can contribute productively towards the nation and economy, leaving a large number of older people at the dependency of youngsters. Another significant consequence of population ageing is the increasing demand for health care by the old aged at a very high cost, as the geriatric medical care is costlier (de Jong-Gierveld and Van Solinge 1995; Holliday 1999). There are growing concerns about the long-term viability of intergenerational social support systems, which are crucial for the well-being of both the older and younger generations (Cliquet and Nizamuddin 1999). More people living for longer periods will require the extension of retirement, pension and other social benefits, which calls for social security systems to change (Bravo 1999; Creedy 1998).

An important consequence of fertility decline is the progressive reduction in the availability of kin to whom future generations of older persons may turn for support. This process is bound to have a significant impact on the well being of older persons, especially in the less developed countries where social support for the older persons is largely provided by immediate family (Hoyert 1991; Wolf 1994). Besides, the social and economic institutions will find it difficult to adjust so abruptly as the impact of population ageing on the society's socio economic institutions may be amplified by the speed at which occurs. When considering the pace at which the dramatic events occur, it will be a serious challenge for the social and economic institutions to adjust. Increasing proportion of the older ages necessarily affects the relative importance of the other segments. These changes in age composition can dramatically affect society's political, economic and social structures. The need for change in pattern of resource distribution and use will be an imperative and there will be intergenerational conflict (Walker 1990; Jackson 1998). The need for support to old aged will be on the increase as a consequence of shift in the population to higher ages structures. Support to old aged is only partly provided through public transfer of resources and the family remains an important source of support to older persons, especially in the less developed regions (United Nations 1994). Population ageing will create a situation in which the young is increasingly in a compelled position to provide care and support, all sorts of support including medical as well as physical, to the old aged in the family. This may perhaps operate as a resource drain on the part of the earning member, due to the reasons mentioned earlier like the higher cost of geriatric medical care. Rapid growth of the oldest group among the older population is of special relevance in terms of public policy as it will create a long-term demand for health and other care systems (Crimmins 1997; Pollard 1995).

The gender dimension of Population ageing is another issue that needs to be focused in public policy. Since mortality rates are usually higher among the male population, even at older ages the percentage of female tends to increase with advancing age. In most countries older women even now outnumber older men, and most of them are widows, with less education, less work experience, and less access to public assistance and other private income sources (Higuchi 1996; United Nations 1999). Hence, while designing public policy due concern towards this segment of older population must be provided.

Another significant impact of the population ageing is to be reflected in the areas of labour force participation and literacy. As Gruber and Wise (1999) observed, in the more developed regions, where social security coverage is nearly universal, decline in labour force participation at older ages primarily reflect changes in public policies regarding early retirement. On the other hand, in the less developed regions, there is large concentrations of old aged population in the agricultural and informal sectors, who have little or no social security coverage. But, lower levels of labour force participation, both in the more and less developed regions, are partly associated with shortage of employment opportunities and obsolescence of skills and knowledge (Drury 1994; Taylor and Walker 1996). As far as literacy of the older generations are concerned, generally in the less developed regions, illiteracy is much high among the older generations. Public policy needs to be geared in such a way that the literacy levels of the older populations be enhanced so that higher levels of literacy among the older generations are substantially to affect their needs, interests and attitude to life as well as will improve their quality of lives.

CONCLUSION

Population Ageing, the inevitable consequence of development gains in the health sector, has emerged as a development challenge, for both developed and developing economies. In fact, it appears to be a tough and formidable challenge to the less developed regions, as it calls for a reversal of several public policies in the context of retreating State and cutting down of welfare and social security measures. The speed and dynamics as well as pattern and timing of population ageing in the developing regions are comparatively different from that of developed regions. One of the major determining factors of population ageing is the sharp decline in fertility that occurred faster in the developing regions. Another factors contributing for the increased number of older people is the gains in life expectancy and consequent mortality rates throughout the world, particularly in the developing world. Asia will be the home of more than 60 per cent of the above 60-year-old population in the coming decades. In the first part of the paper the global scenario of Population Ageing has been examined during the period from 1950 to 2050. It has clearly brought out the regional variation in the pattern, timing and intensity of population ageing. Population ageing, emerged in the more developed regions at an early stage will be moving to the less developed regions with high intensity, placing heavy burdens on them in terms of health care, social security measures and public policy to address the aged. The less developed regions will have higher concentrations of old aged in the coming decades; while the share of more developed regions will be on the decrease. The second part has examined the dynamics and determinants of population ageing from a global perspective. The general trends and determinants of population ageing have been analyzed. The declining fertility, mortality and enhanced life expectancy has been the major determinants of population ageing. One of the major trends in the process is that the growth rates of old aged are much higher than that of total population everywhere. The gender dimension of population ageing calls for special packages and policy designs needed for the increasing female aged in the less developed regions. The third part has examined the consequences and policy implications of the process of population ageing. Population ageing, the unprecedented shift in age structures towards older ages will send unexpected shocks and tremors so far unheard of in the economy. The impact will be profound on a broad range of economic, political, and social conditions and the situation emerging will call for revision and further designing of public policy in the less developed regions. In the fourth part, the region wise picture of the trends and dynamics of population ageing in Asia has been attempted. Eastern Asia, comprising China and Japan, will have to host the largest concentrations of older populations in the coming decades. South Central Asia, in which India is included, will be the second largest host of aged population. Both in the rate of growth of older aged populations compared to total population and concentration of them, these regions stands out.

The next few decades will see the increasing concentration of older generations in the Asian sub continent. On the average one to two out of every five will be above 60 in Asia by 2050. The economies in Asia will have to gear their public policy to address the older generations. At present a few economies and governments have a definite policy and well-organized system to take care of the largest single segment of the aged population. One of the most serious issues the governments will face is the question of support systems required for these older generations. Changing social setup from the agro oriented co-family living to nuclear families results in the loosing the familial support to the old aged people. Increased labour force participation by women in formal and informal sectors has resulted in the loss of presence of women, the ultimate caregiver, in the family.

Migration to the urban and semi-urban areas for employment and better opportunities also accentuates this phenomenon as it forces the youngsters to leave their ancestral homes at their native places with their parents. Even at the urban-based nuclear families, since both the husband and wife have to go out in search of bread, the parents and old aged people living with them are in deep and sustaining agony. All these results in old aged people left uncared and unwanted at homes either in the concrete jungles of urban areas or deserted homes at the rural areas. Now a day, they live as helpless witnesses as well as victims of fast changing world, marginalized and relegated from the mainstream. One of the most serious and significant challenges the Asian economies, particularly China and India, will have to face during the coming decades, is the question of designing an effective public policy to address the problems of old aged population.

NOTES

The terms 'aged' and 'old aged', in this study, refer to those above 60 years of age, unless otherwise specified.

REFERENCES

Bravo, J. (1999), Fiscal Implications of Ageing Societies Regarding Public and Private Pension Systems, In R. Cliquet and M.Nizamuddin (eds.), *Population Ageing: Challenges for Policies and Programmes in Developed and Developing Countries,* United Nations Population Fund; and Centrum voor Bevolkings-en Gezinsstudien (CBGS), New York and Brussels.

Creedy, J. (1998), *Pensions and Population Ageing: An Economic Analysis,* Edward Elgar Publishing, Cheltenham, United Kingdom and Northampton, Massachusetts.

Crimmins, E. (1997), *Trends in Mortality, Morbidity, and Disability: What should we Expect for the Future of our Ageing Population,* In International Population Conference, Beijing, 1997, Vol. 1, Leiege, International Union for the Scientific Study of Population. (IUSSP), Belgium.

Cliquet R. and Nizamuddin, M. (eds.) (1999), *Population Ageing: Challenges for Policies and Programmes in Developed and*

Developing Countries, United Nations Population Fund; and Centrum voor Bevolkings-en Gezinsstudien (CBGS), New York and Brussels.

De Jong-Gierveld, J. and H. van Solinge (1995), *Ageing and its Consequences for the Socio Medical System,* Population Studies No. 29, Council of Europe Press, Strasburg, France.

Drury, E. (1994), Age Discrimination against older Workers in the European Union, In *Studies on the Four Pillars,* Issues and Practice No.73, Geneva Papers on Risk and Insurance.

Gruber, Jonathan and David. A. Wise (eds) (1999), *Social Security and Retirement around the World,* University of Chicago Press, Chicago, Illinois.

Higuchi, K. (1996), Women in an Ageing Society, In *Added Years of Life in Asia: Current Situation and Future Challenges,* Asian Population Studies Series, No.141, Economic Commission for Asia and the Pacific, Bangkok.

Hoyert, D.L. (1991), Financial and Household Exchanges between Generations, *Research on Ageing,* 13(2).

Holliday, R. (1999), Ageing in 21st Century, *The Lancet,* (December) 354 (Supplement 4).

Jackson, W.A. (1998), *Political Economy of Population Ageing,* Edward Elgar Publishing, Cheltenham, United Kingdom and Northampton, Massachusetts.

Mirking, Beth and Weinberger (2001), The Demography of Population Ageing, In *Living Arrangements of Older Persons: Critical Issue and Policy Responses,* Population Bulletin of the United Nations, Special Issue Nos. 42/43.

Peterson, Peter (2001), Quoted in the Preface of *Living Arrangements of Older Persons: Critical Issue and Policy Responses,* Population Bulletin of the United Nations, Special Issue Nos.42/43 2001.

Pollard, J.H (1995), Long-term Care in Selected Countries: Demographic and Insurance Perspectives, *Zeitschrift fur Bevolkenrungswissenschaft,* 20(3).

Tailor, P.E. and A. Walker (1996), Intergenerational Relations in the Labour Market: the Attitudes of Employees and Older Workers, In A. Walker (ed), *The New Generational Contract, Intergenerational Relations, Old Age and Welfare,* University College London Press, London.

United Nations (1994), *Ageing and the Family,* Proceedings of United Nations Inter national conference on Ageing Populations in the Context of the Family, Kitakyushu, Japan, 15-19 October 1990.

United Nations (1999), *Ageing in a Gendered World: Women's Issues and Identities,* INSTRAW.

United Nations (2001), *Inter National Strategy for Action of Ageing 2002,* Draft Text Proposed by the Chairman of the Commission for Social Development acting as the Preparatory Committee for the Second World Assembly on Ageing as its Resumed first Session, New York.

United Nations (2002), *World Population Ageing 1950-2050,* Department of Economic and Social Affairs, United Nations, New York.

Walker, A. (1990), The Economic 'Burden' of Ageing and the Prospect of Intergenerational Conflict, *Ageing and Society,* 10 (4).

Wolf, D.A. (1994), The Elderly and their Kin: Patterns of Availability and Access, In L.G. Martin and S.H. Preston (eds.), *Demography of Ageing,* National Academy Press, Washington DC.

8

GENDER DIFFERENTIALS IN POVERTY

BOITUMELO D. MMOLAWA

INTRODUCTION

Todaro (1994) has observed that in poor communities in the third world women and children experience the harshest deprivation. Furthermore women and children are more likely to be poor and malnourished and less likely to receive medical services, clean water, sanitation or other benefits. From a human poverty or capabilities perspective, women are poorer in most societies in many dimensions of capabilities such as education and health. Resource allocation within households is often biased against girls and women. It is harder for women to transform their capabilities into incomes or well-being. Gender inequalities in the distribution of income, access to productive inputs such as credit, command over property or control over earned income, as well as gender biases in labour markets and social exclusion that women experience in a variety of economic and political institutions form the basis for the greater vulnerability of women to chronic poverty. Across a wide range of cultures and levels of economic development, women tend to specialize in paid production activities. Women's combined paid and unpaid labour time is greater than men's (UNDP 1997). Although it is often stated that labour is the poor's most abundant asset, women are relatively time poor and much of their work is socially unrecognized since it is unpaid.

Women's responsibilities for reproductive labour limit the range of paid economic activities they can undertake. Women are less mobile than men because of their reproductive/caring labour activities and because of social norms that restrict their mobility in public. In the paid sphere, women tend to be concentrated in informal labour activities such as home working, since such activities allow them to combine paid work with unpaid reproductive labour. According to the prevalence of female-headed households and lower income contribute to this disturbing phenomenon. These factors combined ensure that women's financial resources are meager and unstable relative to men's.

FACTORS ASSOCIATED WITH GENDER DIFFERENTIALS

There are many factors that contribute to high incidence of female-headed households and their relatively poor economic position. The factors emphasized as contributing to poverty are different from one discipline to another. Economists have traditionally focused on wage or income differentials between male and female-headed households, education and formal employment. For demographers the emphasis has been on the incidence of marriages while the law discipline has looked at it from the legal status of women.

Some of the factors associated with gender differentials for the case of Botswana are as follows:

Income and Poverty

The income disparities between male-headed households (MHHs) and female-headed households (FHHs) can be explained by wage differences, which exist between males and females. The fact that women do not have easy access to formal employment in private companies or public organizations contributes to income disparities (Mmolawa 2002). Furthermore, as Siphambe (2000: 1) showed using data from the 1993/94 HIES that there is occupational segment of workers by gender in Botswana's labour market in that female workers are generally confined to narrow range of occupations(See also CSO 1999).

As it will be elaborate in the subsequent sections FHHs are also characterized by aspects which aggravate poverty such as larger households and more dependents, less education, more degree of vulnerability to unemployment and fewer assets.

According to the 2002/03 HIES the national mean monthly household disposable cash income was about P2127; that of MHHs was more (P2605) than that of FHHs (P1574). Across all the location and education strata, MHHs had higher mean disposable income than FHHs. For details see Table 1.

These trends are similar to the 1993/94 HIES findings. In that case the mean disposable cash income for MHHs was again higher (P1087) than that of FHHs (P532). For detail see Table 2.

Age of the Household Head

Advanced age appears to have a positive relationship with poverty in general. As Table 1 indicates, at national level, the mean disposable cash income reaches its peak (P2948) in the age group 40-49 years and declines (through age group 50-59 to 60+ years) to P1139. This seems to be the general trend across gender and location strata.

Assets

An asset may be defined as a valuable property that a person, household or company owns which can be used or sold to meet high expenses or pay debts. The poor, in this case, usually lacks assets as well as income. In local economies in which wealth and status come from land, disadvantaged households are typically land poor or landless. Other forms of assets may include houses, various types of cars and in rural areas even livestock especially cattle.

Female-headed households are normally disadvantaged in acquisition and ownership of assets because of their lower income status and cultural and legal systems related to ownership and inheritance of such assets.

Table 1
Mean Disposable Cash Income by Age of Household Head (2002-03)
(In Pula)

Age Group	*Cities / Town*		*Urban Villages*		*Rural Areas*		*National*		
	Male	*Female*	*Male*	*Female*	*Male*	*Female*	*Male*	*Female*	*Total*
<20	1271.86	1654.82	895.55	717.83	164.49	163.62	496.45	603.66	544.22
20-29	1989.28	1759.37	2201.81	1584.70	1005.72	912.78	1755.00	1462.99	1628.06
30-39	4423.98	2825.62	3312.73	2139.77	1527.15	1207.74	3164.63	2046.77	2648.60
40-49	6664.16	3228.42	3340.05	1939.69	1452.39	766.09	3923.05	1828.93	2947.94
50-59	5451.33	3583.62	2972.65	1851.34	1249.68	953.81	2820.71	1739.85	2338.22
60+	4367.18	2443.67	1803.91	1323.21	762.35	450.13	1376.88	901.94	1138.75
Total	4507.20	2694.96	2673.01	1732.93	1136.00	789.84	2604.99	1573.59	2126.62

Source: Adopted from 2002/03 HIES data, Central Statistics Office, CSO [2004:32] .

Table 2
Mean Disposable Cash Income by Age of the Household Head (1993-94)

Age of head	*Urban*		*Urban Village*		*Rural*		*National*	
	Male	*Female*	*Male*	*Female*	*Male*	*Female*	*Male*	*Female*
<30	1137.92	649.76	689.89	587.08	528.36	348.39	836.91	592.18
30-39	2241.33	947.65	1378.28	722.35	708.58	345.58	1674.29	659.34
40-49	2204.95	1255.94	1047.54	541.94	745.10	432.80	1352.39	673.43
50-59	2527.63	544.77	1197.29	449.11	452.82	261.90	1154.43	347.60
>60	1199.81	876.88	603.76	466.55	361.68	232.88	474.11	329.91
Total	1892.09	860.75	934.69	564.73	518.43	357.05	1087.03	532.03

Source: Adopted from the 1993/94 HIES data, Central Statistics Office.

According to calculations based on the 2002/03 HIES the poor have very limited assets. While for instance, about 60 per cent of some high income group households (earning P10000 or more) owned trucks and other types of motor-cars, negligible ratio of households earning less than P600 per month possessed similar combinations of cars.

Another illustration is based on ownership of cattle. Households owning 100 heads of cattle or more were essentially the rich. While about 5 per cent of households with disposable income of P10,000 or more possessed 100 heads of cattle or more almost none of the households earning less than P600 per month owned such heads of cattle (CSO 2004: 118, 120).

Employment Status

In general, the positive relationship between unemployment and income poverty is unquestionable. According to the 2002/03 HIES data the mean monthly disposable income for the heads of unemployed (those actively seeking work) is P820 compared to P3307 for heads of employees paid in cash (CSO 2004:104). That survey also indicates that the overall unemployment rate was 23.8 per cent. The unemployment rate for males and females were 21.4 and 26.3 per cent respectively. Across all regions, unemployment rates for females were higher than those for males (CSO 2004:2). These points lead to the females' vulnerability to poverty.

Education

The distribution of education to income and economic development is well documented in literature (Siphambe 2000:1). Thus households with uneducated or lowly educated heads are likely to be poorer than households with higher education level. As CSO (2004:12) summarizes the mean disposable incomes for households whose heads have never attended school, and those whose heads attended non-formal education, are consistently lower for all regions when compared to those whose heads attended formal education. The relatively poor position of females is reflected in the

Table 3
Households by Head's Level of Education, Income Groups, Gender and Stratum (National) in Percentages

Income Group 1	*Never Attended School*			*Non-formal*			*Primary*			*Secondary*			*Total*		
	T2	*M3*	*F4*	*T*	*M*	*F*	*T*	*M*	*F*	*T*	*M*	*F*	*T*	*M*	*F*
Low-income	81.7	76.3	84.5	70.2	69.5	81.5	62.8	54.0	71.1	37.3	31.2	44.6	59.4	46.7	66.3
Middle-income	17.5	23.0	14.6	29.0	29.9	17.5	34.2	42.0	26.8	49.4	49.3	49.6	35.2	38.3	33.7
High-income	0.8	0.7	0.9	0.8	0.6	1.0	3.0	4.0	2.1	13.3	19.5	5.8	5.9	8.4	3.0
Percentage Household	30.4	32.6	27.8	2.3	1.9	2.8	32.3	29.6	35.4	35.0	36.0	33.9	100	100	100
No. Households ('000)	120	69	51	9	4	5	127	63	65	138	76	62	394	211	183
Mean Disposable Income ('000)	1.2	1.2	1.0	1.3	1.4	1.1	1.9	2.2	1.5	4.1	5.1	2.9	2.4	2.9	1.9
Mean Household Size	5.1	4.8	5.4	5.0	4.9	5.0	4.5	4.2	4.7	3.0	3.0	3.0	4.0	4.0	4.0

Notes:(a) Low income group (0-1500), Middle income group (1501-8000), High income group (8000+) as defined by Central Statistics Office (CSO 2004)

(b)T= Total, M=Male and F=Female

Source: Computed by the author using 2002/03 HIES data, CSO [2004:102]

2002-03 HIES findings that there are more female heads with the highest level of education being primary school in all regions (CSO 2004:1) (see Table 3).

From Table 3 the following salient observations are in order;

- There is a positive relationship between education and income. Mean disposable income increases from about P1200 for households whose heads never attended school to P4100 for households whose heads reached secondary education.
- On average about 59 per cent of total households heads are in the low income groups: 47 per cent of the total male heads and 66 per cent of the total female heads are in that group.
- Only about 6 per cent of the total households are in the high-income group: 8 per cent of the total male heads and 3 per cent of the total female heads are in that group.
- About 82 per cent of the never attended school heads are in the low-income group: female heads being about 85 per cent of the total female heads.
- Only about 0.8 per cent of the never attended school heads are in the high-income group. Female heads being 0.9 per cent of the total female heads. About 37 per cent of heads who attended secondary school are in the low income group; 31 per cent of total male heads and 45 per cent of the total female heads are in that group. This is comparable to Mmolawa (2002) conclusion that heads of poor female households are generally better educated than poor MHHs. This may be because males in that group tend cattle and other activities.
- Only about 13 per cent of heads who attended secondary school are in the high-income group: about 20 per cent of the total male heads and 6 per cent of the total female heads are in that group.

Number of Dependants

Theory stipulates that poor people are usually characterized by large family sizes. This is so because they tend to invest in the number of children they have with the hope that these children will pull them out of poverty when they start working. In addition, even before they can earn income, children can free adults from various domestic tasks. Many poor families who are uneducated usually lack knowledge on family planning activities. According to World Bank (1990), many poor parents reported that they want no more children and their last child was unwanted. The family size along with extended families tends to increase the number of dependants for an individual that is earning income. On the gender front, both the 1993-94 and 2002-03 HIES female/headed households are characterized by large household sizes than male-headed households. This is largely because they are more attached to children. This characteristic points to females' vulnerability to poverty.

Summary of the Factors

The educational attainment by women is more concentrated on the end of the education ladder compared to men. This is mainly for developing countries. The implication is that higher levels of education obtained by men means a greater opportunity to earn higher incomes since education level and income have been found to be correlated.

Men are found to be more likely in formal employment than women. On the other hand, women tend to be self-employed in activities such as beer brewing and other hawking activities whose remunerations are not as high as income from formal employment. The combination of higher educational attainment and formal sector employment by men is found to contribute to higher incomes earned by men as compared to women. Normally female-headed households have more dependants and majority of these dependants are not working.

CONCLUSION

Based on the above, the following policies which may adjust the substantial poverty gap that exist between men and women could be adopted by many developing countries:

- The adult education scheme should be made in such a way that will encourage women to attain higher levels of education. This strategy should also be implemented in rural and remote areas. If adult education is well implemented, it will help women to get better formal employment; they will get better incomes and therefore be in a position to acquire assets. Consequently their poverty status would be improved.
- Government also needs to intensify family planning programmes so that women are given a range of existing options to choose from. Such an effort could contribute to reducing the number of dependants, which adversely affect poverty status.
- Quotas should be introduced in any financial assistance program, in such a way that more women are considered for the programme than men.
- Challenges for enhancing women's participation include making society aware that the rights of men and women are equal under the constitution and ensuring equal participation and representation by women in national and local government decision making bodies. Other challenges are to remove political, legal and economic barriers that have deprived women of equal opportunities with men and ensure that laws, policies and programmes are gender sensitive with proper monitoring and follow ups.

REFERENCES

CSO (Central Statistics Office) (1995,1999, 2004), *Household Income and Expenditure Survey Reports*, CSO, Botswana.

Mmolawa B.D. (2002), *Poverty and Demographic Structure of Households,* Unpublished BA dissertation, University of Botswana.

Siphambe H.K. (2000), Education and Labour Markets in Botswana, *Development Southern Africa*, 17 (1): 105-116.

UNDP (1997), *Human Development Report,* Oxford University Press.

World Bank (1990), *World Development Report*, World Bank, Washington DC.

Todaro, M. (1994), *Economic Development*, Longman Publishing, New York.

9

PROBLEMS OF GIRL CHILD LABOUR

R. MEENAKSHI

INTRODUCTION

Child labourers are those who are deprived of their rights to grow as children and are forced to work for a living. Encyclopedia of Social Sciences defines child labour as 'when the business of wage earning or of the participation in self or family support conflicts directly with the business of growth and education, the result is child labour'. The problem of child labour is not peculiar to India alone as it exists in England also even before the advent of industrial revolution. Karl Marx proclaims that the result of purchasing children at an immature age by the capitalists is not only a physical deterioration but also a social degeneration as well. Though employment of children is more or less a global phenomenon, its incidence is heaviest in South Asia. In these countries employment of child labour has become a conspicuous problem. Whether it is due to the need of assistance in the 'struggle for survival' of the poor families or inclination of employers due to comparative cheapness or many other reasons including less effective application of the preventive legal measures, children in a large number are forced to sell their prospects for petty gains. India stands first in sharing this social evil of child labour.

GENDER DISCRIMINATION

Gender discrimination among children is still continuing in the socio economic structure of India and the third world. Particularly in India, parents generally favour boys economically more than the girls. The economic value of girl child is enhanced further in India where social and cultural taboos restrict women from participating in paid work of family occupational works. In our society girl child is the daughter of denial in traditional culture and gender discrimination is conspicuous and appalling. She is the sad reflection of the society. The problem gets compounded in the case of employing girl children. The gender discrimination resulting in denial of right to those to be born and reduced opportunities for survival, development, protection and participation within the context of structural inequality make the girl child most vulnerable. The discrimination against the girl child is rather all pervasive and begins very early, often even before her birth. It continues as she trudges along the roles of daughter, wife, mother etc. The girl children of India are thus subject to biases and discriminations of various kinds in various measures, forms and degrees. The girl child faces discrimination on all counts as a girl, as a child and as a labourer. The percentage of girls employed in both rural and urban areas is higher than that of boys. Besides girls are often engaged in activities like cooking, cleaning, fetching water, taking care of younger siblings etc., which are non-remunerative and hence not considered as labour.

THE LIFE OF A GIRL CHILD

As a human family, we are doing a really terrible job of taking care of our girl children. While there are many countries where little girls are cherished, loved, and cared for, the vast majority of girls live in countries where this is not so. It is the condition of girls in these countries that is so critical to our future. This is not to deny or diminish the desperate lives led by many of the world's boys. Boys are conscripted as soldiers, trafficked in the sex trade and 40 million boys worldwide are without access to basic education. As appalling and unacceptable as these facts are, they in no way compare to the tragic conditions and mistreatment of our girls. A little girl eats last and least and she is up to three times more likely than boys to suffer malnutrition. She is often not taken to the doctor when she is sick and she is less likely to be immunized.

Girls are often kept out of school and put to work. Whether at home, in factories or in the field, little girls are at work. She starts work at a very young age, and works from dawn to dusk, proving the adage 'A girl is never a child'. If she does go to school, she's still at risk. Rather than being a safe refuge and a source of empowerment, the school situation is often dangerous. A recent study showed that 32% of reported child rapes in South Africa were committed by schoolteachers. This is the life of a girl in the developing world, if she is allowed to live at all. Each and every year, millions of sex-selective abortions are performed, virtually always on female fetuses.

If you go to one of the poorest states in India and take a car from the capital to the most remote village, you will not find health clinics, sanitation or clean water. What you will find is the latest technology to determine the sex of a fetus. It is estimated that annually 1 million female fetuses are aborted in China and 5 million in India, even though laws have been passed to stop this despicable practice. In addition to feticide, there are female infanticide babies killed at birth again, just because they are girls. Infanticide occurs in 17 countries. In India alone, more than 10,000 girl babies are victims of infanticide each year. Many people feel that the actual number is much higher. This is nothing short of murder. In China and India, there are growing disparities between the number of men and the number of women. In some areas, the disparity is as great as 710 women for every 1000 men. If it doesn't kill her by infancy, violence is an ever-present danger throughout her girlhood and throughout the rest of her life. If she is a girl in Africa, the Middle East or other parts of the world, she may be subjected to Female Genital Mutilation. Two million girls, usually between the ages of four and eight, fall victim to this practice each and every year. Early in a girl's life, she is often forced into sexual relations. 50% of all sexual assaults are committed against girl's age 15 or younger. She is married without her consent and becomes pregnant long before her body is ready. The leading cause of death for girls age 15-19 is complications from pregnancy.

Girls are an important sector of our society who lack equal opportunities to develop and who are subject to discrimination that is often a breeding ground for violence against them. This discrimination becomes evident, for example, in school textbooks that present the girl child as an individual, who imitates the traditional roles of adult women and that, at the same time, makes the contribution of women at all levels invisible. At the same time, educational institutions do not give girls the same opportunities as boys to develop and to exercise their rights. Thus, from childhood, the girl child's self esteem is harmed on a daily basis, given that this role, generally, is reinforced by adults, including teachers, parents and in the family environment. This role of only being 'for others' does not prepare girls to defend their space, their integrity, or their human rights on an equal basis as men, not in childhood, nor in the future.

STATUS OF GIRL CHILDREN IN INDIA

The girl child often faces discrimination from the earliest stages of life, through childhood and into adulthood (Thorat 2001). Her low status is reflected in the denial of fundamental needs and rights and in such harmful attitudes and practices as a preference for sons, early marriage, domestic abuse, sexual exploitation, discrimination, less food and less access to education.

- 1 out of every 3 girls does not live to see her 15th birthday
- One-third of these deaths take place at birth
- Every sixth girl child's death is due to gender discrimination
- Females are victimized far more than males during childhood

- 1 out of every 10 women reported some kind of child sexual abuse during childhood, chiefly by known persons.
- 1 out of 4 girls is sexually abused before the age of 4
- 19% are abused between the ages of 4 and 8
- 28% are abused between the ages of 8 and 12
- 35% are abused between the ages of 12 and 16
- 1 out of 6 girls will not live to see their 12th birthday.
- 3 lakh more girls than boys die every year.
- Female mortality exceeds male mortality in 224 out of 402 districts in India.
- Death rate among girls below the age of 4 years is higher than that of boys. Even if she escapes infanticide or foeticide, a girl child is less likely to receive immunization, nutrition or medical treatment compared to a male child.
- 53% of girls in the age group of 5 to 9 years are illiterate.
- Every year 27,06,000 children under 5 years die in India. And the deaths of girl children are higher than those of male children.
- Mentally/physically challenged girls are at a particular risk to violence and abuse.

The persistence of hunger and abject poverty in India and other parts of the world is due in large measure to the subjugation, marginalization and disempowerment of women. Women suffer from hunger and poverty in greater numbers and to a great degree than men. At the same time, it is women who bear the primary responsibility for actions needed to end hunger: education, nutrition, health and family income. Looking through the lens of hunger and poverty, there are seven major areas of discrimination against girl children in India:

Malnutrition

India has exceptionally high rates of child malnutrition, because tradition in India requires that women eat last and least throughout their lives, even when pregnant and lactating. Malnourished women give birth to malnourished children, perpetuating the cycle.

Poor Health

Females receive less health care than males. Many women die in childbirth of easily prevented complications. Working conditions and environmental pollution further impairs women's health.

Lack of Education

Families are far less likely to educate girls than boys, and far more likely to pull them out of school, either to help out at home or from fear of violence.

Overwork

Women work longer hours and their work is more arduous than men's, yet their work is unrecognized. Men report that 'women, like children, eat and do nothing'. Technological progress in agriculture has had a negative impact on women.

Unskilled

In women's primary employment sector-agriculture-extension services overlook women.

Mistreatment

In recent years, there has been an alarming rise in atrocities against women in India, in terms of rapes, assaults and dowry-related murders. Fear of violence suppresses the aspirations of all women. Female infanticide and sex-selective abortions are additional forms of violence that reflect the devaluing of females in Indian society.

Powerlessness

While women are guaranteed equality under the constitution, legal protection has little effect in the face of prevailing patriarchal traditions. Women lack power to decide who they will marry, and are often married off as children. Legal loopholes are used to deny women inheritance rights.

India has a long history of activism for women's welfare and rights, which has increasingly focused on women's economic rights. A range of government programs have been launched to increase economic opportunity for women, although there appear to be no existing programs to address the cultural and traditional discrimination against women that leads to her abject conditions.

CAUSES FOR GIRL CHILD LABOUR

The problem of child labour cannot be attributed to a single factor. Following are the major causes for the emergence of girl child labour.

Poverty

Poor children in India begin working at a very young and tender age. Many children have to work to help their families and some families expect their children to continue the family business at a young age. India has all along followed a proactive policy in the matter of tackling the problem of child labour. India has always stood for constitutional, statutory and developmental measures that are required to eliminate child labour in India. Indian Constitution consciously incorporated relevant provisions in the Constitution to secure compulsory universal elementary education as well as labour protection for children.

Forced Labour

Many of the forms of girl child labour practiced around the world are forced in the sense that children are taught to accept the conditions of their lives and not to challenge them. They find themselves in effective slavery. Girl children are pledged by their parents for small loans. Little girl children are made to work from dawn to dusk everyday severely stunting their growth during formative years.

Commercial Sexual Exploitation

The underground nature of the multi billion-dollar illegal industry in the commercial sex exploitation of girl children makes it difficult to gather reliable data. But NGOs in the field estimate that each year at least one million girls worldwide are lured or forced into this form of hazardous labour, which can verge on slavery. The girl children have to confront serious health risks everyday and are lunged into a distorted reality in which violence; distrust, shame and rejection are the norms.

Domestic Service

Girl child domestic workers are the world's most forgotten class. They are often extremely poorly paid and their terms and conditions are very often entirely at the whims of the employers and take no account of their legal rights. Hey are deprived of schooling, play and social activity and of emotional support from family and friends. They are vulnerable to physical and sexual abuse. They are very often cut off from the community, denied rest and play. Among the most common adjectives used to describe child domestic workers are 'timid' and 'listless'. Thus childhood has been stolen from the girl children.

Industrial and Agricultural Labour

Girl children work n all types of jobs in industrial and agricultural sectors. The number girl children exploited by jobs in these sectors may be just as great and the dangers associated with much of their work are no less appalling. In these occupations, children play a largely invisible role.

Street Work

The street is a hazardous workplace. Children who work on streets often come from slums and squatter settlements where poverty and precarious family situations are common, where schools are poor and where safe places to play simply do not exist. Work for the family may demand too much from children requiring them to labour long hours in income generating activities.

GIRL CHILD LABOUR AS A SOCIAL PROBLEM

As a developing country, India is faced with a multitude of social problems. One such problem, child labour, has disgraced the entire subcontinent giving it the distinction of having the largest number of child labourers in the world. While many are willing to admit that a child labour problem exists, very few people are willing to accept responsibility for the problem. The first step in arriving at a solution is to first recognize the causes of this dilemma: these include poverty, burdens on the family to pay off standing debts, the general Indian attitude toward child labour, the irrelevant and often inaccessible education system, and the inefficiency of protective legislation for working children. A solution to this predicament can be achieved through educational improvements, which will therefore overcome the other factors influencing the Indian child labour crisis.

Effect of Caste System

The rigidity of the caste system in India has, among other things, contributed to the mushrooming of child labour in the country, says the UNICEF. It is felt that dominant cultural group in India might not wish its own children to do hazardous labour but it would not be so concerned if young people from racial, ethnic or economic minorities did it.

Cultural Aspects of Gender Neglect

Although gender marginalization is a widely accepted theoretical concern, one view holds that cultural factors are responsible for entrenched female inequalities. Another view holds that changes in relations of production and in the system of property relations will automatically resolve gender issues. It must be borne in mind that culture is not uni-dimensional. Culture affects the material activity of people and their ideas. Feminists over the past two decades have promoted a generalized consciousness about women and their strategic role in production and reproduction, especially female children. Cultural stereotyping and restrictions on movement subject girls to the authority and control of male children and adult males. Girls are socialized differently and are not encouraged to be autonomous or to use initiative. In the public sphere, girls are used by families to serve household and production needs of the family and other relatives. Working wages for girls are very low, and working conditions are oppressive. The economic status of the household determines allocation of work, access to education, and lifestyle.

CHILD LABOUR LAWS IN INDIA

Through a notification dated May 26, 1993, the working conditions of children have been regulated in all employment, which is not prohibited under the Child Labour (Prohibition and Regulation) Act. Following up on a preliminary notification issued on October 5, 1993, the government has also prohibited employment of children in occupation processes like abattoirs /slaughter houses, printing, cashew nut descaling and processing, and soldering. Children perform a variety of jobs: some work in factories, making products such as carpets and matches; others work on plantations, or in the home. For boys the type of work is very different because they often work long hours doing hard physical labour outside of the home for very small wages. The government has made efforts to prohibit child labour by enacting *Child labour laws in India* including the 1986 Child Labour (Prohibition and Regulation) Act that stated that children under fourteen years of age could not be employed in hazardous occupations. This act also attempted to regulate working conditions in the jobs that it permitted, and put greater emphasis on health and safety standards.

However, due to cultural and economic factors, these goals remain difficult to meet. For instance, the act does nothing to protect children who perform domestic or unreported labour, which is very common in India. In almost all Indian industries girls are unrecognized labourers because they are seen as helpers and not workers. Therefore, girls are therefore not protected by the law. Children are often exploited and deprived of their rights in India, and until further measures are taken, many Indian children will continue to live in poverty.

VIOLENCE AGAINST GIRL CHILDREN

Violence is a major barrier to education for millions of girls across the globe. The prevalence of violence against girls affects both their rights to education and their rights in education. Violence or the fear of violence is an important reason for girls not attending school. Besides being in itself an infringement of girls' rights, violence is also denying girls their right to education. Violence against girls takes many forms including rape, sexual harassment, intimidation, teasing and threats. It affects all girls, regardless of age, race, class, caste or location. Poverty, war and long journeys to school put girls at additional risk. The causes are rooted in male-dominated cultures, which belittle or condone violence against girls and women. Violence is used as a tool for imposing male power. Sometimes Girls themselves often regard violence as inevitable and feel powerless to complain. It has been found that violence against girls takes place in schools, on the way to school and around schools and that the violence itself takes many forms. It includes sexual violence, sexual harassment, intimidation, teasing and the threat of violence. The impact of the violence is immeasurable and includes loss of self-esteem, depression, anger, risk of suicide, unwanted pregnancy, HIV infection and fear of victimization. Combinations of these factors cause many girls to drop out of school. Violence affects all girls regardless of age, race, class, caste or location.

Girls are also very vulnerable when they have to walk long distances to school, particularly in rural and poor urban areas. In Pakistan, girls in secondary school become more vulnerable because secondary schools are few and situated far from villages. In rural areas of India, girls who have to walk long distances to school are at risk of kidnap and trafficking. Violence against girls is not restricted to the classroom or the schoolyard. It happens in many school-related places. Violence against girls manifests its effects in low enrolment of girls in schools, poor performance at school, high dropout rates, teenage pregnancy, early marriage, increasing rates of HIV/AIDS in the 15-24 year old age group and psychological trauma. Violence against girls has its roots in patriarchy and unequal power relations that still exists worldwide Therefore the problem must be seen within this broader framework. It is a symptom and a result of the larger problem of gender inequality that has to be tackled in all spheres.

THE PLIGHT OF THE GIRL CHILD

111 million children of the 250 million child labour force are Indian. Every 2nd child has no access to primary education in India. Every 3rd girl child does not live to see her teen years in India. There are no estimates of the number of children who are subjected to child-trafficking, debt-bondage, forced labour, pornography, prostitution and drugs, in India. Trafficking of persons is the second largest illegal trade after arms sale. In 1997 according to U.N calculations, the procurers, smugglers, and corrupt public officials involved in the international trade in human beings, extracted $ 7 billion in profits from their cargo. There are no accurate statistics of how many people are involved, but it is estimated that in the last 30 years, trafficking in women and children in Asia for sexual exploitation alone has victimized over 30 million people. Everyday about 200 girls and women in India enter prostitution and 80 per cent of them against their will. At the current rate of growth by 2025 one out of every five Indian girl children will be a child prostitute. Keeping in mind the enormity and complexity of the problem, a pledge was made to initiate at the National level, committed and concerted action in developing programs on health, education and a safer environment for children, in partnership with NGOs, Corporate Houses, and Government agencies.

The girl child is perceived as a burden to be passed on to another family. Her contribution in the household economy is unacknowledged. The adverse attitude towards the girl child signals the catastrophe of serious demographic imbalance and degeneration of socio-economic conditions. Unfortunately, the rejection of the unwanted girl begins even before her birth. Prenatal sex determination tests followed by quick abortions eliminate thousand of female foetuses before they can become daughters. Those unfortunate girls who manage to survive till birth and beyond, find the dice heavily loaded against them. In a male dominated society, girls are denied equal access to food, health care, education, employment and even simple human dignity. Her sacrifice and dedicated services ensure the well being of the family, but in return, she receives neglected childhood devoid of proper education and health care.

FEMALE ILLITERACY AND CHILD LABOUR

The factors that affect the well-being and health of female children in India: sex ratio, literacy, food intake, morbidity, mortality, early marriage, maternal mortality, nutrition, prenatal care and delivery, family planning responsibilities, and access to health services. India has recognized within its Constitution and other government documents and programs equality for women, but practices lag behind principles.

Illiteracy and female illiteracy in particular, continues to be a serious problem in India (Barbara Herz 2006). According to the 1991 Census of India, about 60 per cent of Indian women were illiterate, that is, unable to read and write in any language. The inability to read and write has serious consequences for women's health, nutritional status, and skills acquisition over the lifetime. Illiterate persons are unable to read simple pamphlets on health practices, household hygiene, nutrition, their rights in employment or family planning methods. Acquisition of skills beyond the simplest tasks becomes impossible, and thus illiteracy condemns individuals to a lifetime of unskilled and poorly paid work. The problem of female illiteracy in India is compounded by conservative social attitudes that place little value on female education and that stress the desirability of early marriage and motherhood. It must be borne in mind that poverty and social conservatism need not be an obstacle to improving the health, literacy and job skills of poor, adolescent girls.

Elementary education and child labour are intimately linked. A very widely held belief regarding India's poor performance in education is that the demand for elementary education is low because of the large-scale poverty in this country. It is commonly put forward by many, including officials in India that the poor cannot afford to send their children to school. According to this view it is a 'harsh reality' that poor parents simply cannot miss the income of their children as wageworkers or household help in order to make ends meet. The problem is massive. According to official estimates around half of the children between 6 and 14- around 90 million - are not attending school but most probably the number comes closer to 115 million. It is a well-established fact that children in India are working on a large scale in the household, in family enterprises or in income-earning activities outside the home. It is however not so well established how many children are working, how much time they spend on that work and how much is the income thus earned or saved (by allowing parents to earn income). Estimations of the number of working children vary from 11 million to at least 90 million children. The former figure is from the Census of 1991 while the latter is based on the official number of non-school attending children. Unofficial estimates of the number of non-school going children go up to 115 million. Studies have shown that improvement in education leads to diminishing child labour. An example is found through comparing education vs. child labour in Kerala and Andhra Pradesh. In Kerala, where virtually all children attend school, exists the lowest incidence of child labour; in Andhra Pradesh, with one of the lowest school attendance percentages, the highest occurrences of child labour throughout India are found.

EMPOWERING GIRL CHILD

Child development is dependent upon the family and the social environment. Patriarchy establishes the structure, roles, and responsibilities of the family through hierarchies of age, gender, and generation. Males hold authoritative positions because of their control over resources and the assumption of their superiority. Family unity and stability is based on conformity with the community and kinship norms. The Indian family places a low priority on the development of individual family members and children. Female children are a low priority both as children and as girls. Girls carry a heavy domestic workload in the family, but girls do not receive recognition for their contributions. The family socializes children based on norms of gender and age inequalities. Deviation from patriarchal norms results in ostracism. Families without resources are vulnerable to deprivation and exploitation. Gaps have widened between rich and poor, and men and women. Particularly vulnerable groups are women in single-parent families and female-headed households. The combination of patriarchy, increased consumerism, and structural adjustment programs marginalizes girl children. Every family should be considered equal in dignity and worth and have the right to freedom, choices, life, security of person and privacy, and protection from domestic violence. Vulnerable family members need special attention. Every family member should take responsibility for promoting sensitivity and responsiveness, positive communication, companionable relationships, democratic decision making, respect for individual needs and differences, peaceful and non-violent approaches for resolving conflicts, and support in crisis situations.

RECOMMENDATION

It is heartening to note that the working girl child or girl child labour has been considered as vulnerable group in our society. Several disciplines are involved in understanding the growth and development of this vulnerable group. Social workers and educationists have been for a long time concerned more with the girl child labour and have contributed a great deal in focusing the attention of the people to the importance of several factors which should be taken care of in helping them to develop fully. It is, therefore necessary to understand the scientific basis of this ever-increasing problem of girl child labour so that public opinion can be more really contributed in a large measure.

Moreover it has been found that currently of all the girls out of school in the developing world, one-third lives in South Asia. In parts of South Asia, only one girl in four attends primary school. Yet in Bangladesh, India, and Sri Lanka, primary school enrolments are high and rising and gender gaps falling or disappearing. Not all children finish and fewer than half learn effectively, but far more enroll than did fifteen years ago. In secondary school girls' enrolments generally remain low and lower than boys'. Yet progress has occurred, again particularly in Bangladesh, India, and Sri Lanka. Huge challenges remain in increasing enrolment particularly for girls from the poorest families, the most remote areas, or the most culturally conservative settings. But South Asia's own experience shows that when there's a will, there's a way to educate girls. The differences in performance among and within countries prove that effort matters and can make a real impact.

Towards ensuring survival of the girl child, the objectives must be oriented towards (Gopalan and Bhaskar 1998):

- Prevent cases of female foeticide and infanticide and ban the practice of amniocentesis for sex determination;
- End gender disparity in infant mortality rate; eliminate gender disparities in feeding practices, expand nutritional interventions to reduce severe malnourishment by half and provide supplementary nutrition to adolescent girls in need;
- Reduce deaths due to serious illness by 50 per cent among girl children under 5 years and ensure immunization against all forms of serious illnesses;
- Provide safe drinking water and ensure access to fodder and drinking water nearer home. Ensure that a wide

range of prevention programmes, which include information.

- Education and communication in all local languages is available in all countries, and that aims at encouraging responsible sexual behaviour, including abstinence and fidelity, and expanded access to essential commodities, including male and female condoms.
- By 2005, ensure that at least 90 per cent, and by 2010 at least 95 per cent of young men and women aged 15 to 24 years have access to information and education on HIV.
- Develop and make significant progress in implementing comprehensive care strategies to: strengthen family and community-based care, including those provided to infected children, and to monitor treatment.

Protection of the girl child and fulfillment of the above mentioned objectives are to be ensured through the following:

- Relief for those girls who are economically and socially deprived and who belong to special groups;
- Intervention to sensitize various agencies on the need to protect the girl child and adolescent girls from exploitation, assault and physical abuse;
- Education and sensitization of male members of the family to the special needs of the girl child;
- Equal treatment, dignity and respect for girl children in the family and community, as well as providing support and help in their day-to-day work so that they get time to avail of the opportunities for self-development;
- Rehabilitation services to reduce the growing instances of exploitation of girl children and adolescent girls.
- Protection of girl children and adolescent girls from prevalent social evils such as dowry, child marriage, prostitution, rape, incest, molestation etc., through appropriate legislation and proper enforcement.

CONCLUSION

The tale of the girl child in India is one of immense tragedy. Out of the 400 million children (the largest child population in any one country) in India, at least 63 million are out of school, two-thirds of them are girls. India is home to at least 100 million child labourers. Although separate figures on girl labourers are not available, it is estimated that at least 42 million girls under the age of 18 years belong to the category of child labourers. The number equals the population of countries like Burma and South Africa. Many are tortured and exploited by their employers or even the police. One estimate indicates that 50 to 60 per cent of the crimes against girls and women involve girls between 2 and 16 years of age.

Undoubtedly, the structural gender inequalities of our society make the girl child very vulnerable. The practice of child marriage is still common in western Indian states like Rajasthan. Even in New Delhi, at least 18 per cent of mothers who live in the slums are between 12 and 14 years old. Over 45 per cent of under-18 girls today are illiterates. Most poor families choose first to send their sons to school while daughters help in chores at home. If the family is slightly better off, the son is sent to a private school while the daughter goes to a government school.

Poverty is not the main reason for child labour and low elementary school participation in India. It is rather the absence or very low quality of elementary education; as well as to some extent the direct costs of schooling, which drives children to work. Parents are generally keen to have their children educated, although somewhat less so for girls. The fact that a lot of children are neither working nor going to school gives further evidence that the government school system is not providing education of a basic quality. The poverty constraint at the household level, where it exists, can be overcome by appropriate interventions as for example the state of Kerala and the work of the MV Foundation have shown. While incentives like free mid-day meals and free books might be of help, they are not a substitute for good primary education. Girls spent on average much more time on work than boys. Most of this work is domestic work. The higher returns from girl's labour for parents, traditional beliefs regarding marriage as the ultimate goal for girls, the practice of early marriage and insufficient awareness of the social benefits of educating girls, make them the most difficult group to wean away from work and get them into schools. Although the number of working hours of many non-school going children seems to be relatively limited, there is still a large group of children trapped in child labour. While child labour might partly be 'default activity' as a consequence of ineffective education, the vested interests and social norms related to child labour also are themselves a factor leading to marginalization of the school system and an excuse for the state not to take its responsibility. Mobilization for the elimination of child labour is, besides for obvious other reasons, therefore an important instrument to put pressure on the state to take its responsibility for elementary education seriously.

REFERENCES

Gopalan, S and Bhaskar, V. (1998), Response of the Government to the Problems of the Girl Child, *Women's Link,* 4(3): 2-6.

Barbara Herz (2006), *Educating Girls in South Asia: Promising Approaches,* United Nations Girls' Education Initiative (UNGEI).

Thorat, S. (2001), *Data Base on Child Labour in India: An Assessment with Respect to Nature of Data, Period and Uses,* A Part of the Research Carried out within UCW (Understanding Children's Work), A Joint ILO, World Bank and UNICEF Project.

10

WOMEN ACCESS TO ONLINE BANKING FACILITIES

SIDDHARTHA SARKAR

INTRODUCTION

India's participation in net is new compared to the other major Asian countries. The net working of resources by innovative information and communicative technology is making limitless opportunity for accessing all available modes of social learning and intelligence. The net has been called for special attention because of its potentiality to generate wealth, foreign exchange and employment. With the advent of cyber media the hurdles regarding space and reproducibility have totally been shifted. Accordingly India's partaking into online brings about a basic change in the value system, quality of life, thought and vision and ultimately leads to acquire a status of developed country.

The Internet banking in India is in the infancy stage of development though many banks initiate to adopt it. In developed economy it has already become user friendly and cost effective. Compared to the American households to use net banking, India's participation is detrimental. Still in India most of the customers have to go to the neighbour bank, stand in a queue to verify their account statements and wait for sometimes while bank personnel provide a new chequebook. With the evolving of online banking and financial programme like Microsoft money and Intuit Quicken, customers can say goodbye to calculator, never ending paper bank statements and numerous account registers. The facility of online banking is more than a PC link to the banks. Online permits customers access the net and then log on to the web sites of bank of interest. To go online banking, customers must have an account with the bank and a computer with Internet facility. Then the customers fill up an application to notify the acceptance of terms and conditions to the bank for accessing the online account. Once this is done an exclusive login user name and a password would be handed over to the user by the bank in order to use the online portal. Some banks might ask for a monthly charge from its customers. Banking portals offer basic services like online bill payment, change of address, account summary, viewing past bills, searching for a specific charge, customer support, application for Credit /Debit cards, add on cards, application for loans, life insurance or home mortgage transfer funds electronically between accounts and FAQ. Unlike the actual physical banks, online banking sites are available 24 hours a day, seven days a week (excluding the small down time taken for site maintenance). Online banking portals ensure that customers can access their accounts from anywhere. Online bank sites accomplish and confirm transactions quicker than the tellers at a real bank. Customers can access and manage all of their bank accounts from one secure site. One of the major hurdles for the lack of trust with online baking is the 'security and privacy' issue. Users should feel assured in the first place that the online banking portal they are using is indeed the authentic site. For this to happen, the bank must provide evidence to prove its identity. In most cases this is achieved by the banking website requesting for a username or password in order to proceed with the transactions/user actions. The issue of unauthorized access to the online banking system is also important. This is controlled via authentication of username/passwords and encryption. Even while these security features are implemented, unless the users see them on the online portal they will be cautious about using the online channel. Placing the privacy and security information on the prime location of the website is essential. Content organization of the website should be such that the user need not search through for important information such as the security and privacy policy.

Internet banking has created new ways to provide banking services. It allows customers to avoid a long queue and give then flexibility of doing their banking at any time. For bankers it is an opportunity to avoid establishing more bank branches and cut management and administrative expenses. In India more than five dozens of banks are presently offering any sort of net banking facilities. Among others the ICICI bank, City bank and Indus Ind bank are the net banking premiers who offering a series online. Apart from that many foreign banks are offering online banking facility. In India the banks with online services offer account details, transfer of fund, submission of application of loan etc. In the 1990s banks laid great thrust on Internet banking drawing from the estimates of very lower cost of transactions in Internet banking. An interesting development of the growth of Internet banking is that it could promote more of brick and mortar banking as well. A recent report observed that in virtually every market, it is the traditional, established brick and mortal banks that are attracting the biggest audiences. A large majority of online customers are most likely also customers of the in-person bank branches. Another report says that in the height of Internet boom, big banks declared bank branching dead and were aggressively investing in technology instead. They hoped to win over customers to their new electronic systems and cut back on expensive bricks and mortar. So they spent heavily on call centers and website and also opened less costly mini branches in grocery and discount stores. It is noted that not only banks, even software companies are taking steps to further net banking. Several research studies discloses that in general the foreign and private banks are far ahead of public sector or cooperative banks in terms of number of sites and their level of development. The private banks with futuristic management have been playing a pathfinder role in Indian net banking.

ONLINE BANKING: INDIAN EXPERIENCE

The Internet banking is changing the banking industry and is having the major effects on banking relationships. Internet banking involves use of Internet for delivery of banking products and services. Advantages previously held by large financial institutions have shrunk considerably. The Internet has levelled the playing field and afforded open access to customers in the global marketplace. Internet banking is a cost-effective delivery channel for financial institutions. Consumers are embracing the many benefits of Internet banking. Access to one's accounts at anytime and from any location via the web is a convenience unknown a short time ago. Thus, a bank's Internet presence transforms from brouchreware status to Internet banking status once the bank goes through a technology integration effort to enable the customer to access information about his or her specific account relationship.

The banking industry in India is facing unprecedented competition from non-traditional banking institutions, which now offer banking and financial services over the Internet. The deregulation of the banking industry coupled with the emergence of new technologies, are enabling new competitors to enter the financial services market quickly and efficiently. Indian banks are going for the retail banking in a big way. However, much is still to be achieved. E-banking utilizes technology to allow a bank's customers and other stakeholders to interact and transact with the bank seamlessly through a variety of channels such as the Internet, wireless devices, ATMS and physical branches. Internet banking is one component of a comprehensive e-banking offering. E-banking has exploded onto the web and the Internet is a powerful and cost effective medium for business to interact with and service their customers. The number of online banking services to customers continues to grow and the Internet offers enormous opportunities for banks, and other financial services to fundamentally reshape their organizations. Banks can generate revenue through increased account, access fees and benefit from promotional opportunity to cross-sell products such as credit cards and loans (Yerkes 1988). Jeevan (2000) observes that the Internet enables banks to offer low cost, high value added financial services. US web-corporation argues that finally banks are finding that a comprehensive online banking strategy is essential for success in the increasingly competitive financial services market. Competition and changes in technology and lifestyles have changed the face of banking and banks in the present environment are seeking alternative way to provide and differentiate their services. For enabling either information access or transactions, banks have to put up a web site. There is data to suggest that most hacking activity that happens is targeted at breaking into web-side security (Infosys). Banks as well as consumers view the security threat as perhaps the most serious threat; Denny (2000) observes that the security of Internet access to client account is the biggest challenge facing banks. For success in the increasingly competitive financial services market, banks are finding that a comprehensive online banking strategy is essential which also provides the essential security requirements. Security policy should include management commitment, technological support and effective disseminations of the policy and the security awareness of all users. Cronin (1998) observes that the implementation of SET, the standard for secure electronic transactions on the Internet and its widespread adoption including security measures like encryption, digital authentication, and verification of on-line identity, increase consumer confidence. Stamoulis (2000) adds that the advances in Internet security and the advent of relevant protocols such as Integrion, SET, etc, put banks in perspective again as financial intermediaries and facilitators of complete commercial transaction via electronic networks. To compete in a market transformed by globalization and technological revolution, banks have been forced to seek alliance and establish joint ventures to maintain their competitiveness and efficiency (Denny 2000). Banks are engaged in a battle to maintain their supremacy and consolidation offers the banks a chance to create organizations that are both larger and more streamlined. Also, consumers are increasingly looking for services they can access from a singly entry point. The urges to merge mainly arise from cost reduction through elimination of overlaps or through greater reach at more economic costs. Banking mergers like Chase, Chemical NationsBank, Million Bank and Bank of America were largely driven by the abolition of the antiquated inter state barriers to banking in the US. Mergers in Europe have been driven more by the trend towards universal banking whereas the recent merger in Japan is more a strategy of survival in a mounting NPA scenario. The opportunities for banks in the Internet arena are varied as they can become technology providers by spinning off technology resources to start up new business stream, become content providers for information regarding products, indices, etc and enablers by providing back bone systems to support multiple payment system alternatives. Also, banks examining the cost and maintenance of conventional bricks and mortar facilities see tremendous value in an international web presence whose globalization costs seem minuscule by comparison. Thus, e-banking will offer a transparent environment to compare the cost and quality of services offered by a variety of financial institutions. As a result the focus is going to shift from generic banking service to customized banking services.

India is still in the early stages of e-banking growth and development. Competition and changes in technology and lifestyle in the last five years have changed the face of banking. The changes that have taken place impose on banks tough standards of competition and compliance. The issue here is where India stands in the scheme of e-banking. E-banking is likely to bring a host of opportunities as well as unprecedented risks to the fundamental nature of banking in India. The impact of e-Banking in India is not yet apparent.

Many global research companies believe that e-banking adoption in India in the near future would be slow compared to other major Asian countries. Nair (1999) observes that Indian e-banking is still nascent, although it is fast becoming a strategic necessity for most commercial banks, as competition increases from private banks and non banking financial institutions. According to Nasscom's Internet survey in 2001 on the Internet usage trends, the number of active Internet subscribers in India is expected to increase to over 18 million and the user base to over 30 million by 2004-05. It also found that more than 200 cities and towns in India have Internet connectivity. The Nasscom - McKinsey study in 2002 revealed that despite the global economic challenges facing the IT software and services sector, the outlook for the Indian industry remains optimistic. The Reserve Bank of India has also set up a 'Working Group' on e-banking to examine different aspects of E-banking. The group focused on three major areas of e-banking i.e. technology and Security issues; legal issues and regulatory and Supervisory issues. RBI has accepted the guidelines of the group and they provide a good insight into the security requirements of e-banking. The importance of the impact of technology and information security cannot be doubted. Technological developments have been one of the key drivers of the global economy and represent an instrument that if exploited well can boost the efficiency and competitively of the banking sector. However, the rapid growth of the Internet has introduced a completely new level of security related problems. The problem here is that since the Internet is not a regulated technology and it is readily accessible to millions of people, there will always be people who want to use it to make illicit gains. The security issue can be addressed at three levels. The first is the security of customer information as it is sent from the customer's PC to the web server. The second is the security of the environment in which the Internet banking server and customer information database reside. Third, security measures must be in place to prevent unauthorized users from attempting to long into the online banking section of the website. From a legal perspective, security procedure adopted by banks for authenticating users needs to be recognized by law as a substitute for signature. In India, the Information Technology Act, 2000, in section 3(2) provides for a particular technology (viz., the asymmetric crypto system and hash function) as a means of authenticating electronic record. Any other method used by banks for authentication should be recognized as a source of legal risk. Regarding the regulatory and supervisory issues, only such banks which are licensed and supervised and have a physical presence in India will be permitted to offer e-banking products to residents of India.

CASE STUDY

ICICI is one of the leading private sector banks in India, which combines financial strength with a reputation for innovation and a universal culture that embraces change. On March 31, 2002 ICICI formally merged with ICICI bank and emerged as India's first Universal Bank. ICICI banks retail distribution network continues to expand and it now has 409 branches and extension counters and 1,066 ATMS across about 240 locations (ICICI 2002). The strategy of ICICI bank after the merger with ICICI Ltd. is that of building a diversified portfolio. The merged entity will continue to be into project finance and the focus will be to tap the potential in retail financing. ICICI bank offers a wide spectrum of domestic and international banking services to facilitate trade, investment, cross border business, treasury and foreign exchange services. ICICI bank has been quick to realize that e-banking has changed from a somewhat experimental delivery vehicle into an increasingly mainstream one for delivery of broad spectrum of banking products and services. Basic e-banking services are rapidly changing from competitive differentiator to competitive necessity. The group has leveraged on a number of tie-ups to come up with its various offering. For its Internet banking offering the ICICI bank uses Infinity from Infosys, for its credit card business its uses Vision Plus from Pay Sys, USA, for WAP services the tie-up with cellular service providers Orange and Airtel helps reach out to these users, while the WAP technology is being implemented by the in-house ICICI Infotech service. To leverage the Net for its marketing initiatives ICICI bank and Satyam Info way have jointly set up a 'COM' company to promote banking products on the Net. The bank has also entered into agreements with leading corporate like BPL, Rediff.com. Usha Martin and Tata Communications for B to C solutions in a bid to further strengthen its Internet banking product offering and services. Also ICICI has joined hands with a consortium led by Compaq to take the lead in offering a solution to the Indian e-commerce community. This consortium offers a B2B and B2C ecommerce payment gateway within India. The Bank has been offering phone banking free of charge and was first to launch an Internet Banking service in the country named Infinity (ICICI 2000). Infinity now provides a host of online banking solutions to retail as well as corporate customers. ICICI's constant endeavour in providing more value to the customers has resulted in Infinity being the front-runner amongst online banking offerings in the country. Also, in keeping with the customers need for increased security, Corporate Infinity now provides multiple levels of authentication besides user ID/ password and includes security tokens (ICICI 2000-01 Annual Report). ICICI also strives to be a center for leading research on financial engineering in India, particularly in the area of valuation of securities, risk management and derivatives. By leveraging on the groups resources ICICI provides custom tailored solution that can support even the most complex business strategy (ICICI 2000). ICICI is now moving all its operations into the era of 'virtual integration'. Not only has this drastically reduced costs, but it has also increased and improved its services to customers.

Money India offers a unique facility by ICICI of transferring funds to India. Additional modules were added-gifting and reminders to broaden its scope and enhance ICICI's relationship with customers (ICICI Annual report 2000-01).

Internet banking for the retail segment is a recent phenomenon that has generated a lot of interest in the Indian banking industry. Private and foreign banks have been the early adopters while the PSU banks are also beginning to latch on to the bandwagon. As per IDC estimates, the total number of registered users for Internet banking in India is over two million. But this figure needs to be adjusted for dormant users and multiple accounts (a user having accounts with more than one bank). India has a little less than a million active Internet banking users. And though this is just 0.096 per cent of the total population, it represents 15 per cent of the India's Internet user population. Thus indicating that the concept of Internet banking is surely catching on. Impressive as these figures might be, the truth is that India lags behind other countries in Internet banking. In the US, the number of commercial banks with transactional websites is 1,275 or 12 per cent of the total number of banks. Of these, seven could be called 'virtual banks.' Ten traditional banks have established Internet branches or divisions that operate under a unique brand name. At present, in the US approximately 78 per cent of all commercial banks with assets more than $5 billion, 43 per cent of banks with $500 million to $5 billion in assets, and 10 per cent of banks under $500 million in assets have transactional websites. From the Asian market experience, it is clear that Internet banking is here to stay and will be a major channel to acquire and service customers. Markets like Korea and Singapore have nearly 10 per cent of their population banking over the Internet. Though, these markets are way ahead of India both in terms of Internet penetration and online banking penetration, India is a big potential market and is fast catching up with its Asian counterparts.

In contrast, Indian banks have an insignificant Internet banking record. ICICI Bank kicked off online banking way back in 1996 and a host of other banks soon followed suit. But even for the Internet as a whole, 1996 to 1998 marked the adoption phase, while usage increased only in 1999 due to lower ISP online charges, increased PC penetration and a tech-friendly atmosphere.

After ICICI, Citibank, IndusInd Bank and HDFC Bank and Timesbank (now part of HDFC Bank), were the early ones to bite the technology bullet in 1999. According to head, information technology, HDFC Bank, 'our vision was very clear, we were not enamored by the concept of Internet banking but looked at it more as an add-on service which our customers should gradually adopt'. In line with this strategy, initially the Net banking facility was provided in order to meet the information requirements of the customers and gradually it ventured into fund transfers and third party transfers.

Though adoption of Internet banking by Indian banks and their customers would not set the Arabian Sea on fire, no one can deny the obvious benefits that this service offers. Costs of banking service through the Internet amount to a fraction of the costs through conventional methods. Industry estimates assume teller cost at Re 1 per transaction, ATM transaction costs at Re 0.45, phone banking at Re 0.35, debit cards at Re 0.20 and Internet banking at Re 0.10 per transaction. The president, information technology, UTI Bank, argued that 'no wonder, the cost-conscious banks in the country are now actively considering using the Internet as a channel for providing services. People were skeptical about even ATM at the beginning, but look how it has picked up today'. However, he warns that banks cannot expect instant returns, unless the Internet population itself does not reach a critical mass. Besides, he also feels that fully computerized banks, with better management of their customer base are in a stronger position to cross-sell their products through this channel.

The head, consumer banking, ABN-AMRO Bank, feels that the prohibitive costs of real estate would always make Internet banking a much more viable option in the long run than physical banks. In today's environment besides their physical branches, banks need to grow non-branch delivery networks as a part of their growth strategy. ATMs are currently the hot favourite for most banks, but Internet banking definitely has the potential to leave the rest behind. Therefore, on the whole, Internet banking increases operational efficiencies and reduces costs, besides giving a platform for offering value added services to the customer, thereby fulfilling all the essential prerequisites for a flourishing banking industry.

As in all forms of technology innovations, PSU banks have remained laggards in the race for adopting Internet banking practices. There are very few nationalized banks like State Bank of India, Bank of Baroda, Allahabad Bank, Syndicate Bank and Bank of India that offer Internet banking services. Some others like Union Bank of India, Canara Bank and Punjab National Bank are on the verge of doing so. SBI's Internet banking initiative, launched in July 2001, is in fact doing quite well and has over 18,000 registered customers across 150 branches. The enthusiastic response has encouraged the SBI management to extend the service to an additional 500 branches. But despite positive news like this, PSU banks still have a lot of catching up to do on the Internet banking services front.

However, not many are willing to buy the argument that it's the lack of regulations that is preventing the PSU banks from taking the Internet plunge. 'More than a lack of regulatory framework, it is lack of zeal and a mindset attuned towards resisting any new technology that is holding back the nationalized banks. On top of this, the highly politicized unions are also an impediment as they feel that Internet banking would expose the low productive levels of the workforce'.

The average customer profile of PSU banks is also comfortable with the traditional banking system and is not too keen on adopting an online model. Typically, most PSU banks have the majority of their customer base in the smaller cities or towns and even in remote villages. Even in bigger cities, a large proportion of their customers are either senior citizens or at least 50+ who have a natural aversion towards adopting new technology. This not the case with private or

MNC banks, where the clientele is mostly urban-based falling in the 20-40 age group and who have a higher exposure to technology.

Even the IDC survey seems to confirm this premise. Among the elite Internet banking users, that is, those customers who belong to Socio-Economic Class A1 (SEC A1) in the top five cities, it has been found that people access their account through the Internet once every week. Similarly users visit their ATM centre on an average of two times per week. The workplace happens to be the most favoured place to access Internet for banking purposes. The home comes to a close second while cyber cafés take the third place. ATM in the close vicinity to the office is the most preferred place among users for banking. The users (24 per cent) who access the ATM near their office mostly go during the first half of the day, between 9 AM to 12 PM, but most preferred time by all users (41 per cent) is between 6-9 PM.

This probably explains why more and more banks are looking at Internet banking as another attractive addition to their bouquet of delivery channels. At least in urban areas, ATMs are already fast becoming the most popular mode of banking, while phone banking and mobile banking are also on the upswing as the user base grows. Internet banking now seems to be the perfect model to complement the whole system. 'In fact, currently telephone banking is much more popular than Internet banking. But HDFC Bank is working on a strategy to integrate various channels like the telephone, ATM, Internet, mobile, branches, etc. Customers have real-time access in all wherein any action in any of the above mentioned channels would be immediately reflected in the account of the account holder'. All these initiatives taken by banks are part of their channel diversification strategy, where they intend to put the strategy matrix in place. This will be done through sprucing up the channel strategy in depth and width in which width would mean the various varieties of channel and depth would mean the value added services in each channel. What is ultimately emerging is that though there is certainly a high level of importance attached to

Internet banking, it is at present not necessarily a priority for all banks. As far as banks are concerned, migrating customers to any self-directed channel is the main goal. However, the future of banking will be one in which customers can address most of their needs through self-directed means and the key differentiator will be how effective a bank is in getting its customers online and deriving measurable value from this presence. One can sum up the whole Internet banking scenario with the adage, 'For while winners may not see massive gains, the losers will fade from view as their ability to compete is eroded with every mouse click' (Indian Express Group 2002).

WHY WOMEN?

Since 2004-05, the percentage of online users has increased by 54 per cent to 38.5 million users-male online users increased in absolute numbers but dipped from 72 per cent (2004-05) to 68 per cent (2005-06) and women numbers increased from 28 per cent in 2004-05 to 32 per cent in 2005-06 [12.32 million]. The estimate for the male female ratio in the next two years is that it will be closer to the 60:40 ratios but will still result in the absolute numbers of men being higher than women.

This research was conducted by the Internet and Mobile Association of India in collaboration with Cross tab Marketing Services that surveyed 6365 respondents in December 2005. The research was undertaken with a view to ascertain the gender parity online with a primary focus on understanding the female demographic and their activities online giving marketers a better perspective while designing their marketing and promotional programs to cater to a defined online Target Audience (IAMAI 2006). With India's Internet population poised to reach 100 million by 2007-08 the online male female ratio is estimated to change to 60:40 by 2007-08 from the current 68:32. The IAMAI (2006) study reveals that 73 per cent of women own an ATM Card, 36 per cent own a Credit Card, 41 per cent own a Debit Card (figure 1). 14 per cent of women use their Credit Cards online, 10 per cent of women use their Debit Cards online and 8 per cent of women use both Credit and Debit Cards Online (figure 2).

Figure 1: Credit Card/Debit Card Ownership

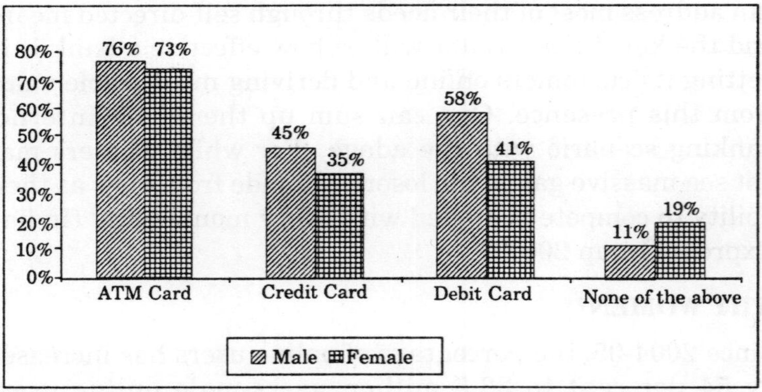

Figure 2: Credit Card/Debit Card Usage Online

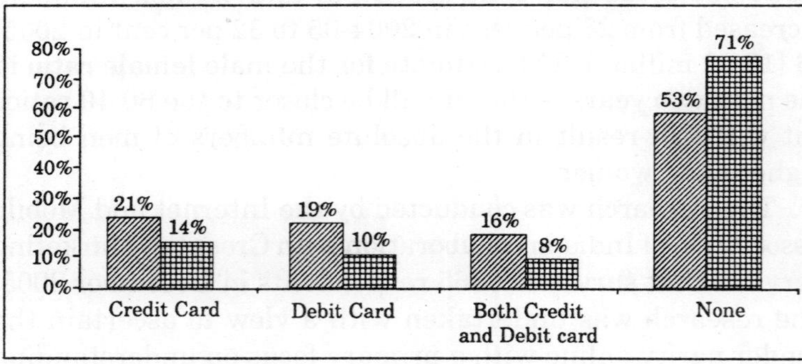

Various Online Activities by Women

- 96 per cent of women use the Internet for e-mailing for personal use and 92 per cent for work purposes. Increasing communications related activities especially for personal use would over a period of time make Internet extremely integral in a user's day to day life.
- 63 per cent of women use the Internet for Surfing for personal purposes and 50 per cent surf the Internet for work related issues.

- 65 per cent of women use search engines for their personal requisites and 66 per cent use search engines to find work related information.
- 29 per cent of women use the Internet for personal research and 37 per cent use the Internet for work related research.
- 51 per cent of women look up news online as a personal activity whereas 38 per cent look up news online for their professional requisites.
- 55 per cent of women use the Internet to Search for Jobs. This is 5 per cent higher than men at 50 per cent.

Online women in India are cautious about their online financial transactions as clearly seen by the below mentioned statistics:

- 11 per cent of women use the Internet to participate in an Online Auctions.
- 9 per cent of women use of the Internet for Online Stock Trading.
- 12 per cent of women use the Internet for Online Bill Payments.
- 24 per cent of women the Internet for Online Banking.
- 22 per cent of women use the Internet for Online Shopping.

WOMEN AND INFORMATIONAL TECHNOLOGY

Information technology (IT) has become a potent force in transforming social, economic, and political life globally. Without its incorporation into the information age, there is little chance for countries or regions to develop. More and more concern is being shown about the impact of those left on the other side of the digital divide the division between the information haves and have-nots. Most women within developing countries are in the deepest part of the divide further removed from the information age than the men whose poverty they share. If access to and use of these technologies is directly linked to social and economic development, then it is imperative to ensure that women in developing countries understand the significance of these technologies and use them. If not, they will become further marginalized from the mainstream of their countries and of the world. It is essential that gender issues be considered early in the process of the introduction of information technology in developing countries so that gender concerns can be incorporated from the beginning and not as a corrective afterwards. Many people dismiss the concern for gender and IT in developing countries on the basis that development should deal with basic needs first. However, it is not a choice between one and the other. IT can be an important tool in meeting women's basic needs and can provide the access to resources to lead women out of poverty. Getting reliable statistics on women's Internet use in developing countries is very difficult. The standard indicators are not disaggregated by sex, and the available data are not very reliable or comparable. However, it is clear that the numbers are small and the distribution limited. Most women Internet users in almost all developing countries are not representative of women in the country as a whole, but rather are part of small, urban educated elite. In many developing countries, less than one per cent of the population male or female access Internet. By regions, women are 22 per cent of all Internet users in Asia, 38 per cent of those in Latin America, and six per cent of Middle Eastern users. No regional figures by sex are available for Africa. Most women in developing countries who use information technology use it at work. Except in upper-income enclaves, home access to a computer and the Internet is not a phenomenon. Users at work generally divide up between those who use it as a tool of production (routine office work, data entry, manufacturing, computer industry jobs, programming, and related work) and those who use it as a tool of communication (creating and exchanging information). As a tool of communication, the most prevalent application is networking for political advocacy on behalf of women. This came about because the nongovernmental organizations that promoted electronic networking and worked in political advocacy were the early adopters and is continuing users of the technology in developing countries. Also, developing country women have used electronic communication for networking to promote their business interests. This area is far less developed than that of politically activist networking, but it represents an interesting area with possibilities for further development. E-mail is the major information technology application that women's organizations and individual women in developing countries use. But, time constraints as well as bandwidth limitations make Web use difficult for women. Few women are producers of information technology, whether as Internet content providers, programmers, designers, inventors, or fixers of computers. In addition, women are also conspicuously absent from decision-making structures in information technology in developing countries. A series of factors, including literacy and education, language, time, cost, geographical location of facilities, social and cultural norms, and women's computer and information search and dissemination skills constrain women's access to information technology. Science and technology education is necessary for women to work in IT at the level of computer programmers, engineers, systems analysts, and designers. Women's low enrollment in science impedes this globally. In developing countries, there is a great deal of variation in the percentages of women in natural sciences, computer science, and engineers. There are indications that young women in developing countries are not as affected as U.S. women by attitudes that computer science is not an attractive field to enter. For example, women comprise between 30 and 50 per cent of students in computer science and other natural sciences in a number of developing countries. Africa remains the area of greatest concern; however, as African women have the lowest participation rates in the world in science and technology education at all levels. Uses of information technology to assist women in their current economic activities, including farming, trade, and entrepreneurship, are detailed in the following sections. For instance, women farmers could greatly increase productivity using information on improved technologies, agricultural inputs, weather, and markets. Traders and other entrepreneurs need to find marketing information and disseminate information about their businesses. Schoolgirls from the local communities who generally learn computer skills rapidly could be trained to serve as information intermediaries for the older women. The new information economy offers many possibilities for new IT-enabled businesses that women could establish or in which they could work. Most numerous are the service jobs outsourced by major corporations in the U.S. and Europe. At the low end of the skill level and largest in number are jobs in data entry and data capture. Software programming, GIS, and systems analysis jobs require much higher skills and education, but women are moving into these jobs in several developing countries. While the business-to- consumer e-commerce area has generated a great deal of excitement, it can be a difficult field to enter. Women's handicrafts can find niche markets, but marketing and management skills are needed, and supply and delivery problems must be addressed. Some successful developing country e-businesses have targeted their diaspora markets and taken advantage of local delivery. More profitable opportunities exist for women's small-scale enterprises in business-to-business and business-to-government markets. Availability of credit, particularly in the form of micro-credit, is a necessity for women to enter such businesses. While micro-credit is increasingly popular, its availability falls far short of demand. For employment in core sector information technology jobs, women in developing countries need to acquire the necessary training to move into more technical, better paying, cognitively oriented jobs. While degrees in science and technology are the entry tickets to the higher end of using and producing information technology, women can master many aspects of computer use and maintenance with much less training, with much of it available outside the formal education system. Information technology can offer significant opportunities for virtually all girls and women in developing countries, including poor women living in rural areas. However, their ability to take advantage of these opportunities is contingent upon conducive policies, an enabling environment in their countries to extend communications infrastructure to where women live, and increased educational levels. Out of enlightened self-interest, women in developing countries need to involve themselves in the area of information and communication technology policy and regulation. Information technology has become a potent force in transforming social, economic, and political life globally. There is little chance for countries or regions to develop without their incorporation into the information age. More and more, development strategists see the need for developing countries to embrace information technology both as a way to avoid further economic and social marginalization as well as to offer opportunities for both growth and diversification of their economies. The uneven distribution of these technologies within societies as well as across the world has been termed 'the digital divide'. It reflects a division between the information haves and have-nots on many lines that often overlap within countries by race, ethnic group, class, age, region, and gender; between countries; and globally, between those who have access to abundant information resources and those who do not have this access. Women within developing countries are in the deepest part of the divide, further removed from the information age than are the men whose poverty they share. The gender gap in the digital divide is of increasing concern; if access to and use of these technologies is directly linked to social and economic development, then it is imperative to ensure that women in developing countries understand the significance of these technologies and use them. If not, lack of access to information and communication technologies becomes a significant factor in the further marginalization of women from the economic, social, and political mainstream of their countries and of the world. Without full participation in the use of information technology, women are left without the key to participation in the global world of the twenty-first century. It is essential that gender issues be considered early in the process of the introduction of information technology in developing countries. Despite frequent claims to the contrary, information technology is not gender neutral. Gender needs to be considered at the early stages of the diffusion of IT in order for women to participate fully in their use. Gender influences factors such as income, time constraints, literacy, education, language, and cultural contexts that affect access to facilities, training, and employment in the information technology area. Seemingly gender neutral, national level decisions about infrastructure can impact gender and affect women's opportunities to use new technologies including decisions about what systems to put in place (at what cost to the consumer?), which suppliers of communications services (will they have universal service obligations?), and where facilities will be located (will they be available in rural areas?). These aspects of technology choice impact whether women will have equitable access to the new technologies. At the same time, failing to consider gender issues (such as sexual division of labour, cultural definitions of women's activities, women's paid and unpaid labour, and women's multiple roles) from the early stages of technology diffusion may unwittingly generate unintended negative effects on women. This happened with the Green Revolution where technology and technological change brought significant costs for rural women. In the case of information technology, the potentially adverse impact on gender may be even more pervasive than with the Green Revolution because information technology is a meta-technology that cuts across virtually every economic sector and geographical area. As with all new historical trends, the advent of information technology has been accompanied by a tremendous amount of hyperbole about its transforming powers. Information technology in itself will not bring about an end to poverty or transform the lives of women in developing countries. At the same time, IT can threaten the livelihoods of women, when, as part of economic globalization, it eliminates the jobs they were performing or puts them in new jobs under harsh conditions and with low pay. It can even be a tool of sexual exploitation. While IT brings threats, it also brings the promise of new and better jobs and businesses, of fuller participation in the political process, of communication with worlds outside the boundaries of home and community, of easy access to information and resources that can change lives, and of the ability to acquire education and skills and to transcend social restrictions all of which can empower and enhance the quality of women's lives in developing countries. Taking advantage of the opportunities will also take awareness and action because most women in developing countries have neither the access to the new technologies nor the prerequisites for their use. Programs will have to be designed and put in place that ensures women's access to the technologies that can empower them in many aspects of their lives. Many critics dismiss the issue of information technology and gender in developing countries because of the more pressing needs that women in developing countries have for safe water, adequate food, improved health, and better education: The debate centres on prioritizing need: how important is Internet access in an area without safe water or even affordable telephone services? While some health workers praise the satellite system that has brought them e-mail connections and cheap access to health information, others complain that Internet connections will not pay for aspirin or syringes. Health, water, food, education, and information technology are not in opposition to each other in the drive to empower women in developing countries. They are all needed. Simply ending the isolation that many women face in rural as well as urban areas through improved communications will go far toward promoting economic growth and alleviating poverty. Information technology can be a tool for bringing education and improved health services to women. There is no longer a choice. The forces of globalization have made this one world and one economy. While there are risks in joining the global information society, the greatest risk of all is in not joining in it. The new technologies are a lifeline that can enable women in developing countries to join the battle for economic, social, and political empowerment. In order to describe the situation of women and information technology in developing countries and measure the extent of the gender digital divide, we will look at women's use of new information technologies in developing countries how many women are using them, who these women are, what they are using them for, and what roles women have within the information technology industry and its governance.

OBJECTIVE AND METHODOLOGY

The available literature on online banking in India does not provide women customers' perception and attitude about the system operating by banks. The present study has been designed to understand the women customers' willingness to avail the Internet banking facility offered by Indian banks and level of satisfaction in present banking services. The study aims at finding out perceptions of the female customers regarding accessibility of e-banking opportunity and to identify their interest on it.

The data for the study were collected using non-random opportunity sampling of 100 working female customers dealing with either private/ foreign and public banks in West Bengal. Several information on female customers has been gathered from survey of field investigation and primary data collection was carried out by obtaining individual responses to questionnaire. While survey instrument was primarily focused mainly on attitude and perception of female customers, a number of demographic characteristics and socio-economic questions were also asked to the respondents. Each potential respondent was provided a brief explanation as to the purpose of the study and they were assured that their responses to the questionnaire would be anonymous.

FINDINGS

The socio-economic and demographic profile of the women customers indicates that majority of the respondents (62 per cent) were in the age group of 25-35 and 33 per cent belonged to the age group of 36-45. Most of the women operated bank account for more than 8 years. 42 women were married at the time of survey and 3 such women were widow. Most of the women were graduate and seven women were found to be postgraduate. The most of the respondent women (74 per cent) had some knowledge about online banking operation and other knew the concept but never tried.

The study reveals that still the respondents come to the bank, stand in a queue, issue a cheque and withdraw the money. Table 1 shows perception of individual female customers on net services provided by the banks.

Table 1
Women Perception on Online Banking

Percentage

Issues	*Strongly Agree*	*Agree*	*Disagree*
Getting ready for using e-banking facility	23	53	24
Launching net banking literacy programme by bank	64	32	04
Promoting ATMs and Credit cards advantage all over the country	57	42	01
Downloading and printing online accounts	03	02	95
Safety and security of online banking operation	22	52	26
Excellence response time of online banking	14.9	9.5	75.6

Source: Field Study.

The survey discloses that 23 women were agreed strongly and ready to keep pace with Internet banking system prevailing in India. Most of the respondents were in favour of launching any kind of net banking literacy programme by the banks. Although a few of the sample customers enjoyed ATMs and Credit cards facility at the time of survey and 57 per cent argued strongly in favour of ATMs, Debit/Credit cards facility all over the country. Meanwhile it is found that 95 per cent of women participants were not in favour of downloading their accounts balance from the Internet sites thinking the cost associate with it, but in order to save productive time sometime they had to do it. It is found that among 74 women those having some experience with online banking operation most of the women (75.4 per cent) disagreed with the issue relating to excellence response time of online banking and 74 per cent argued strongly in favour of safety and security of online banking.

So far as the customers' satisfaction with the online banking system is concerned it is important for any banking strategy in present competitive environment. Satisfaction is relative terms and may vary from one situation to another. Customers' satisfaction cannot be measured directly. It can be measured indirectly through their opinion and responses to various aspects of banking services. The opinions of the respondents had been recorded on five-point scale of satisfaction containing twenty items relating to various aspects of online banking services. The most desired response is given five score and the least is zero. Thus the customers' satisfaction scale holds a maximum score of 100. The sample respondents had been grouped into three categories based on their level of satisfaction as low, medium and high. The customers with less than twenty per cent of total score fall into low satisfaction category, customers with total score between twenty-one and sixty per cent under medium satisfaction category and the respondents with above sixty per cent of the total score under the high satisfaction category.

It is observed that customers' satisfaction score ranges from 37 to 84 for online operating banks most of which was foreign/private banks and average satisfaction score is 56.4. It has been found that customers' satisfaction score of the respondents is 34.6 in private banks most of which in the infancy stage of online banking infrastructure and individual score range from 21 to 45. The respondents opined that although computerized system exist in most banks but lack of operational efficiency from the part of the banking personnel system often collapses. The respondents were classified into three categories on the basis of their individual satisfaction score. In case of online facility provided by foreign/

private and public banks, the respondents were classified into three groups on the basis of their individual satisfaction score. It is found that as far as foreign/private banks offering online facility no respondents fall in the category of low satisfaction and there were 81 female representing in the high satisfaction group. Besides in case of public banks the number of customers belonged to the low, medium and high satisfaction group being 32, 54 and 04 respectively.

CONCLUSION

With the increasing user participation in accessing Internet banking, banks face the challenge of making their customers feel satisfied with the process of accessing the required information right the first time, every time. Banking sector evidence proves that usability is a critical success factor in improving customer satisfaction and retention, which is very important for online banking portals since the competition is only a click away. Though implementing safe usability design principles reduce the potential usability problems, it is very difficult to predict the reaction of users and prevent their unexpected misinterpretations. With a plethora of technology available to evolve online banking portals, banks have no doubt started realizing the importance of customer satisfaction gained from using these online channels. Since there is a huge amount of uncertainty that looms over users' reaction and expectations, it has become essential to have usability testing performed on online banking portals. Usability testing will definitely go a long way in enhancing customer satisfaction that will ultimately result in enhancing the users trust in the bank.

The greatest potential of technology is the fact that it offers possible solution to the hurdles and challenges. The answer to the strategic challenge posed to the banks by Indian financial market essentially stands on cyber retail networks connected through the very small aperture terminals. This will offer viable solution via customers browsing points. In order to face future challenge posed to the banks, following options are available:

- Getting ready for change and adoption to fast moving customers needs.
- Launching literacy campaign to define online strategy of bank to the customers.
- Managing different product portfolio of bank systematically.
- Generating synergy in conventional and multiple distribution channel.
- Expending product and service range offering.
- Selecting the targeted web properly.
- Defining a set of standard practices or policies to coordinate participants' activity.
- Investing a basic corporate online infrastructure and e-banking infrastructure.

Online banking has become a necessary survival weapon and is fundamentally changing the banking industry worldwide. To day, the click of the mouse offers customers banking services at a much lower cost and also empowers them with unprecedented freedom in choosing vendors for their financial service needs. No country today has a choice whether to implement online banking or not given the global and competitive nature of the economy. Banks have to upgrade and constantly think of new innovative customized packages and services to remain competitive. The invasion of banking by technology has created an information age and commoditization of banking services. Banks have come to realize that survival in the new e-economy depends on delivering some or all of their banking services on the Internet while continuing to support their traditional infrastructure. The rise of e-banking is redefining business relationships and the most successful banks will be those that can truly strengthen their relationship with their customers. Without any doubt, the international scope of e-banking provides new growth perspectives and Internet business is a catalyst for new technologies and new business processes. With rapid advances in telecommunication systems and digital technology, e-banking has become a strategic weapon for banks to remain profitable. However, banks are uncertain about the regulatory framework for conducting e-business and the regulatory and taxation issues for governing cyberspace presents formidable problems. Developing such a system is not easy as the Internet is not organized geographically and it is almost meaningless to refer to a website as national or local. Any successful attempt at governing cyberspace will involve significant international cooperation. The Indian experience of e-banking is gradually merging with its international counterparts. While the private sector and foreign banks have been fast in adopting Internet technology in client servicing, there is a gradual trend for the major public sectors and numerous cooperative units to move in the same direction. A mix of policy support and security assurance should propel further e-banking adoption in India. What ever be the options selected the long run success of the banks on the web largely depends on adopting a web mindset, taking senior management initiatives to transform the organization from inward to outward looking, redesigning optimal channel portfolio, aligning roles and value proportions with customers segments, ability to do multiplicity with simplicity, recognizing major competencies, acquiring new capabilities through strategic alliances and catching on the fast mover's benefits.

REFERENCES

Cornin, Mary, J. (1998), *Defining Net Impact: The Realignment of Banking and Finance on the Web*, Banking and Finance on the Internet, John Wiley and Sons, New York.

Denny, Stephanie (2000), The Electronic Commerce Challenge, *Journal of Internet Banking and Commerce,* November, 3(3).

Indian Express Group (2002), Internet Opens New Vistas for Indian Banks, Mumbai.

ICICI (2000), Available at http://www.icici.com/icicibank.

ICICI (2002), Available at http;//www.icici.com/icicibank.

ICICI Annual Report 2000-01.

Internet and Mobile Association of India (IAMAI) (2006), *IAMAI Report on Varied Activities of Women Online 2006.*

Jeevan, M.T. (2000), *Only Banks: No Bricks, Voice and Data,* Available at http://www.voicendata.com/ content/convergence/ trends/ 10011102.asp.

Nair, A. (1999), Indian Internet Banking Still Nascent, *Asia Internet News,* December 5.

National Association for Software and Service Companies (2002), Nasscom-McKinsey Report 2002, New Delhi.

Stamoulis D.S. (2000), How Banks Fit in an Internet Commerce Business Activities Model, *Journal of Internet Banking and Commerce*, June, 5(1).

Yerkes, Lesha (1998), *Growing with Technology: The Benefits of Internet Banking*, Available at www.bankinfo.com

11

GENDER DIMENSIONS OF HIV/AIDS EPIDEMIC: RELATING THE ISSUES OF HIV/AIDS SCOURGE TO GENDER EQUALITY AND DEVELOPMENT

N. Narayana

INTRODUCTION

HIV/AIDS is among the greatest development and security issues facing the world today. It is the most devastating new disease to have emerged in recent history. Although, worldwide, approximately as many women as men suffer from HIV, this aggregate figure conceals marked differences in the implications of the disease for men and women. Some of these results from biological differences in sex between men and women, but more result from socially defined gender differences.

The consequences of HIV/AIDS can be far-reaching for women. Not only does HIV disease have terrible consequences for the individual, causing serious illness and eventual death, it has the potential to trigger negative social reactions. Across the world, people with HIV/AIDS experience discrimination and stigmatization. Children and young people who are orphaned by the epidemic, and who themselves may be infected, are sometimes left without the support of adults. For women and adolescent girls, the consequence of AIDS can be particularly dire and women may be blamed for HIV disease even in circumstances where they have been infected. There is also evidence to suggest that infected women are less likely to receive the kind of care and support made available to male household members. Moreover, where the male head of household has died there may be loss of social support for young head of household has died there may be loss of social support for young women and lack of legal protection to inherit land and property. Some young women may find themselves unwelcome in the extended family (Aggleton and Warwick 1998).

This work discusses some broad gender issues in the context of HIV/AIDS epidemic and prevailing general relations and attitude of people towards women infected by HIV. It also examines how development processes can be understood by means of a gender equality approach. The chapter provides some useful insights into the impact of the HIV epidemic on men and women and how the epidemic is intensifying poverty in general and poverty among women in particular. Further it reviews issues in order to identify the relevant lessons to be learnt for policy formulation.

THE PROBLEM OF HIV/AIDS

Around 65 million people have been infected with HIV and AIDS has killed more than 25 million people since it was first recognized in 1981 (UNAIDS 2005). The vast majority of the 38.6 million people living with HIV are unaware of their status. As shown in the Table 1, at around 17.3 million, women make up almost half of the total number of people living with the virus, 13.2 million of which live in Sub-Saharan Africa (76% of all women living with HIV). Sub-Saharan remains the most affected region in the world. Two thirds of all people living with HIV are in Sub-Saharan Africa where 24.5 million people are living with HIV in 2005. Growing epidemics are underway in Eastern Europe and Central Asia where 220, 000 people were newly infected with HIV in 2005 (UNAIDS 2005). Declines in HIV prevalence have been noticed in Kenya Zimbabwe, urban parts of Haiti and Burkina Faso and some states in India.

Table1
People with HIV/AIDS- Regional Figures- 2005

Region	*People living with HIV*	*New infections 2005*	*AIDS deaths 2005*	*Adult preva-lence %*
Sub-Sahara Africa	24.5 million	2.7 million	2 million	6.1
Asia	8.3 million	930, 000	600, 000	0.4
Latin America	1.6 million	140, 000	59, 000	0.5
North America & Western & Central Europe	2 million	65, 000	30, 000	0.5
Eastern Europe & Central Asia	1.5 million	220, 000	53, 000	0.8
Middle-East & North Africa	440, 000	64, 000	37, 000	0.2
Caribbean	78, 000	7, 200	3, 400	1.6
Oceania	78, 000	7, 200	3, 400	0.3
Total	38.6 million	4.1 million	2.8 million	1.0

Source: UNAIDS [2005] Report on the Global HIV/AIDS Epidemic.

On the costs side, HIV/AIDS prevention has been consuming scarce resources, as most of the developing countries cannot afford to spend huge amounts to contain the epidemic. However, in view of its serous adverse effects on socio-economic development countries can no longer remain with out pursuing the problem and allocating resources to prevent the spread of the infection.

In terms of resources needed, in 2005, a total amount of US$ 8.3 billion was made available for AIDS funding. As indicated in the Table 2, this figure is estimated to rise to US$ 8.9 billion in 2006 and US$ 10 billion in 2007. But it falls short of what is needed- US$ 14.9 billion in 2006, WS$ 18.1 billion in 2007 and US$ 22.1 billion in 2008. For treatment and care, about 55% of these resources will be needed in Africa, 20% in Asia and the Pacific, 17% in Latin America and the Caribbean, 7% in Eastern Europe and 1% in North America and the Near East (UNAIDS 2005).

Table 2
AIDS Resource Needs (US$ billion)

Activity	*2006*	*2007*	*2008*	*Totals for 2006-08*
Prevention	8.4	10.0	11.4	29.8
Treatment and Care	3.0	4.0	5.3	12.3
Orphans & Vulnerable children	1.6	2.1	2.7	6.4
Programme costs	1.5	1.4	1.8	4.6
Human resources	0.4	0.6	0.9	1.9
Total	14.9	18.1	22.1	55.1

Source: UNAIDS [2005].

WOMEN WITH HIV

Although HIV/AIDS is a global problem, the majority of people living with HIV/AIDS reside in African continent. In sub-Saharan Africa, out of 28.5 million HIV infected people, 15 million were women living with HIV/AIDS in 2001. This constitutes 58% of adults who are living with the virus. HIV positive African women constitute 88% of the world's women with HIV/AIDS. Sub-Saharan Africa is the only region where HIV prevalence and AIDS deaths are higher for women than men, bearing in mind that AIDS is a leading cause of death in this region (UNAIDS 2005). These aggregates mask key age/sex differences in HIV prevalence. For example, for every 15-19 year-old boy that is infected, there are five to six girls infected in the same age group. Women under 25 years of age present the fastest-growing group with HIV/AIDS in Sub-Saharan Africa, accounting for nearly 30% of all female HIV/AIDS cases in the region (UNAIDS 2002).

The Southern African Development Consortium (SADC) region is the most affected, accounting for nearly 37% of all infections in the world. Four countries represented in this meeting are in the epicenter of the epidemic. These are Botswana, Lesotho, South Africa and Swaziland, which together account for 20% of all people living with HIV/AIDS in the SADC region (UNAIDS 2002).

Gender has been found to be a critical factor in contributing to high HIV/AIDS prevalence and has been blamed for the HIV/AIDS epidemics in sub-Saharan Africa. Research studies suggest that the risk and vulnerability to HIV/AIDS are substantially different for men and women as shown the marked age and sex-differentiated HIV prevalence rations. For example, in South Africa the age and sex distribution of HIV infection shows that prevalence level rise more quickly in women and then decreases with age whereas with men the peak prevalence levels occur at an older age (Nelson Mandela/HSRC Study of HIV/AIDS 2002). Gender norms and expectations play a significant role in exacerbating women's and girl's risk of HIV infection. Within familiar, men's illnesses are often perceived as more important than women's illnesses because they have a greater impact on wage earning. The contribution of women's work to family survival is usually undervalued, and women's illnesses may be ignored until they are unable to perform daily tasks. Again women receive an average of 30 to 40% less pay than men doing the same work (Albertyn 2000).

Women are often blamed for the spread of HIV to their partners and HIV/AIDS is incorrectly perceived as a woman's diseases and many parts of the world, causing women to refrain from HIV testing and seeking out care in order to avoid being ostracized and abused. Using antenatal data from pregnant women to estimate the HIV prevalence in countries has contributed to the perception that women bring HIV to their partners, yet it is the synergistic effect of gender, biology, socio-economic factors and behaviour that increase women's risk of HIV infection (Albertyn 2000). Some of the factors that account for differences in vulnerability and risk for men and women are behavioural or social and even biological.

UNEQUAL GENDER RELATIONS

One of the most significant causes of the increasing rate of HIV infection among females is the subordinate role accorded to women in the family and public life. The marital power bestowed upon men in some societies makes it difficult for women to negotiate for many things. For example, in a study done in Swaziland, it was found that women's vulnerability to HIV/AIDS infection increases. This increase is because of economic, social and cultural factors and different forms of violence that place them at a disadvantage within relationships, family and the economy at large (Whiteside *et al.* 2003). Women's economic dependent on men, which include their high poverty level and lack of access to opportunities and resources, contributed of their vulnerability to HIV/AIDS infection. And the reason for this is because men can withdraw their economic support if women do what they want. In addition to the economic factors, cultural expectations and practices are found to contribute to women's vulnerability to HIV/AIDS.

Importantly, there has been increasing awareness that prevailing gender relations affect not only the development of the epidemic, but the manner in which individuals, groups and communities respond. Unequal gender relations can be seen in many ways but are particularly visible in the special vulnerability of women to HIV/AIDS in developing countries. Economic and social vulnerability, as well as stereotypical gender roles influence women's and men's vulnerability to HIV infection, while fuelling the overall course of the epidemic (Ankrah and Attika 1997).

As the epidemics of HIV/AIDS developed over time, governments, international organizations and non-governmental organizations (NGOs) have recognized that social inequalities and power relations have an important impact on HIV transmission. Factors such as poverty, migration and urbanization have a key role to play in facilitating HIV infection. Other variables known to influence the vulnerability of individuals and groups include social background, age, race and gender. Frequently, these different variables interact with one another so as to render some groups, especially women, systematically more vulnerable and other groups more protected.

Policies and programmes to promote greater equality between men and women are considered to be crucial to HIV prevention (Rao Gupta 1995). Despite increasing recognition of the importance of more equal gender relations, many programmes continue to work solely with women in an attempt to help empower them. As Wood and Jewkes (1997) point out, however, this focus is often based on an erroneous set of assumptions about women's ability to control and sustain their health. In the field of international development, several programmes have recently altered their terminology from 'women in development' to 'gender and development'. However, the majority of initiatives to challenge and transform prevailing gender relations still focus on women alone (White 1997). Numerous HIV prevention programmes and interventions have focused on women. This over-emphasis on reaching women who are particularly vulnerable to HIV infection has led to inadequate participation of women in programmes and programming and broader social circumstances.

Some commentators have called for increased male participation in work towards greater gender equality and improved reproductive health. Concern has also been expressed about shifting the focus and resources from women to men. The key may lie in involving men in ways, which are more supportive of both men and women's concerns. Empowering women depends on policies for change that involve men in a woman-centered and gender-sensitive perspective, not just taking men's perspectives or needs into account.

STIGMATIZATION AND ATTITUDE TOWARDS WOMEN WITH HIV/AIDS

Stigmatization and blame have characterized the HIV/AIDS epidemic. The manner in which people are blamed has consequences for the provision and receipt of care. Research studies clearly demonstrate how men are much less likely to be blamed for HIV infection than women, and are more likely to be afforded care by their partners, families and communities (Aggleton and Warwick 1998; de Bruyn *et al.* 1995). It is suggested that women living with HIV do attract guilt and blame partly because they are perceived to have failed in their roles as nurturers and careers. In addition to the increased stigmatization of women who have become infected with HIV, the burden of care for people with HIV/AIDS also falls on women. Women are central to the provision of care for people with HIV/AIDS.

Attitudes and responses towards people with HIV/AIDS, including the provision of care are strongly influenced by gender and gender norms (Aggleton and Warwick 1998). In some countries, however, levels and quality of care is also influenced by perceptions of innocence. When women needed HIV-related care, they generally did not expect or receive the same level of care and support as men. Women who were sick often return to their parents for care since they are unlikely to receive this from their male counterparts.

Even in cases where men did offer some support and care, gender norms influence the nature and amount of care that men offer. Evidence suggests the existence of clear double standards governing the care given to men and women. Whereas men with HIV disease were little questioned about how they became infected and were generally cared for by women, women with HIV-related conditions were frequently castigated and blamed and received lower levels of support. Women also had to balance responsibility for provision of care with the need to support the family financially. In spite of such problems, women continued to provide care as mothers, wives, neighbours and volunteers (Aggleton and Warwick 1998).

Differences in attitudes towards women and men with HIV, and patterns in the provision of care for people with AIDS, are related to dominant versions of masculinity and femininity. Women who become infected with STDs or HIV are often viewed as blameworthy. Blame is less likely to be ascribed to men however, who are assumed to have little control over their behaviour. In addition, women traditionally provide care for family members who are sick, while a care-giving role is not consistent with dominant versions of masculinity.

INVOLVING MEN IN THE PREVENTION OF HIV INFECTION

Most gender sensitive programmes are aiming to reduce levels of HIV-related risk behaviour of women. However, programmes and interventions involving men are also needed to reduce the impact and outcomes of HIV.

The following are some of the issues, which are helpful in formulating programmes in the prevention of HIV infection by involving men.

- It is necessary to recognize gender inequalities that intersect with other social inequalities such as those organized around class, age, race and religion. Programme design needs to be sensitive to these patterns of interaction if gender and sexual inequalities are to be properly addressed.
- Given the intersection between gender and other inequalities, the elimination of poverty for men and women through programmes of social development and other means, is crucial to the prevention of HIV transmission.
- In needs assessment and in programme design, it is important to allow men to express their needs, while keeping in mind that work will also need to be undertaken to ensure that all work is sensitive to the gender inequalities which serve to silence and disadvantage women.
- The concern, which many men express about the health and welfare of their children, may provide a useful way of gaining attention in relation to HIV-related work.
- Since women are more likely to be blamed for HIV infection, work to counter the stigmatization and discrimination associated with such blame needs to take place with men as well as with women.
- It is crucial for HIV-related health promotion to encourage men to take a more active role in the care of people with HIV-related illnesses.

Poor working conditions and risks of work-related injury and mortality may facilitate sexual risk taking and HIV transmission. These issues need to be addressed through programmes to promote improved working conditions as a part of a broader commitment towards social development.

Given what has been said, it is clearly important to involve men more fully than hitherto in work linked to the prevention of HIV infection. However, responsibility for HIV infection is not just a matter for the individual. Broader social policies and actions are needed to inhibit the growth of the epidemic. Unequal gender relations, as well as other inequalities facilitate HIV transmission and the growth of the epidemic. In the long term, greater social and gender equality must be the aim of those seeking to enhance reproductive health among both women and men in developing as well as developed countries. However, given the entrenched nature of existing gender roles, beliefs and expectations, it is unlikely that enormous advances can be made in the short term. In the light of the global pandemic of HIV/AIDS, it is important to think realistically about what is attainable, and on what timescale.

Although greater equality between men and women must be the ultimate goal, this may take a long time to achieve. In the interim, however, it is important that risks to the sexual health of people in developing countries are reduced. An incremental approach, which seeks to reduce the immediate risks of HIV infection within a gender sensitive framework, may therefore be most helpful. In the first instance, ensuring greater male participation in programmes to promote sexual and reproductive health is crucial.

Where possible, it is important to tackle gender inequalities and the socio-economic and other inequalities with which they intersect, at a structural level as well. Policy-makers need to be encouraged to develop structural and environmental interventions to help women and men; make changes in their behaviour which might help them to protect their sexual health. These interventions might include changes in laws to protect women against male violence. Both of these actions would render more visible the circumstances in which HIV-related risks may be particularly acute, and could lead to the development of more effective programmes for prevention. The provision of education for girls, and increased opportunities for participation in the labour market, will help to reduce both widespread poverty and the economic dependence on men, which renders women vulnerable to sexual exploitation. Labour laws, which enforce improved working conditions and reduce injury and death in the workplace for men may also help men change their orientation towards certain forms of risky sexual behaviour.

Much existing information about men's behaviour and beliefs comes not from men themselves, but from women. We still know little about what men think, and what they might respond successfully to, in terms of HIV prevention. Although in the case of domestic violence, it may be difficult to generate accurate accounts from men themselves, it is important to engage men in discussion to gain an enhanced understanding of their perceptions, attitudes and practices.

It is important to get accurate and up to date information on men's beliefs and practices in relation to gender and sexual health. This is especially true in those contexts where the risk of HIV infection is high. Since risk-taking appears to be an important part of dominant ideologies of masculinity in a number of societies, it is important to develop a better understanding of risk-taking behaviour among men, especially among those who work in dangerous and/or isolated environments.

GENDER, HIV EPIDEMIC AND DEVELOPMENT

HIV epidemic has a deeper impact on development. The global epidemic of HIV was seen initially as a crisis in public health and was considered as a health issue that required a health response. But now it is seen much more complex issue influencing the social, cultural and economic determinants. The epidemic is not simply about public health but is concerned with development in all of its dimensions.

The problem of the epidemic is increasingly perceived as developmental in its origins, in that the determinants are fundamentally structural and creating gap between a deepened perception of the problem and a commitment to effective action. It is increasingly clear that the issues that prevent a more effective and multi-sectoral response to HIV and AIDS are bound up inextricably with the failures of development in the last few decades.

An effective response to the epidemic entails more than redefining it as a developmental problem. For that relevant and effective policies for development are needed. Precisely, the failures of development that generated the conditions in which the HIV epidemic has thrived also constrain effective responses to its deepening socio-economic impact. The epidemic has made social and economic divisions within countries, of poverty, inequality of wealth, social, political and economic exclusion and differential access to basic services such as health, education and housing.

Underlying these conditions and often central to the weakness of the policy and programme response to development and to the epidemic is the issues of gender. So, not only is development at the core of the problem of the HIV epidemic, but at the centre of the issues of gender. It is, therefore, the failures of development, which remained largely untouched issues. Worse still is the fact that unwillingness to deal with gender issues in any fundamental sense has bedeviled the national response to HIV and AIDS in many countries. Little progress is possible unless the core role of gender is understood in relation to the epidemic, and until gender issues are addressed through general development policies and programmes.

So issues of gender are central to epidemic processes and are also critical for sustained human development. Addressing gender through effective policies and programmes is the way forward if development objectives are to be realized. It is also necessary if HIV transmission is to be reduced and if societies are to be able to respond effectively to the widening range of social, cultural and economic effects of the epidemic.

What is understood by development includes improvements in development activities directly to achieve the objectives that include poverty reduction, more equal distributions of wealth and income, better access to improved public services, and greater gender equality.

The development process has to be fundamentally transformed by the introduction of gender analysis, as it is now no longer possible to construct an analysis of an economy ignoring gender equality issues. This is because men and women have different social and economic roles, differential access to income and resources and different economic behaviours, including different patterns of consumption and expenditure. To attempt to understand economic and social change without incorporating an explicit gender analysis is therefore an exercise in futility.

Gender analysis must pervade the development process in order to arrive at an understanding of socio-economic change. The advent of the HIV epidemic should transform development thinking as the epidemic directly affects most households. This is also because of its implications, which are far-reaching for every aspect of people's lives now and in the future, and its effects are felt in every sector at every level. It is negatively affecting life expectancy and dramatically reducing the national capacity in every sphere. It is also reducing national output, exports, savings and investment, and is also crippling the capacity of the educational system, the agricultural extension system and the health system. Rarely has there emerged a single phenomenon with such powerful consequences to undermine decades of development achievement. The development debate and development thinking has to change in this direction.

The most essential aspect in gender analysis understands the significance of the HIV/AIDS epidemic since the epidemic has been intensifying the socio-economic inequality of men and women. In attempting to understand how the HIV epidemic is affecting social and economic life, it is vital to have a way of analyzing systematically the contributions and demands made by men and women to the society and to the economy. Traditional economics devotes much energy to the measurement of economic activity in terms of gross domestic product, income per capita, labour force etc. But these are very inadequate and inaccurate as reflections of reality. A great deal has to be considered about the omission from standard economic measures of the vast amount of unpaid labour contributed by women in all economies.

In rural Africa, for example, the unpaid work of women in gathering fuel wood, collecting water and processing food contributes immensely to the survival of households and to the well being of present and future workers. Yet rarely are such activities accurately measured in the context of collecting standard national income data. Furthermore, the caring work that women undertake, the need for which has risen dramatically in the context of the HIV epidemic, is also generally omitted from economic data. However, there is another dimension, which relates to the failure to take full account of paid work, often but not exclusively undertaken by women. In all developing countries there is a vast array of paid domestic service, sometimes paid in kind (food, shelter) and sometimes in cash. However, there is also a vast, uncounted casual agricultural labour force involving men and women, boys and girls, in all areas of rural production, including ploughing, sowing, weeding, harvesting, pruning and processing.

While analyzing the interaction of gender, development and the HIV epidemic, it is essential to understand the potential of the HIV epidemic for much greater social and economic disruption than traditionally assumed. This is more important when we take in to account the unmeasured contributions to social and economic activity particularly of women and young girls. It is also necessary to know the effects of the epidemic through the erosion of social capital that is caused by morbidity and mortality, such that the scale of the losses is compounded because of the losses of human resources and the disruption of social and economic systems. Given the critical social and economic roles that women play, it is essential that they are empowered through a restructuring of social and economic relationships and addressing the multiple challenges of the HIV epidemic

POVERTY, GENDER AND HIV

HIV is highly contagious and is threatening to undermine economic, social and political structures, and reversing economic development in many parts of the world. The epidemic is threatening the lives of the rich and poor alike in all countries.

Changes have to take place at the level of communities, to support prevention programmes and to care for those affected, including support for poor people. However, in order to be effective in society as a whole these micro changes need to be complemented by changes at the macro level. Macro level changes must include shifts in the structure of public expenditure, probably involving significantly increased levels of expenditure for prevention of HIV infection. In order for these to occur, support is needed from among the politically and economically powerful sections of the society. They need to recognize that HIV/AIDS threatens to undermine their own future and that of their children just as much as it will undermine the future of the poor and the powerless.

In developed countries huge amounts of resources are being devoted to the development of drugs, but relatively little to the development of effective vaccines. But the drugs while they are available in rich countries to those with access to health systems under private or public insurance are still not available to all especially many of the poorest and those who are among the working poor. Since the poorest populations cannot display their needs through market demand so the market ignores their needs. The absolute neglect is the poorest living in the developing world who cannot afford to purchase ARV drugs and for whom there is effectively no functioning health care system in operation.

It is necessary to consider the deeply rooted social and economic bases of poverty and the relationship between HIV and poverty. Something must be done about underlying causes such as lack of employment, appalling housing conditions, poor education and few training opportunities, vastly under-resourced health services, environmental decay and a social and economic environment which destroys community social capital. Unless the structural determinants of poverty, exclusion and hopelessness are addressed, HIV will continue to spread and the socio-economic consequences intensify, with all of its implications. In the process, the rich and powerful cannot both ethically and practically avoid having to deal with the problems of HIV and AIDS. It is a well-known policy rule that it is better to deal with a problem earlier rather than later, since delay leads to cumulatively greater problems that could have been avoided, with much higher costs.

It is a fallacy to believe that ARV drugs represent a solution to the HIV epidemic even in the rich countries. This is also the case in the developing world where budgets constrain what under-funded health systems can provide and where the poorest living with HIV and AIDS are excluded from access to even the barest forms of care as a result of their poverty. In so far as anyone has access to ARV therapy and other quality medical care in developing countries, then it is those who are the wealthy and those who manage to gain access legally or otherwise to public budgets. This being so, it is still a matter which is deeply puzzling that the rich and powerful in developing countries are not doing more to prevent the further spread of HIV which is killing their children and their close relatives just as it is killing the poor. The epidemic is also undermining economic development as even the children of the rich will be facing at best an uncertain future and at worst a set of social and economic conditions that represent a reversal of development.

Furthermore, there is plenty of evidence that HIV infection is high even amongst those with secondary and higher levels of education. Not only does HIV/AIDS threaten the human capital stock of the country and the capacity to maintain and advance development, but it also has direct costs for those educated people infected with HIV. Thus the rich, educated and the poor in developing countries, and especially men, are not only exposing themselves to a deadly virus but also their partners and their children. Hence the importance of gender and its inter-relationship with poverty and wealth in the processes are internal to the HIV epidemic. As noted above this is not confined to only poor men and indeed there is enough evidence now to believe that infection rates as noted above are in many countries positively correlated with socio-economic class.

What is needed, at least, is a dramatic transformation in the economic relationships between men and women, in order that women would have sufficient economic independence to choose. This is not to suggest that such a transformation will occur by economic change alone. Economic change must be seen as necessary but not a sufficient condition. This is because women's subordination and HIV transmission are indissolubly linked. Apart from changes in the economic position of women, are improvements in access to education and training and adjustment of labour markets so as to enhance both employment and pay conditions are required. For women this would involve investment in new skills through training etc. to improve their capacities. Corresponding changes would also be needed in the labour market to open up economic opportunities from which they are presently excluded. Such exclusions are not always simply a result of differential access to skills but often because jobs have been set-aside for males in industries and other organizations in many countries.

For most women, given the effective access, which they have to education and training, choices are extremely limited. Large numbers work as domestic workers at home or abroad with the worst and most exploitative working conditions, which are totally unregulated and frequently exposed to abuse. It follows that changing the conditions of women lives through gender sensitive and focused policies and programmes is at the core of effective and relevant responses to the HIV epidemic in all developing countries.

Concurrently, countries have to invest equally in the education of men and women. This would help to understand fully why equitable social arrangements are needed. There should be a situation where everyone could gain from social and economic transformation. If the opportunity is grasped to make those changes to the organization of social and economic activity that are worth to bring transformations that is in fact the whole point and purpose of human development.

LESSONS TO BE LEARNT IN THE FORMULATION OF POLICIES AND PROGRAMMES FOR GENDER EQUALITY

Learning the lessons in policy areas and applying these to the global response to HIV is clearly desirable. The outcomes should reflect much of what is needed if we have to structurally change the conditions of women lives in ways that will make a fundamental difference to the global experience of HIV and AIDS. It needs to be recalled that learning the lessons is not the same as assuming that these are directly transferable from one area of human experience to another. But at least they point the way forward and provide evidence of what is achievable through policies and programmes that are relevant and effective.

There is general agreement that large size of the family imposes unreasonable burdens on women. There are benefits to be derived from reductions in family size, for all members of the family, in the form of improved standards of living. Of course, there are also gains for society in general through reductions in the level of poverty, better-educated and healthier children who grow into more productive adults. The state will be benefited in the form of faster economic growth and lower rates of public expenditure in areas such as education and primary health care. So it has long been argued by demographers that there are bigger social returns from investment in population control than from other competing uses of savings and that a smaller and healthier population is both feasible and desirable.

The policies for HIV and AIDS should be effective in supporting women, and to some extent men, in limiting family size. To do so meant changing a world in which women have traditionally had little or no voice over matters relating to fertility for whatever reasons. The argument quite simply is that if women were given more voice and more power they would choose lower rates of fertility. As a result of which there would be profound outcomes for women and children and substantial social benefits. The basic structural conditions have to be eliminated to derive beneficial outcomes (Cohen and Elisabeth Reid 1996).

- Social and economic constraints such as high levels of female illiteracy and little or no economic independence including weak attachment to labour markets.
- The existence of cultural and social pressures that reinforced other factors so as to leave women with the belief that continuous child bearing was required as part of their social and familial duties.

As long as the above elements are present in many developing countries, it is difficult to bring change. It is now evident that appropriate policies relating to female literacy, female employment and access to credit, and changes in property rights and so on can make a huge difference to the lives of women. With demonstrated effects that are sustained in female fertility such that women, children and their communities are better off than they would otherwise have been in the absence of the changes, which brought about the fertility decline.

Of course, the increases in real income are not a pre-condition to attain changes in family size. If supportive policies and programmes are put in place and made available to women then they are perfectly capable of controlling family size. This would bring an enormous shift in the burdens that they and their families have faced for generations. These are very relevant and point the way forward in developing more effective policies and programmes for dealing with the HIV epidemic. For example, in India fertility rates have fallen substantially from six children per couple, a few years ago, to three today. Of course, fertility rates vary a good deal from district to district in India. In some districts in India fertility ratios are even lower than they are in USA or UK or China although in the aggregate replacement ratios are still above two for India as a whole. In the States where the fertility declines have been fastest, Kerala, Tamil Nadu and Himachal Pradesh, the key factors in producing these declines seem to have been female literacy and female employment. Rapid improvements in these two areas seem to have catalyzing impacts on women's lives through improving their standard of living and in enhancing their voice within families and communities. Contrariwise those states in India with the highest levels of fertility are precisely those with the worst records on female literacy and female employment.

Also there is evidence that cultural and religious variables are not immune to change. A good example can again be drawn from Kerala, which has one of the largest Muslim populations in India, but in spite of such a high percentage of Muslims amongst its total population Kerala has seen the largest fertility decline of any state. It seems from the data as if Indian Muslims have fertility levels not dissimilar from other communities in their region in fact much lower than in Pakistan. Similarly in Bangladesh which has a very large Muslim population. There has also been significant reduction in fertility rates associated with widespread public discussion of the need to reduce gender inequity, enhanced access to family planning facilities and advice and improvements in women's economic position through such programmes as micro-credit. Today Bangladesh's fertility rate is much closer to that of India than it is to Pakistan's in spite of the fact that they both have predominantly Muslim populations (Cohen 1999).

It is clear that many factors operate to change fertility. Nevertheless there are elements in the process of fertility decline, which seem to be common to all societies. What seems to be needed is a coherent and general understanding of fertility decision making within families and the development and delivery of policies and programmes that change the conditions relating to fertility. These include a) greater access to girls for education; b) better employment opportunities for girls and women; c) enhanced access to labour markets through changes in the conditions that restrict and constrain women's participation; d) and access to better health care and to enhance family planning facilities. Each of the above is self-reinforcing and all are necessary for a sustained decline in fertility, which has at its core the aim to enhance gender equity.

The sine qua non of effective policies for population has been an improvement in the position and power of women, pursued through policies and programmes that are seen as mutually self-supporting. It is evident that much has been achieved already through recognizing that policies and programmes need to address all of the structural factors that contribute to decision making within families and communities. This has entailed changing the conditions and attitudes of both men and women through activities that are social, economic and cultural in their content and by doing so to bring about sustained changes in fertility. What is now clear is that similar changes can also contribute to the kinds of changes in behaviour that are so desperately needed if the transmission of HIV is to be contained and reversed. The recent evidence in India shows that fertility can be brought down even in communities, which are amongst the poorest in the world.

DEVELOPMENT PERSPECTIVES TO THE HIV EPIDEMIC

Experience of the HIV epidemic tells that the HIV epidemic is not simply an issue of public health, but it is much more than health and is generally about development. Hence the need to ensure that the development community is actively involved in national responses to the epidemic in terms of the integration of HIV and AIDS in core areas of development, such as poverty reduction, gender and social sector development. It is to ensure that HIV/AIDS should become an integral part of developmental programmes.

The development community needs to understand that if HIV and AIDS are not integrated in development activities then in many countries such programmes are unlikely to succeed. It is inconceivable that targets of primary education for all in Africa could possibly be achieved given the erosion of human capital due to HIV and AIDS in many countries. It is also due to the intensification of poverty because of AIDS experienced by many families. Under these circumstances sectoral programmes, such as health and education need to be revisited by all concerned with development. This will help to realign policies and programmes with the new conditions due to the impact of HIV and AIDS on the economic and social systems.

HIV-specific and HIV-related projects and programmes need to reflect the reality of local conditions. There is little point in designing and implementing activities that are unrelated to local needs and yield few if any benefits. To avoid this outcome, various processes are needed to ensure that the design of projects is undertaken with local inputs that actively involve beneficiaries. Fundamental to improvements in their relevance and performance is a capacity to undertake and utilize applied research. Where this research capacity is weak then it will need to be strengthened through sustained programme support.

As far as possible local institutions should be involved in the design and implementation of projects and programmes and they should be assisted in strengthening both their own capacity and in undertaking activities to strengthen the capacities of other collaborating organizations. It should be recalled that the HIV epidemic systematically destroys human capital and undermines organizational structures. So, there is a need not merely for a strengthening of capacity but also for its maintenance.

Gender equality has to be seen as central to the development effort and as with HIV should be integrated in all development programmes. This follows from the proposition that the empowerment of women is fundamental for all development. Women and female-headed households are over-represented amongst the poorest in all societies. Effective policies for reducing poverty amongst women are worthwhile because of clear evidence that poverty is a major determinant of HIV transmission. Poverty also constrains the capacity of families to cope with HIV-related illness. Women also play a critical role in all social and economic life although their contribution is systematically underestimated by standard economic and social analysis. It is now clear that achieving development entails empowering women. Putting in place programmes for HIV that are effective in addressing issues of prevention, care, social support and mitigation of the socio-economic impact of the epidemic will depend crucially on the mobilisation of women.

Policies and programmes need to be geared towards women's empowerment. These would include improved access to education and training, adult literacy, access to credit, improvements in health and reproductive services, legal changes to property rights and enforcement of women's civil and political rights. Not only is the empowerment of women central to issues such as fertility decline and the consequential benefits of this but also in ensuring that the next generation are better educated and healthier. As we have seen these are precisely the conditions that need to be created if countries are to cope with the multiple challenges of the HIV epidemic.

CONCLUSION

Effectively reducing new infections and reversing the rapid spread of HIV infection is crucial to the government and civil society. The concern is to create a social environment that discourages people from engaging in risky behaviour that puts them and consequently women at risk of HIV. It is necessary for governments to ensure that women do not remain subservient to men. This is possible by repealing all the discriminatory customary laws that dis-empower women in property ownership, land ownership and inheritance.

It is necessary to use education system to change social norms that increase vulnerability to HIV for men and women. This involves changing the curriculum in primary school and introducing new positive roes to men and women. This might include defining gender as a subject in primary schools to address the behaviours that expose men and women to risk not necessarily only from HIV/AIDS. It is essential to mainstream gender in to HIV prevention, care and treatment activities. Evidence that gender has been mainstreamed will be apparent when policy planners analyze the gender perspectives and no can identify the conditions that affect women more than men. They should also identify the risk factors for men and women for each of their conditions and develop different interventions for men and women accordingly. When this approach is used in developing health policies and plans, then gender will have been mainstreamed (Shisana 1999).

It is suggested that involving men more fully in HIV prevention work is essential if rates of HIV transmission are to be reduced. This is likely to require a considerable scaling up of existing efforts. While such a move may not be universally popular, it seems necessary if we are to ensure that men take on greater responsibility for their own health, and that of their partners and families. It can no longer be assumed that by working with women we will be able to redress the profound social inequalities of gender that exist in the world today. If men are not properly involved in work to challenge the complex inequalities of gender which facilitate and reinforce the transmission of HIV, women are likely to have to take on responsibility for changing men's ideologies and practices as well as their own. Policies and programmes are needed to transform existing agendas of prevention, health promotion and development so as to make women more sensitive to HIV-related vulnerabilities.

REFERENCES

Aggleton, P. and Warwick, I. (1998), *A Comparative Analysis of Findings from Multi-site Studies of Household and Community Responses to HIV and AIDS in Developing Countries,* UNAIDS, Geneva.

Albertyn, C. (2000), *Prevention, Treatment and Care in the Context of Human Rights,* Presentation at the Expert Group Meeting on the HIV/AIDS Pandemic and its Gender Implications, Windhoek.

Ankrah, M. and Attika, S. (1997), *Adopting the Female Condom in Kenya and Brazil: Perspectives of Women and Men,* Family Health International/AIDSCAP, Arlington, VA.

Cohen Desmond and Elisabeth Reid (1996), *The Vulnerability of Woem: Is this a Useful Construct for Policy and Planning,* UNDP Issues Paper No. 28.

Cohen Desmond (1999), *Responding to the Socio-economic Impact of the HIV Epidemic,* UNDP Working Paper, Available at www.undp.org

de Bruyn, M. *et al.* (1995), *Facing the Challenge of HIV/AIDS/STDs: A Gender-based Response,* Royal Tropical Institute, Southern Africa AIDS Information Dissemination Service and WHO Global Programme on AIDS, Amsterdam.

Nelson Mandela/HDRC Study of HIV/AIDS (2002), *South African National HIV Prevalence Behavioral Risks and Mass Media Household Survey 2002,* Human Sciences Research Council Publishers, Cape Town.

Rao Gupta, G. (1995), *Integrating a Gender Perspective in UNAIDS Policies and Programmes: A Proposed Strategy,* UNAIDS, Geneva.

Shisana, O. (1999), *Gender Mainstreaming in the Health Sector, in United Nations: Women and Health Mainstreaming the Gender Perspective in the Health Sector,* Report of the Expert Group Meeting 28 September-2 October, Tunis.

UNAIDS (2002), *Gender and AIDS Almanac,* UNAIDS, Geneva.

UNAIDS. (2005), *Report on the Global HIV/AIDS Epidemic,* July, UNAIDS, Geneva.

White, S.C. (1997), Men, Masculinities and the Politics of Development, In C. Sweetman (ed.), *Men and Masculinity,* Oxfam, Oxford.

Whiteside, A., Hickley, A., Ngcobo, N. and Tomilinson, J. (2003), *What is driving the HIV/AIDS Epidemic in Swaziland, and what more can we do about it,* Swaziland Press, Durban.

Wood, K. and Jewkes, R. (1997), Violence, Rape, and Sexual Coercion: Everyday Love in a South African Township, In C. Sweetman (ed.), *Men and Masculinity,* Oxfam, Oxford.

12

GENDER INSTABILITY: A THREAT TO HUMAN SUSTAINABILITY

ARUP KANTI KONAR

INTRODUCTION

By any criterion, human being ranks highest in the scale of species. Human life, which is exceptionally dynamic, moves through periods of relative stability and instability. Human life has basically three dimensions, which are natural dimension (*ND*), ecological dimension (*ED*) and social dimension (*SD*). This trinity determines the trend pathway of human civilization. This means that the relative stability/instability of the three dimensional human life determines the relative stability/instability of the trend path of human civilization. According to Oakeshott (1962:304), 'Civilization (and particularly ours) may be regarded as a conversation being carried on between a variety of human activities, each speaking with a voice, or in a language, of its own...And I call the manifold which these different manners of thinking and speaking compose, a conversation, because the relations between them are not those of assertion and denial but the conversational relationships of acknowledgement and accommodation'. The *ND*, *ED* and *SD* of human life respectively indicate the interaction of human species with the nature, ecology and the humans themselves. Each of the three dimensions has two aspects such as (i) impact of humans on the nature, ecology or human society and (ii) the impact of nature, ecology or humans on the human society. Thus three dimensions have six aspects. Again each aspect of any dimension has two sides such as (*a*) positive side and (b) negative side. So, the three dimensions of human life have twelve sides. The preferred examples of four sides of *ND* are as follows:

- The life support system of nature is the positive side of the natural impact on humans. This is called natural stability (or, sustainability).
- The natural catastrophes/calamities are the negative side of the natural impact on humans. This is called natural instability (or, un-sustainability).
- Humanly induced afforestation is the positive side of the human impact on the nature. This is called positive humanization/socialization of nature.
- Humanly induced deforestation is the negative side of human impact on nature. This is called negative humanization/socialization of nature or denaturing/ denaturalization.

The preferred examples of four sides of *ED* are as follows:

- Humanly induced premature extinction of non-human species is the negative side of human impact on ecology. It is called decolonization, ecological instability or negative humanization/socialization of ecology.
- Defending, revival, renewal or reinvention of non-human species is the positive side of human impact on ecology. It is called positive humanization/ socialization of ecology or ecologization.
- The existence of biological diversity for sustainability is the positive side of ecological impact on humans. This is called ecologization of human society.

- Various human diseases created by the diverse non-human micro-organisms are the negative side of the ecological impact on humans. This is called the de-ecologization of human society.

The *SD* of human life shows the interaction of humans among themselves within the human species. The *SD* has multitude of sub-social dimensions (SSD_S), the preferred examples of which are economic, political, philosophical, religious, spiritual, moral, ethical, cultural, psychological, sociological, scientific, technological, communicative, informational, sexual, marital, familial, ritual, gender, private, public etc. The set of SSD_S of *SD* is not exhaustive, rather illustrative or indicative. Each *SSD* has two sides such as positive side or stability and negative side or instability. The stability and instability of each *SSD* are represented by their respective sets of indicators. All the sets of stability or instability- indicators are not necessarily mutually exclusive. All the SSD_S have both common set of stability- indicators and common set of instability- indicators. If the former is stronger or weaker than the latter we have social stability (or, social sustainability) or social instability (or, social un-sustainability). The sample examples of common instability-indicators of all the SSD_s are poverty, inequality, malnutrition, illiteracy, hunger, premature death, sickness, crime, violence, terrorism, warfare, corruption, hegemony, oppression, exploitation, kidnapping, rape, child-sex, murder, killing, gender-discrimination, inequality and fundamentalism, child labour, prostitution, all kinds of sub-social fundamentalism, smuggling, illegality, fraud, misconduct, aggressiveness, power-hungry, power-dominance, power-supremacy, illicit trade of goods and people etc. On the other hand, the sample examples of the common set of stability-indicators of all the SSD_s of *SD* will be opposite to those stated just earlier. The social stability/instability does not necessarily imply that all the SSD_S of *SD* of human life must exhibit stability/instability simultaneously with the same intensity within a given period of time. It may happen that some SSD_S of *SD* exhibit stability, while the remaining SSD_S

exhibit instability with same or different intensities. The comparison of intensities of human dimensional/sub-dimensional instabilities becomes possible only when their indices can be constructed by any means. Every instability index should have three values such as lowest value (say, 0), highest value (say, 10) and a critical value (say, 5). The critical value determines whether the concerned instability is socially tolerable or not. Any value less than or equal to critical value is treated as socially tolerable value, while any value greater than or equal to critical value is treated as socially intolerable value. The social instability index can be constructed by the weighted arithmetic mean of all the sub-social instability indices.

NEW INTERPRETATION OF SUSTAINABILITY AND UN-SUSTAINABILITY

Sustainability is both the euphemism and euphuism for survival of only human species, which should be regarded as an enlightened self-interest. True or real sustainability implies the simultaneous stability of all the three dimensions in human life such as *ND*, *ED* and *SD*. But since natural instability is exogenously and autonomously given, so sustainability should be redefined as the coexistence of ecological stability and social stability, ceteris paribus. On the other hand, un-sustainability should mean the coexistence of both the ecological instability and social instability, given the natural instability. The notions of sustainability and un-sustainability will be amply clear from the following points:

(a) Given the ecological and social stability, un-sustainability may occur if the natural instability index exceeds its critical point.

(b) Given the natural and social stability, un-sustainability may occur if the ecological instability index exceeds its critical value.

(c) Given the natural and ecological stability, un-sustainability may occur if the social instability index exceeds its critical point.

(d) If all the natural, ecological and social instability indices simultaneously exceed their respective critical points then also un-sustainability may occur.

(e) If at least any sub-social instability index assumes extremely high value, ceteris paribus, then also un-sustainability is inevitable. For example, if the global warfare is undertaken by the militarist *SSD* of *SD*, then the question of sustainability becomes utopian. Further if intensifying terrorism is encouraged, sooner or later un-sustainability will emerge. So, only one or two sub-social extreme instabilities are sufficient to bring about absolute collapse of sustainability. But at present our human civilization is going through the stage of socially tolerable un-sustainability, since all the three human dimensional instability indices have not exceeded their critical limits.

Recently some scientists and scholars are suffering from both natural fundamentalism and ecological fundamentalism. Fundamentalism means tradition defended in traditional way, while tradition refers to the customs, beliefs, practices, ceremonials, rituals etc. by which the past can be substituted for the present. Fundamentalism can arise wherever traditions are under threat/challenge or are being eroded. Fundamentalism can be created or reinvented in all the dimensions and SSD_S of *SD* in human life. It is much dangerous to the society, since it does not accept the dynamic and varying nature of tradition. Like nature and ecology tradition should be defended but not in the traditional way. As both the nature and ecology have been denaturalized/ denatured and de-ecologized respectively owing to intensifying socialization of the whole universe, similarly tradition has been de-traditionalized losing its traditionality. Nature, ecology and tradition are equivalent in the sense that all are erroneously treated as pre-given and independent of human activities. And it is also presumed that they should/ can be defended/ revived in the traditional way. Return to original state of nature and ecology is a healthy fetishism, utopianism and elusive. Yet both should/can be defended/ revived, but not in the traditional way. Today's nature and ecology should be conceived as humanized, socialized or re-moulded nature and ecology respectively. Further in the world of unprecedented socialization the pristine notion of sustainability can never be restored. What can be realized is the surrogate or renewed sustainability, not more than that. Excessive emphasis on natural and ecological restoration with least attention toward the stabilization of intensifying instabilities of the multiple SSD_S of *SD* in three-dimensional human life may be received as a sophisticated nostalgia. It needs reiteration but not exaggeration that social stability can generate both the ecological as well as natural stability through the human 'rational, conscious and moral' pathway, but the converse can never be true. That is why the present paper has been designed not to create a hubbub of heated controversy about the gender instability, which is only one of the multiple sub-social instabilities of social dimension in human life, but to offer an analytic perspective of gender instability for its potential stabilization through policy recommendation.

GENDER WARFARE

While sex is the biological dichotomization of human species into male and female, gender is the socialized version of sex. Sex is a matter of biology, while gender is a construct, something learned or acquired rather than natural. Gender is of two types such as masculine and feminine. Gender instability is one of the important sub-social instabilities of social dimension in three-dimensional human life. The gender instability has basically two vital indicators such as (i) gender fundamentalism and (ii) male violence against women, which has boldly been renamed as 'war against women' by French (1992). Male violence against women is of two types such as indoor violence and outdoor violence. Indoor violence may be renamed as domestic, private, familial or internal violence, while outdoor violence may be treated as public, foreign or external violence. Each of the indoor and outdoor violence can be classified into (a) physical violence, (b) psychological violence and (c) sexual violence. The preferred means of violence are rape, divorce, separation, murder, molestation, torture, kidnapping, female foeticide, extra-marital relation, oppression etc. Leftists argue that violence is ruled out in socialist society, while the rightists and conservatives are of the opinion that violence is not only a necessary and endemic feature of human life, but also generic to the human condition. Violence and the threat of violence in social dimension of human life can destroy or cripple the lives of millions. It is the means whereby individuals, groups or states can impose their will on others. Clash of values and interests can be resolved through the usage of violence. Clash of interests and jousting for power act as the origin of violence. According to Galtung (1990) violence refers to a wide set of conditions, which inhibit the development of individuals' life chances, i.e., it is any social barrier that vitiates the realization of potential. The nature, intensity and real cost of male violence against women will be obvious from my preferred works such as 'Women and War' of Elshtain (1988), 'Rape' of Tomaselli and Porter (1986), 'War against Women' of French (1992) 'Understanding Sexual Violence' of Scully (1990), 'Women's Oppression Today: Problems in Marxist Feminist Analysis' of Barret (1980) and 'Societal Change and Family Violence from 1975-1985' of Stauss and Gelles (1986). French (1992:200) has described the nature of violence as: 'In personal and public life, in kitchen, bedroom and halls of parliament, men wage unremitting war against women...men start repressing females at birth: only the means vary by society. They direct female babies to be selectively aborted, little girls to be neglected, underfed, genitally mutilated, raped or molested...the climate of violence against women harms all women. To be female is to walk the world in fear...women are afraid in a world in which almost half the population bears the guise of the predator, in which no factor-age, dress or colour distinguishes a man who will harm a woman from one who will not'. She adds that up to six thousand years ago, the status and power of women was either equivalent or superior to that of men. Women become male dominated with the establishment of first states. She also argues that when women are not available, men turn other males into women. So male prisoners regularly rape other male prisoners, and many ministers and priests betray the trust of little boys or male teenagers by molesting them. Even the Greek Philosopher Plato (427-347 BC) without hesitation remarked that women is inferior to men...since women is not the complement of man, she is in no special sense fitted to be his companion. The sole objective of marriage is the propagation of children (See Stace 1972: 224-225). Plato was also the supporter of homosexuality, for he added that 'the natural companion of man is not a woman, but another man'. Gilder (1974:114) remarks that men without women are destructive both to themselves and society. If men can not be providers, they have to resort to the muscle and the phallus. Segal (1990:317) says that 'It is just as easy to envisage a world free from fears of the interpersonal violence, rape, and child sexual abuse which, in their most dangerous and prevalent forms, are the violent acts of men'. Maleness/masculinity are intrinsically embedded in violence ranging from casual street violence to large-scale war. Sarcastically speaking, a time will come when the women, by assuming the designation of 'species', will successively go through the four stages of rare species, vulnerable species, endangered species and eventually extinct species. For the woman-man ratio, which is now less than unity, is diminishing at an increasing rate. Violence is a concrete expression of aggressiveness of masculinity. This means that means of violence is the monopoly of men. In other words, violence has been universally masculinised. Most feminists claim that the war against women originates from patriarchy. Patriarchy is persisting for about millennia. The monopoly of the means of male violence has sustained the patriarchy. Patriarchy is still being sustained by the male violence not only against women, but also men. Among various forms of male violence against women, the sexual violence should be prioritized. The important factors responsible for the occurrence male violence against women are gender fundamentalism, familial instability, misinterpretation of marriage, lack of emotionally dialogic communication, erosion of moral values and lack of consciousness and rationality. According to Kristol (1983:77), family is one of indispensable pillars of a decent society. Further Goldsmith (1988) argues that family is the basic unit of human behaviour, without which there can be no stable society. Beyond doubt family acts as a moral regulator of its members. The deficiency and erosion of moral values should be conceived as the vital factor for social instability. Tom Wilkie in the book 'Perilous Knowledge' (1993) writes '...that human beings retain a moral value which is irreducible'. But unfortunately that irreducibility of human moral value is being threatened by the endless change of the global society. Marriage should not be treated as a patriarchal and economic relationship between the marital couple, rather it should be regarded as the collusive union and emotional tie that can be established and sustained through personal attraction, sexuality, morality, intimacy and love. However it can not be denied that sexuality is innately ingrained in the marriage. Marriage becomes pointless if it is not backed up by fair sexuality of both the partners. Similarly most of the male violence against women is sexuality-intensive. No society can be discovered that is devoid of male violence against women and where violence has not been masculinized. Recently violence and crime are being substituted with terrorism and war. The diverse forms of crime, violence, terrorism and war are the indicators of various sub-social instabilities that threaten the social stability or sustainability and thereby accentuate the global un-sustainability-syndrome.

FEMINIST FIGHT FOR FAIR FUTURE

The women's movement of the 1960s should not be treated as the start of feminism. It has diagnosed the problem of women's inequality in the society and proposed solutions. In the book 'Sexual /Textual Politics' (1985), Toril Moi remarks that while 'feminist' is 'a political position', 'female' 'a matter of biology', then 'feminine' 'a set of culturally defined characteristics'. According to Peter Barry (1999:139), '...that not all literary criticism written by women is feminist, that not all books about women writers are feminist, that feminist writing need not be by women, and that feminist criticism is directed exclusively at a female readership'. Elaine Showalter in the book 'A literature of their own' (1977) writes that in the history of women's writing the following phases are noticed (i) Feminine phase (1840-1880), in which women writers imitated dominant male artistic norms and aesthetic standards, (ii) Feminist phase (1880-1920), in which radical and separatist positions are maintained and finally (iii) Female phase (1920 onwards) which looked particularly at female writing and female experience. Feminism originated in the struggle for women's rights which began late in the 18th century, more particularly with Mary Wollstonecraft's 'A Vindication of the Rights of Women' (1792). Later on John Stuart Mill's 'The Subjection of Women (1869) and Margaret Fuller's 'Women in the Nineteenth Century' (1845) brought about enormous popularity and prestige of feminism. Feminism is a protest against the means, mechanisms and methods of patriarchy. The 'Patriarchal Society' was coined by Virginia Woolf, who is famous for his classical work 'A Room of One's Own' (1929). Noteworthy that Dorothy Richardson had invented the term 'psychological sentence of the feminine gender' in his 'Pilgrimage' (1915). Simone de Beauvoirs' 'Le Deuxieme Sexe' (1949) questioned the whole position and the role of women in the society. Mary Ellman's 'Thinking about Women' (1968) depicted the ways women are represented in literature. Kate Millett's 'Sexual Politics' (1969) examines how power relations work and men manipulate and perpetuate male dominance over women. Academically feminism is also a protest against the still persisting 'phallogocentricism' coined by Jacques Derrida. Phallogocentricisation means masculinisation of language. The question arises whether there is a form of language, an *ecriture feminine* which is inherently feminine and whether this is available to man. Virginia Woolf argues that language is gendered and there is no common sentence ready for women's use. Dale Spender in the book 'Man Made Language' (1981) says that language is not a neutral medium but the one that contains many features reflecting its role as the instrument, through which patriarchy finds expression. Kate Millett condemns Freud as a prime source of patriarchal attitudes against which feminists must fight. Feminism was bolstered up in the 1970s and 1908s. There is a vast literature on feminism which basically deals with the protest against women's oppression, objectification, subordination, exploitation, violence etc. that can be encapsulated by 'war against women'. The developments in feminism are classical feminism, neo-feminism, modernism, foundationalism, structuralism, poststructuralism, postmodernism, psychoanalysis, Frankfurt School, discourse theory, semiology, deconstructionism, women's studies, cultural studies, gender studies, reductionism, essentialism, American feminism, French feminism, socialist feminism, lesbianism, gayism, lesbian feminism, radical lesbianism, libertarian lesbianism, queerism, communalism, super-essentialism, anti-essentialism, blackism, etc. The preferred examples of the works on pornography, lesbianism and gayism are Coward and WAVAW (1987), Dworkin (1981), Griffin (1981), Merck (1987), Rich (1980) and Winship (1987). In fine, feminism is developed only to adopt necessary precautions and preconditions for feminizing the patriarchal global society. In other words, feminism seeks to bring about social stability (or sustainability) through correcting or reducing the gender instability indicated by gender fundamentalism and gender warfare or male conducted war against women under the patriarchal society. Despite the increasing growth of feminism, the degradation of feminity is still persisting in the global society.

LESBIANISM AND GAYISM

While lesbian means homosexual woman, gay is the homosexual man. Both the lesbianism and gayism are concerned with the sex and sexuality, while feminism basically deals with anti-patriarchal means, mechanisms and methods. Both the lesbianism and gayism act as the resistance to homophobia (which means fear and prejudice against homosexuality) and heterosexism. Lesbianism emerged in the 1980s as a kind of appendix of feminist criticism, before acquiring disciplinary independence in the North. In fine, both the lesbianism and gayism indicate the denial of and departure from the 'perpetual screen of heterosexism'. Classical feminism had marginalized or ignored lesbianism. Radical lesbianism believes in the 'woman identified woman'. Recently heterosexual feminists and lesbians are going through the period of heated contradiction, conflict or controversy. Genital sexuality is ruled out from lesbianism and gayism. Lesbians boldly claim that women can realize integrity only through lesbianism, which is a stable and 'transcendental signifier'. Nowadays there is an emerging trend in the sexual relationship between the lesbians and the gays, which is treated as a part of 'Queerism', a term iteratively used by the gays. According to Barry (1999:142), 'This concept of 'lesbian continuum' therefore designates a wide variety of female behaviour, running, for instance, from informal mutual help networks set up by women within particular professions or institutions, through supportive female friendships and, finally, to sexual relationships'. Lesbianism should be conceived as a mode of female sexuality, rather than a mode of female bonding designed to resist patriarchy. Both the lesbianism and gayism are the new version of gender instability. For if the whole human species is lesbianised and gayised then the unending chain of human generation must be interrupted and eventually the sign of humans will be erased from the tiny little islet of life amid the infinite ocean of lifelessness. Lesbians and gays claim that homosexuality, which was first used in 1869 in Germany, is a matter of naturalness. They should be reminded that if homosexuality were a natural phenomenon then either the still existing spectrum of biological diversity would be wiped out much before or the concepts of nature, natural and naturalness should be redefined obeying the principles of lesbianism and gayism.

No species was/will be sustainable without genital or reproductive sexuality. Thus unipolar or unilateral sexuality should be regarded as a grave threat toward the much bandied about term 'sustainability'. For due to only sexual eroticism, enjoyment, fascination or fetishism, any kind of sexuality or sexism (hetero-sex, homo-sex, oral-sex, anal-sex, vaginal- sex or whatever sex one desires) can be adopted with discretion (and ignoring moral, religious, ethical or spiritual sanctions and taboos).

CONCLUSION AND POLICY RECOMMENDATION

Though gender instability is one of the multitudes of sub-social instabilities of social dimension in three-dimensional human life, yet it can bring about absolute or unprecedented social instability (or un-sustainability) leading to un-sustainability-syndrome of global society. The single most important indicator of gender instability is the perpetuation of socially undesirable means, mechanisms and methods of the patriarchal society for women's oppression and ousting, despite the natural or God gifted complementarily between the masculinity and feminity. The sole objective of patriarchy is to bring about full fledged masculinization backed up by violence of the three dimensional human life, the inevitable and eventual consequence of which is that the 'woman species' (speaking sarcastically) is under the serious threat of un-sustainability. The salient features of patriarchy are gender fundamentalism, war against women, male domination over women, women's oppression, subordination, exploitation, misogyny, militant eroticism and the like. The sexual intensity of male violence against women has reached such a point where the feminist protesters do not hesitate to exhibit public demonstration with completely naked body. Even the war-participating female-soldiers are raped through the male war against women. Realization of gender stability is possible only through the pathway of the trinity i.e., 'consciousness, rationality and morality' of humans. Feminization of the whole social dimension of human life may be a partial solution, not an exhaustive one, since feminization is a unilateral process. For the stabilization of gender sub-social dimension, what is needed is the bilateral dialogic exchange or communication, since the feedback which is absent in unilateral feminism, is congealed in bilateral communication or understanding. If gender instability is to be reduced or ruled out, then the whole masculinity should achieve a state of 'informed ignorance' coined by Nicholas of Cusa (1401-1464) (See May 1964), which implies that the more one knows, the more aware he will be of his ignorance. Thus the further men penetrate into informed ignorance, the closer they come to the truth itself. Even if it is assumed that men are superior to and stronger than women in all respects, then the superior and stronger actors (men) should obey the 'Veil of Ignorance' principle of Rawls (1971) for the common good (i.e., sustainability). The stronger actors (men) should adopt 'benign attitude' toward the weaker actors (women) to attain the global goal of secularly renewed sustainability in the tiny little spaceship of life. In fine, Rawls's 'Veil of Ignorance' suggests that the stronger or super actors (men) should always stoop to the weaker or inferior actors (women) for conquering mutual benefit (here global sustainability). Further my witty comment is that male violence against women will continue owing to the operation of 'Vicious Cycle of Violence' leading to perpetuity of violence. For more violence against women gives rise to the lower female- male ratio owing to large scale premature death of female population which will induce/encourage the males to commit more violence (specially sexual violence) for the satisfaction of sexual eroticism, due to deficiency of females. Thus the cycle is completed. Feminine and gay sexuality involves a new addition to the still persisting threat to social sustainability that may lead to global un-sustainability-syndrome. If feminism is continued to be backed up by lesbianism or the alliance between lesbianism and gayism then the objective for which feminism was initiated will be vitiated. The missions, means, methods and mechanisms of feminism should be directed in such a pathway so that lesbianism and gayism can be effectively separated from the mainstream feminism. The family and marriage concepts should be reinterpreted on the basis of 'irreducible moral value' of Wilkie. Gender fundamentalism and French's 'War against Women' can be reduced or ruled out if the maxim of Confucius that 'Expand knowledge as much as possible' and the advice of Thirteenth-century Sufi author Saadi of Shiraz that 'However much you study you can not know without action' is deliberately and consciously obeyed. Gender instability is closely interrelated with other diverse sub-social instabilities to which our attention should also be directed for their stabilization. The feminism, which was born to fight against the evils of patriarchal masculinisation (i.e. gender instability), is intensifying that instability owing to embeddedness of newly invented two kid-instabilities such as lesbianism and gayism in mainstream feminism on the grave anxiety that the matured kids may topple the optimism of feminism leading to de-immunization of existing sustainability of the global society. The necessity and norms of restoration of ecological stability or sustainability end in a fiasco when multiple sub-social instabilities are ready to eclipse the immunity of the existing relative sustainability. All arrangements in the society in which men and women are the only actors who are treated as both the ends and means are executed for those actors. But if the means in the society itself is instable due to the irrationality of the actors then the eventuality of such end can be brought under question. For only rational being is capable of doing something irrational.

REFERENCES

Barret, M. (1980), *Women's Oppression Today: Problems in Marxist Feminist Analysis*, Verso, London.

Barry, Peter (1999), *Beginning Theory,* T.R. Publications Private Limited, Chennai.

Coward, R. and WAVAW (1987), What is Pornography? Two Opposing Feminist Viewpoints, In R. Betterton (ed.), *Looking on: Images of Feminity in the Visual Arts and Media*, Pandora, London.

Dworkin, A. (1981), *Pornography: Men Possessing Women, Women's* Press, London.

Elshtain, Jean Bethke (1988), *Women and War,* Basic, New York.

French, Marilyn (1992), *The War against Women*, Penguin, London.

Galtung, Johan (1990), Violence and Peace, In Paul Smoker *et al.* (eds.), *A Reader in Peace Studies*, Pergamon, Oxford.

Gilder, George (1974), *Naked Nomads: Unmarried Men in America,* Quadrangle, New York.

Goldsmith, Edward (1988), *The Great U-turn,* Green Books, Hartland.

Griffin, S. (1981), *Pornography and Silence,* Women's Press, London.

Kristol, Irving. (1983), *Reflections of a Neoconservative,* Basic, New York.

May, Kenneth O. (ed.) (1964), *Ways of thought of Great Mathematicians*, Holden-Day, San Francisco.

Merck, M. (1987), Pornography, In R.Betterton (ed.); *Loking on: Images of Feminity in the Visual Arts and Media,* Pondora, London.

Oakeshott, Michael (1962), *Rationalism in Politics and other Essays,* Methuen, London.

Rawls, J. (1971), *A Theory of Justice,* Belknap Press of Harvard University Press, Cambridge, MA.

Rich, A. (1980), Compulsory Heterosexuality and Lesbin Existence, *Journal of Women in Culture and Society*, 5(4): 631-660.

Scully, Diana (1990), *Understanding Sexual Violence*, Unwin Hyman, London.

Segal, Lynne (1990), *Slow Motion,* Virago, London.

Stauss, M.A. and Gelles, R.J. (1986), Societal Change and Family Violence from 1975-1985, *Journal of Marriage and the Family*, 48: 445-479.

Stace, W.T. (1972), *A Critical History of Greek Philosophy,* Macmillan, London.

Tomaselli, S. and Porter, R. (1986), *Rape*, Blakewell, Oxford.

Winship, J. (1987), *Inside Women's Magazine,* Pandora, London.

13

GENDER DIMENSIONS OF TRADE LIBERALIZATION AND DEVELOPMENT

M. RATHEDI

INTRODUCTION

The differences and commonalities between women and men are set by conventions and other social, economic, political and cultural forces. In recent years, there has been increased interest in the gender dimensions of trade among development analysts and policy-makers in different countries. While the complex relationships between trade and gender equality are not completely unknown, the gender issues need to be taken in account in order to achieve all round development. The key issues that ought to be analyzed are: how does trade advance or impede gender equality? What effects does gender equality have on trade? What are the implications of these effects for policy formulation? What strategies are available to make trade policy and practice more gender-equitable?

It is evident that trade has positive effects on employment, economic growth and empowerment and can therefore increase wealth and well being of people. It can also have negative effects, particularly on the lives of poor people and those marginalized by gender, race and class. However, many gender advocates have argued that, despite the evidence, the policies and institutions which govern trade at national, regional and international levels have tendency to ignore gender relations and gender-based differences.

This chapter aims to identify the possible ways and means for ensuring that the trade and gender equality agendas support each other. This is particularly relevant in the context of understanding the implications of trade liberalization and globalization and the role of trade policy in the achievement of gender equality. It highlights how gender-aware trade policies and institutions can effectively support the achievement of gender equality goals and accelerate economic growth and sustainable development. In this chapter it is also discussed the relationship between gender, trade and development by looking at the implications for gender equality and gender relations of trade agreements along with the key features of the development policy environment. It provides some ways forward in promoting a gender-aware framework for trade policy with the hope that globalization puts people first by respecting human dignity and equal worth of every human being.

TRADE AND TRADE LIBERALISATION

Trade is an activity of exchange of not only goods and services but also resources that appears in different forms, and takes place in different locations. It could be two regions or two nations trading their products on the international stage. Moreover, those indirectly participating in trading activities can be paid or unpaid workers, business-owners, importers, exporters and consumers. The actors from the small to the large scale are all economic agents but have different roles and different levels and types of power and influence. Trade policy in terms of rules and mechanisms influences at the national level for cross-border trade activities. It is intertwined with domestic fiscal, monetary and labour market policies. It is also linked to other policies at the macro level such as foreign aid and investment, structural adjustment, debt and development.

Trade liberalization entails the deregulation of foreign investment through the reduction of barriers to international trade, such as tariffs. Reducing tariffs has two major implications: (i) cheaper goods come onto national markets from overseas, affecting existing indigenous producers but also providing cheaper options for consumers, and (ii) Tax revenues previously collected from tariffs on imported goods are now curtailed with an effect on national expenditure. Liberalization also means instituting macroeconomic reforms such as export promotion. With trade liberalization, countries are encouraged to specialize in particular goods and services according to their own comparative advantage.

The trade policy of a country is guided by the agreements of Multilateral Trading System (MTS) as they are the legal ground rules for international trade. At the heart of the MTS are the World Trade Organisation (WTO) agreements, negotiated and signed by the majority of the world's trading nations, and ratified in their parliaments. Essentially, these are contracts, guaranteeing member countries their important trade rights. They also bind governments to keep their trade policies within agreed limits to everybody's benefit. The agreements were negotiated and signed by governments and their purpose is to help producers of goods and services, exporters and importers conduct their business effectively.

Development Dimensions of Trade Liberalization

There are several different versions of the role of trade and trade liberalization. Some argue that trade liberalization should be conducted for all countries. This 'free trade' perspective would mean that the movement of goods and services was entirely dictated by market forces (Williams 2003a); and that all impediments to trade such as tariffs should be removed to allow countries to specialize in producing what they are 'good' at producing. This leads to greater overall production, which results in growth and poverty reduction. However, others argue that some countries need protection to develop the capacity to produce– particularly developing countries with less developed industries. On the other hand, 'protectionism' is where countries are allowed to protect their own markets through the imposition of tariffs on imports and the support of domestic producers through subsidies. The current situation is some where between these two perspectives as negotiations continue on the direction and pace of liberalization.

The development dimensions of the MTS and its global trade rules have been a continuing source of disagreement between developed and developing countries since the coming into force of the WTO. Initially, the conventional wisdom simply assumed that trade liberalization was itself the key factor that would automatically ensure the growth and development of poor countries. However, the relationship between the openness of an economy (something that is necessitated by trade liberalization) and the degree of its economic growth is analyzed. While some studies found a positive relationship between openness and growth (Sachs and Warner 1995; Winters 1999; Ames, Brown, Devarajan and Izquierdo 2001), other findings point to a negative relationship. Still other studies found the relationship unclear and not straightforward (UNDP 2000).

The fact that developing economies are less well placed to immediately benefit from trade liberalization and the need for them to be involved in formulating international trade policy, was first recognized in 2001 in the Doha round of WTO negotiations. What became increasingly evident was that the scope of world trade was not simply a neutral issue of macroeconomics, but that it covered strategic development areas such as agriculture, services, and intellectual property rights and investment. This had implications for people's jobs, livelihoods, well being and human rights. Trade agreements affect individuals through their impact on prices, employment and production structures. This will have varying impacts on different groups of people due to differential positions in the economic system. These different positions arise not only from different national contexts but also from social and cultural factors such as gender, ethnicity and class or caste.

Importance of Gender in the Context of Trade Liberalization

Gender refers to the socially constructed roles and behaviours of, and relations between men and women. Gender relations are characterized by unequal power. Gender norms assign specific entitlements and responsibilities to men and women. As such, they determine the distribution of resources, wealth, work, decision-making and political power, and the enjoyment of rights and entitlements within the family as well as in public life (UNDAW 2005). Gender roles and relations vary according to context and are constantly shifting. The different roles given to men and women constitute what is called the 'gendered division of labour', in which certain forms of work (physical labour, cash-crop farming and managerial roles) are seen as men's work. On the other hand, childcare and works relating to house keeping are highly feminized activities that are directly related to women's responsibilities within the home and the extension of their domestic tasks. Such work is characteristically underpaid and non-regulated (UNIFEM 2005).

In all countries of the world, women continue to exist in roles and relationships that make them subordinate to men. These inequalities severely limit their capacity to engage in and benefit from trade. Acceptable gender roles, including the division of labour, create a society where these hierarchies are translated into economic policies and activities. As underlying gender systems in most countries are grounded in biases and discrimination against women, shifts in trade policy in accordance with global trade rules will inevitably impact on the underlying system of gender relations.

Most often, it is simply assumed either that trade rules are gender neutral in their outcomes and impacts, or at least have a positive outcome for women as compared to men. As a result, national priorities for trade policies and negotiations have been determined without any gender analysis. The supposed 'gender neutrality' of trade both undervalues women's work and obscures women as economic actors. But, in fact, women play many key roles in trade, as producers, employees and consumers, and in reproducing and caring for the labour force. The invisible contribution of women to the economy is estimated to be at least US$11 trillion a year (UNDP 1995).

Feminist economic analysis argues that due to different gender roles, the relationship between women and men in society and women's unequal access to economic resources such as land, credit and technology, macroeconomic policy will have different impacts on men and women. Thus, the conventional assumption that trade policy and trade liberalization are gender neutral in their formulation and impact must be rejected in favour of much more in-depth examination of their gendered impact. Feminist economic analysis seeks to understand the impact of the gendered division of labour on women's empowerment, their well being and the types of work they undertake. It also looks at women's unpaid work and how the intensification and expansion of trade may impact on this (Elson *et al.* 1997).

Trade, Economic Growth and Gender

A number of studies have analyzed the relationship between gender, growth and development. Both micro studies and macroeconomic analysis (Elson *et al.* 1997; FIAS/IFC GEM GGA 2005) indicate that gender inequality directly and indirectly limits economic growth.

The relationship between growth and gender equality is largely due to three factors:

1. Gender differences in access to assets limit women's options.
2. Gender differences in labour remuneration lead to conflict in households and affect labour allocation at the domestic level.
3. Gender differences in labour and other factors of productivity limit economic efficiency and output (Elson *et al.* 1997; Klasen 1999).

In fact, gender inequality seems to account for 15 to 20 per cent of the difference in growth performance between sub-Saharan Africa and East Asia. It is argued that addressing structural gender-based inequalities in education (total years of schooling) and in formal sector employment could allow Uganda to gain up to two percentage points of gross domestic product growth per year (Klasen 1999). The 2004 Ugandan Poverty Eradication Action Plan (PEAP) put this at 5 per cent of GDP (FIAS/IFC GEM GGA 2005). However, some studies also point out that gender inequality in wages stimulated growth in semi industrialised economies such as Thailand. In these cases, the pressure for flexible prices leads to an increase in employment for women, who have lower wages than men since they have less bargaining power. This implies that export-led growth is achieved at the expense of women.

Given the centrality of women's work, not only in the international trade system but also for poverty reduction, an approach to poverty that sees trade as gender neutral is likely to have a negative impact on women's well-being and on their ability to claim entitlements and rights (Jackson and Palmer-Jones 1998). However, trade policies continue to affect men and women differently due to gender inequalities in access to land, information, economic resources and decision-making (Fontana, Joekes and Masika 1998).

The institutional framework of the MTS is based on the assumption that trade policies and agreements are class, race and gender neutral. This underlying assumption has led to the neglect of gender as a variable in trade policy-making, while women and other groups affected by trade policies have been excluded from the decision-making processes related to the WTO as well as at the regional and national levels. The inclusion of development issues in the agenda holds great potential for the integration of gender as a crosscutting theme.

GENDER IMPACTS OF TRADE POLICIES AND LIBERALISATION

Trade liberalization has different outcomes for men and women. These differential impacts are related to many of the most fundamental aspects of livelihoods and well being, including employment, income, food security and access to health services. The outcomes will differ across countries and regions and are based on the type of economic area and specific sector, measures, timing and sequencing of trade policies. They will also cut across different sectors and sub-sectors of trade liberalization: agriculture, services, clothing and textiles, and intellectual property. It is critical that policy-makers and others interested in gender equality, poverty eradication and sustainable economic growth and development are sensitized to the full range of opportunities, challenges and constraints of the liberalization of these sectors (Fontana, Joekes and Masika 1998). This section will look at the practical ways in which trade policies affect men and women differently and therefore affect gender equality. It will firstly address broad impacts on production, employment, income and unpaid work, before going on to look in detail at the various sectors of liberalization: agriculture, services and entrepreneurship.

Production Structures and Employment

Practically, the impacts of trade are felt by individual men and women as fluctuations in price (and hence availability of goods) and through changes in output (what people work to produce, how and under what conditions). The main argument of the proponents of free market policies, including some gender advocates, is that increased trade and investment liberalization can improve economic growth, which in turn can increase women's participation in the labour market. There have been increased employment opportunities in non-traditional agriculture such as cut flowers and clothing and textiles, and also in the electronics-oriented Export Processing Zones (EPZs) and the services sectors. In the year 2000, almost 35 per cent of the manufacturing workforce was women in Latin America and 41 per cent in Asia, where as women account for more than 80 per cent of the workforce in the export industries of South-East Asia. Much of this increase is concentrated in export-oriented industries where electrical components are assembled, textiles are processed, and garments and shoes are produced (Sexton, Nair and Kirbat 2004). Paid employment can improve women's autonomy as well as their economic and social status. It can also shift power relations between women and men, including at the household level, and can improve women's well being, negotiating power and overall status (Fontana, Joekes and Masika 1998). Studies have shown that work in the garment industry in Bangladesh has had a positive effect on women's self-esteem and decision making within the family (Kabeer 2000). In the modern business services such as finance and software have proved to hold great potential for higher pay and more jobs for educated and middle-class women (Joekes 1999 cited in Williams 2003a).

However, the picture is not as clear-cut as this might suggest. The structure of domestic labour markets and global production chains is highly gendered. Despite the advantages, in many contexts trade liberalization is coupled with persistent occupational segregation by sex, both vertical and horizontal. The examples above are of industries that require large numbers of low-cost workers. These industries depend on pre-existing inequalities between men and women Women not only supply a cheaper workforce, but are also supposedly more docile. And, because of the gendered division of labour, work with textiles, for example, fits in accordance with existing gender norms. Women therefore tend to have less skilled jobs than men and most of the time their wages are lower than men's, and they often work in unhealthy and exploitative conditions.

Overall, there has been increasing deregulation of labour markets and casualization of work across regions as a result of global competitiveness and technological innovation. In many African countries as well as in Eastern Europe, trade liberalization has in fact led to increased unemployment (GERA Programme 2000; UNIFEM 2004), as it leads to the contraction of some sub-sectors and the expansion of others which may require different skills and/or fewer workers.

Women tend to work in industries such as the footwear industry in which capital is more mobile. These industries are more sensitive to foreign competition and are most likely to contract at periods of economic downturn. Women are more affected by retrenchment than men, who are perceived as the breadwinners in society.

The liberalization of tariffs in the South African footwear and leather sub-sectors has led to retrenchments and dramatic changes in production processes in local factories. In addition, there has been a direct relationship between company restructuring in the footwear industry and the growth of the informal sector. This has become the last resort not only for the increasing number of retrenched women workers, but also for factories through subcontracting to the informal sector in order to cut labour costs. South Africa's informal sector has increased from 1,136,000 workers in 1997 to 1,907,000 in 1999. There are about 193,000 African women compared to 28,000 white women working in the informal sector. These figures show that it is the social groups with the least power and resources who are most highly represented in the informal sector (ILRIG 2001). This example also shows the importance of noting the differentiated impact among women, due to differences based on class, race and geographical location or ethnicity. It is generally the poor and marginalized groups of women who are negatively affected by unemployment and the restructuring of labour markets.

The Gender Wage Gap

According to the World Bank, if the wage and employment differences between men and women were eliminated this could lead to a one-time increase of approximately 6 per cent of GDP and overall greater economic efficiency (World Bank 2001). Research has shown that intra-household dynamics are affected by who contributes resources and that women's involvement in wage employment increases their control over how household budgets are spent. Moreover, resources controlled by women can have additional benefits, including increased efficiency in subsistence agriculture and a rise in allocations towards health and education (Quisumbing 2003). Although there are significant gains in some areas, in others there is ample evidence that despite the fact that more women may be earning a wage external to the household, the gap between their wages and those of men (the gender wage gap) is far from being closed (UNCTAD 2004; UNIFEM 2004). Industries that began by employing lots of low-cost women workers may begin to embrace new technologies, at which point women are laid off and more men are employed at higher wages due to the skills required. Women's wages will continue to remain lower than those of men while they lag behind in education and training opportunities (Joekes 1999). Even when the available data suggests a reduction in wage differences, this may be the result of a decline in men's wages rather than an increase in women's wages (Kabeer 2003). The persistent gender wage gap undermines the long-term sustainability of women's livelihoods.

Small and Medium Enterprises and Women Entrepreneurs

Market access and enterprise development have been touted as fundamental policies through which developing countries will be enabled to engage in international trade. However, in general, liberalisation under the WTO rules has not significantly increased women's access to credit, nor has it provided more opportunities to use domestic savings for entrepreneurial activities. This is because structural gender inequalities in property rights and ownership mean that women have fewer assets that can serve as collateral. Rather than introducing policies to support women's access to credit, profit-driven liberalisation policies have perpetuated the discrimination against poor women in the mainstream financial market by focusing on urban areas and the more profitable economic sectors. This excludes poor women who are concentrated in the informal sector and operate mostly in small and medium enterprises (SMEs) (Randriamaro 2001). As a result, poor women and other disadvantaged groups have to rely on the informal financial sector for both their survival and economic activities.

An additional challenge is the fact that changes in investment regimes mean that foreign investors are not held to particular performance requirements by the governments of the countries in which they operate. They are therefore able to produce goods at highly competitive prices, which can lead to the displacement of weaker economic actors, most of whom are women, from their segments of the domestic markets. This is likely to have adverse impact on women-owned and other SMEs (Williams 2004). Along similar lines, while competition policy focused on transparency and a 'level playing field' for all businesses may open up space for SMEs, it can likewise expose them to harsh competition from foreign suppliers in areas that were previously protected. Some case studies (Carr 2004) suggest that regional trading arrangements are likely to offer opportunities that are best suited to women, who are mostly small-scale producers and traders. This is because they do not necessarily need large export markets and may find neighbouring markets more familiar and easier to deal with. This is particularly relevant in the case of regions where many women have been historically involved in informal cross-border trade. Focusing on inter-regional/sub-regional markets is also a possible response to the overarching issue of global competitiveness that confronts many small exporters (UNCTAD 2004).

Impact on Services and the Household

The policy reforms induced by trade liberalisation and the WTO regime have also resulted in a shrinking policy space that has altered the role of the state in profound ways. Some argue that trade liberalisation has endangered the fiscal basis of the state as a result of tariff reductions combined with the tight constraints on budgets imposed by IFIs. Trade taxes are an important source of revenue for African countries. For the last decade, they have provided around 28% per cent of the region's total current revenue, compared with 0.8 per cent for Organisation for Economic Co-operation and

Development (OECD) countries (UNECA 2004). In sub-Saharan Africa, as a result of tariff reforms and efforts to reduce fiscal deficits, public investment fell from 6.4 per cent in 2000 to 5 per cent in 2001 in continuation of trends observed through the 1980s and 1990s (UNECA 2004). The most common policy response to these fiscal problems has been to increase domestic indirect taxation on goods and services, with a focus on value added tax (VAT). VAT can be particularly detrimental to women, both as consumers and in relation to their reproductive role, as it is often levied on goods for the household and labour-saving devices such as domestic appliances.

Fiscal austerity also has implications for spending on services such as health and education, which are essential for all, but particularly for women in their role as careers. Fiscal austerity can also constrain the ability of governments to put in place social protection measures and safety nets to offset some of the negative impacts of liberalisation. These negative impacts are compounded by the undermining effects of international trade rules on national commitments to gender equality. Trade liberalisation also therefore has an impact on women's unpaid labour. In addition to having to take on added caring responsibilities with the reduction in social spending, the pressure to produce for export drives people out of subsistence farming where caring responsibilities could often be incorporated into productive work or shared among family members (Mukhopadhyay and Sudarshan 2003). Finally, during periods of economic downturn, women's unpaid work within the household further increases. When household incomes fall and there is less money available for assistance in caring roles for children or the elderly, women move in to make up the shortfall. These are also the times when women are more likely to take on informal work to boost domestic finances.

Women's heavy burden of household responsibilities and their weaker property rights to land and other resources are likely to have contributed to the weak supply response of African agriculture to export opportunities in countries such as Burkina Faso, Tanzania and Zambia (Smith and Chavas 1999). Moreover, women's participation in new opportunities created by trade is only possible when other female household members are available to take on household duties (Newman 2001).

GENDER IMPACTS BY SECTOR

Agriculture

Agriculture plays a significant role in the lives of men and women in the global economy, but particularly so in developing countries, where it is still a significant part of total domestic output as well as a source of employment for a large proportion of the population. Agricultural policies, including those around trade of agricultural produce, have major implications for food security within the household and sustainable livelihoods (Williams 2004).

Gender issues in agriculture cover a broad range of areas that are critical for the maintenance of families and communities in developing countries. Women tend to dominate in the agricultural sector in most developing countries. A decade ago, agriculture accounted for 62 per cent of all female employment in southern countries, and in India it now accounts for about 84 per cent of the total female workforce in rural areas. In Uganda, the percentage of women working in the agriculture sector is also very high. However, most female workers are unpaid family workers or self-employed in the informal sector. In most countries, men are responsible for production of cash crops and women mainly produce domestic staples and involve in small-scale trade of domestic food items (Williams 2003a).

Until the start of agricultural liberalisation in developing countries in the early 1990s, the majority of women producers were still able to meet household subsistence needs and to earn a living income in subsistence farming (FAO 2000). In theory, they could have benefited from trade liberalisation in agricultural products, as it could expand food production, attract investments and boost farm productivity. But the majority of poor farmers have not necessarily seen these potential benefits.

Non-traditional Agricultural Exports in Sub-Saharan Africa

It is often argued that non-traditional agricultural exports (NTAEs), such as horticulture and organic farming, which generate significant revenues, have the potential to redress the bias against women elsewhere in the agricultural sector. For example, while the lack of access to credit remains a major constraint for women who produce 80 per cent of NTAEs in Uganda, it has been found that most women entrepreneurs have been able to access credit and expand their businesses because they own land (ITC 2003). In contrast to the prevailing view, the current situation underlines that in general, it is the male, better-off farmers with large-scale plantations, equipment and capital who have benefited from NTAEs in sub-Saharan Africa. The majority of women are involved in NTAEs as waged labour in large-scale enterprises organized along quasi-industrial lines. Over 65 per cent of workers in Kenya and Zambia are women, and women constitute 91 per cent of horticultural employees in Zimbabwe (Kabeer 2003). In reality, the production of NTAEs varies along the lines of many other forms of agricultural production, from small farms to large-scale commercial enterprises. Differences in gender roles and the gender inequalities that exist in production of commodities other than NTAEs also apply here. For example, Ugandan women involved in horticulture can have difficulties in meeting the EU's environmental regulations because they have less access than men to the required information on organic farming, which is a growing segment of NTAEs in northern markets (Sengendo and Tumushabe 2003).

In reality, there are differentiated outcomes for women in their different roles and locations. For instance, in Ghana, women consumers in urban centres have benefited from the availability of cheaper foodstuffs because they are the net buyers of food. However, women farmers in rural areas, as the net producers of food, have been negatively affected by export-promotion policies that have mainly benefited men and large-scale farmers. They have also suffered, as have men farmers, from declining household incomes due to the increased competition with imports, reduced farmgate prices (price of goods as they are sold where they are produced) and declining commodity prices in international markets (Vander Stichele 1998).

There is clearly a need to rebalance rules that are biased against women's needs and strategic long term interests, and undermines their livelihoods in a context where they constitute the majority of the poor. Governments need to address supply-side constraints facing women and low-income producers such as access to resources, training and extension services and to childcare.

GENDER TRADE AND DEVELOPMENT STRATEGIES

Approaches to Gender and Trade

Work on gender and trade has largely followed key developments in work on gender equality. These include Women in Development (WID) to Gender and Development (GAD) approaches. These approaches are not mutually exclusive, nor are they each limited to one set of 'actors' or to a specific point in time. They also often overlap or coexist within interventions at different levels.

The WID approach, developed in the 1970s and 1980s, focuses on targeting women with specific policies or programmes. In the context of trade, this means policies and programmes that aim to alleviate the negative impacts of trade on women or support their entry into the labour market. This approach does not necessarily address the larger framework of trade reform, but instead addresses a specific set of concerns about women's roles and contribution to the development process at the micro level. In so doing, it appears to recognize and accept that free trade is basically good, and that the issue at stake is merely how to ensure that women can take advantage of its opportunities. This has certainly been the case with many development cooperation programmes and agendas, as well as NGO-oriented service delivery and advocacy of the 1980s and early 1990s. In the mid-1990s, these critiques of WID led to the development of the GAD approach in an effort to integrate an understanding of gender roles and relations of unequal power.

The GAD approach to trade aims to acknowledge the unequal power relations between women and men in terms of access to the resources needed to participate in trading systems, as well as in terms of distribution of their potential benefits. Related to the GAD approach is gender mainstreaming, a process by which an understanding of gender roles and relations of unequal power is incorporated into the design and implementation of all policies and programmes. In spite of its broader focus, like the WID approach, this approach does not necessarily address the conceptual framework underlying current trade policies, institutions and projects. Hence, it can fail to address the conceptual issues related to the neoliberal macroeconomic framework of the WTO, focusing at the macro level instead of micro-level issues to offset the negative consequences of gender-blind processes at the macro level. Moreover, the GAD approach tends to overlook the systemic issues of imbalances in trade agreements between developing and developed countries, as well as structural problems in the global governance of macroeconomic policies in general and trade in particular. In order to redress these inequalities between men and women, and between countries, many gender advocates have turned to the concept of human rights as a way of promoting a more just and 'people-centred' approach to trade policy and programmes.

Macroeconomic policies are closely intertwined with other economic and social policies. It is important to remember that what happens in trade is likely to be much less important for reducing poverty than the other national policy and economic conditions that influence how the opportunities from trade are transmitted to different groups especially women in the economy. Even direct poverty-reducing trade may not produce a favourable outcome if the government does not want to improve income distribution.

Poverty Reduction Strategies (PRSs) have become the framework for the co-ordination of macroeconomic policy as well as development cooperation in a number of developing countries. Moreover, PRSs are meant for the achievement of the MDGs. The funding packages of PRSs include a range of conditionalities related to trade liberalisation that have significant gender implications. For instance, conditionalities related to tariff reduction could directly affect the agricultural products that are important to women, both as producers and managers of food security.

In some instances, the trade reforms driven by IFIs are potentially undermining the progressive content of the WTO provisions (Caliari 2002; Ladd 2003), as is the case for many African countries. Women, who form the great majority of small producers, can be disproportionately affected by such PRSP-driven trade reforms, given their central role in agriculture, food security and social reproduction. Since the launch of the PRSs, efforts have been made to integrate gender perspectives and concerns with mixed results. But there is a very little incorporation of gender in macro policy, including trade policy (Zuckerman and Garrett 2003). Only Rwanda's and Zambia's PRSs addressed the hard issue of budgeting for gender equality, beyond the soft issues of girls' education and maternal healthcare that were the focus of most PRSs.

The New Aid Mechanisms

The primary responsibility of national governments for ensuring gender equity and promoting women's empowerment in trade is much emphasized. For the large majority of developing countries that are debt and aid-dependent, this does not preclude the fact that bilateral and multilateral donors have a decisive impact on the effectiveness of national strategies for gender equality in the context of trade as a critical element of poverty reduction. Human rights, sustainable development and gender equality are at the core of their respective mandates. Therefore the new aid mechanism that are being established as part of the global partnership for poverty reduction will have an important impact on the implementation of the gender equality agenda in all areas, including trade.

The new aid mechanisms are increasingly integrated into national planning processes such as Country Strategy Papers (CSPs). The underlying principles of the new aid mechanisms are donor harmonization, the building of effective partnerships, national ownership and internal accountability. The main mechanisms are sector-wide approaches (SWAPs) and support within the framework of countries' PRSP processes as direct budget support (DBS). SWAPs involve the coordination of donor agencies and national ministries on programmes within a specified sector such as trade. These are accompanied by 'policy dialogue' between development cooperation agencies and national ministries. In the context of trade, this means capacity-building programmes and financial support for trade ministries to promote more effective engagement with international trade policy processes.

However, despite the opportunities to integrate gender into high-level policy dialogue, the potential of SWAPs in promoting gender equality has been limited as it addresses the underlying causes of gender inequality in access to and control over goods and services, particularly significant in the area of trade policy. Many gender advocates recommend a 'twin-track' approach to gender and development policy-making, involving both the allocation of resources to a specific sector dedicated to gender equality issues, and consistent gender mainstreaming in each of the other concerned sectors including trade.

The Millennium Development Goals (MDGs)

The MDGs have taken centre stage in the international development agenda as well as in national development planning, and they are expected to become the mechanism to assess economic policies. The establishment of gender equality and women's empowerment as an independent goal

(MDG 3) is an important development. However, concerns have been expressed about its restrictive interpretation as reflected in the selected targets and indicators. The existence of a gender-specific goal may hide the failure to fully integrate a much-needed gender perspective into the other goals (UNDAW 2005). MDG 8 encompasses macroeconomic policies that have critical implications for gender equality and poverty reduction.

Of major concern is the fact that trade is addressed in MDG 8–to develop a global partnership for development which is not subject to the MDG reporting processes at the national level, because the monitoring of MDG 8 is deemed to be relevant only at the international level. This automatically excludes any analysis and discussion of critical gender issues at the national macro level related to trade, while the MDG process could be a golden opportunity to boost the production of the much needed gender-disaggregated data and indicators on gender and trade. The major recommendations of the Millennium Project Report to the UN Secretary-General for achieving the MDGs include 'a breakthrough in global trade', by ensuring 'improved market access and terms of trade for the poor countries' and 'improved supply-side competitiveness for low-income country exports' (UN Millennium Project 2005). They also include specific interventions to address gender inequality and it should be an intrinsic part of all MDG-based investment packages (UN Millennium Project 2005).

A landmark event in the gender and trade agenda was the WTO yearly public Symposium in June 2003, during which 'the Director General of the WTO, who was the keynote speaker at the plenary, Women as Economic Players in Sustainable Development, acknowledged by his presence and in his remarks the importance of women's contribution to development and global trade' (Williams 2004).

Integrating Gender Perspectives in to Trade Policies

The national trade policy arena is a key to understanding the dynamic relationships between gender, trade and development. Therefore, the starting point for engendering trade policies is at the national level, where the strategies of engagement of the different actors and institutions are defined and implemented.

At the national level, there can be conflict between the various stakeholders between civil society and women's organizations and governments, as well as between the state departments/ministries themselves. The conflict is over to what extent a trade agenda can be developed that serves development and equity. Related to this is the domination of finance ministries in trade policy decision making, which is deemed to be their exclusive territory. This allows little or no input from other sectoral ministries, especially the national gender machineries. Shifting these power dynamics by ensuring the equal participation of citizens in the establishment of social and economic policy priorities would make women more visible and foster the promotion of gender-aware trade policies. In this regard, some initiatives represent important steps in this direction. Work on gender mainstreaming by women's organizations, gender advocates within development agencies has been important in efforts to promote more gender equitable governance.

One major step forward in bringing a gender perspective to national economic policies has been the institution of multi-stakeholder mechanisms and gender-responsive budget initiatives (GRBIs) conducted in an increasing number of countries. The Women's Budget Initiative in South Africa looked at the impact of trade liberalisation policies as part of its overall analysis of the South African budget. While trade liberalisation policies around customs and excise in South Africa may benefit women consumers due to the reduction in prices of basic commodities. But they have led to the contraction of labour-intensive industries such as fruit farming and vegetable canning, where women made up a large percentage of the workforce. This provided an entry point for gender advocates to propose anti-dumping measures in sectors that are important employers of women, together with a social clause on non-discrimination (Goldman 2000).

A major obstacle to the integration of a gender perspective in trade policies is the complexity of the global trade system. It is important to recognize the inherently technocratic and legalistic nature of trade policy processes and the urgent need to challenge a trade policy culture that tends to favour the most powerful players and elites by placing 'a premium on technical information and knowledge' (McGee 2004). Given the existing gender inequalities in terms of access to technology and information, it appears that trade policy processes are imbued with gender relations of unequal power, making them male dominated and restricting possibilities for the participation of women.

Participating effectively in trade policy processes is primarily about accessing, interpreting and acting on information. Thus, the key role of information, knowledge and learning processes in successful strategies cannot be over emphasized. Feminist economists, together with civil society and women's organizations, have greatly contributed to the research and policy analysis with the support of development agencies such as the UK Department for International Development (DFID) and the Swedish International Development Cooperation Agency (SIDA). The establishment of the Inter-Agency Task Force on Gender and Trade is an encouraging development that demonstrates the positive impact of the work done thus far at the policy level. It also has the potential to ensure the effectiveness and continuity of interventions, especially since the different members are increasingly involved in activities related to gender and trade work. The availability of processes for monitoring and assessing the impacts of trade rules on the day-to-day lives of children, men and women is a key to engendering trade policy processes.

The various forms of support to medium-sized, small and micro-enterprises run by women in the formal and informal sectors have proved to be a necessary preliminary step to bring women's businesses to the levels required for their effective engagement in trade. It is based on the recognition that women can play an important role in trade policy, negotiations and export development in African countries, given their daily involvement in the practical aspects of trade. This also means they are likely to be more affected by the results of trade and trade negotiations (UNCTAD 2004). The best practices are integrated programmes that build on specific needs assessments, and address not only the technical gaps but also seek to develop entrepreneurial and managerial skills in product diversification, marketing and trade.

An Approach Towards Gender-aware Trade Policies

There is a need for comprehensive approach to gender and trade issues, together with greater coherence between the macroeconomic environment and processes at the national levels, as well as between trade agreements and commitments to development and gender equality.

An approach build on a clear understanding of the role of local women producers and workers in trade, and more specifically, of their existing and potential contributions to export earnings is most essential (Carr 2004). There is a crucial need for more independent and good quality gender research and analysis. Because they are primarily knowledge-based processes, the nature of trade policies is dependent on the type of knowledge production, which informs their conception. The complexity of the global trade arena combined with the overwhelming agenda of negotiations facing trade officials and negotiators might not be conducive to the integration of a gender perspective. Therefore, gender analysis should be included in a clear and practical way, and perceived as adding value to their work. Research should focus on how to enhance women's capabilities and should also take into account the impact of gender-based barriers to market access on the patterns of growth at different levels. In particular, it needs to look at the social and economic costs of gender inequality and the consequent trade-offs.

Further work on gendered value chains is also needed to better establish the impact of gender-based exclusions and inequalities in market access on local, national and regional growth patterns, as well as the nature and dynamics of micro-macro linkages. Understanding how women access markets as producers and workers will be critical for ensuring pro-poor and inclusive economic growth. The studies on gender and trade underline the critical importance of establishing an enabling policy environment, including macroeconomic frameworks that take into account development, social policy, and gender equity concerns. At the international level, certainly there is scope within the information-gathering process for women's groups and gender experts to be consulted and their reports to be integrated into policy processes.

Engendering Trade Policies

At the national level, the MDGs and PRS processes offer strategic entry points that could be used for gender integration if some preconditions are met. Chief among these is the need to address the root causes of poverty and gender inequality that is not addressed in policies at the macro and micro levels. Because macroeconomic policies, including trade policy, determine the resource flows and investments required to address not only public and private poverty, but also gender inequality, they are key determinants of the achievement of MDGs. Therefore, the links between trade and the different MDGs need to be spelt out, together with the intersecting effects of gender inequality with other factors that determine whether or not the goals are achieved.

The PRS process may provide the opportunity to take into account women and men's different experiences of poverty, including the implications of household structure, composition and organization, and intra-household resource allocation and control. This would involve the inclusion of gender and human development concerns and analysis in the prioritizing of macroeconomic, structural and poverty reduction objectives. There would also be the need for gender-disaggregated statistics along with broader and more comprehensive gender-sensitive, social and human development indicators (Williams 2003a). PRSP reform may also provide an opportunity to move away from the narrow focus on micro credit and small income-generating activities for better structuring of economic and social incentives to support poor women and men's livelihood strategies. This would require setting priorities and designing policies based on gender and equity concerns, with inputs especially from women's groups (Williams 2003b).

Working towards Gender-sensitive Trade Programmes and Institutions

Development interventions on gender and trade have focused on the micro level in areas such as provision of small-business training and micro credit projects. There is now a need for more support for gender mainstreaming at the institutional level. Gender-sensitive institutions are required to remove the structural barriers to improved women's participation in markets and to ensure their rights are upheld as producers and consumers. Gender mainstreaming needs have to be implemented in organizations working on trade-related issues, in order to address women's gender-specific disadvantages. Support from trade unions and other employment institutions for labour rights that take into account different gender roles and relations of unequal power are critical. Women require specific assistance, especially in the areas of trade development, policy and regulation, in order to fill the gaps in their knowledge of the rules governing international trade transactions and standards for specific export-market access. Entrepreneurship promotion, fair trade and market-access initiatives also therefore need to mainstream a gender perspective to ensure that women are able to take up the opportunities they offer. At times, women-focused initiatives such as women's business associations and organizations of women workers can support women in situations where their involvement in mainstream organizations may be problematic. These organizations can also be good starting points for subsequent gender mainstreaming within broader institutions. However, even if such initiatives are orientated specifically to women, they must ensure that they build in an understanding of women's gender roles rather than replicating mainstream organizations or programmes.

RECOMMENDATION

- WTO should ensure the progressive interpretation of existing trade rules recognizing gender equality and women's human rights as a central part of the development process.
- Establish a Task Force on gender and trade in the WTO and engage in capacity-building on gender and trade within its relevant divisions and training programmes for its staff including the national gender and women machineries
- Strengthen interaction with more international agencies concerned with gender and development such as ILO, the World Health Organization, and Regional/sub-regional trade institutions in order to review and update existing gender policy frameworks to cover issues and commitments regarding gender and trade.
- Establish a continuing dialogue on gender issues with trade policymakers and negotiators in the national and international arenas by creating institutional framework for advancing gender equality, include gender focal points in each sector/sub-sector.
- Provide support for the promotion of regional/sub-regional networks of women entrepreneurs and exporters, with special attention to SMEs and the informal sector.
- Recognize the gender-differentiated impacts of trade liberalisation, and the central role of gender equality in achieving favourable trade outcomes by ensuring the integration of systematic gender analysis in trade policy-making and negotiations.
- Support the creation of women's cooperatives and enterprises in order to facilitate their access to information, communication technologies and trading networks.

- Use a rights-based approach to strengthen the policy analysis of and advocacy on gender and trade issues in their work on the PRS and MDG processes.
- Enhance the existing programmes with specific components targeted at women and focusing on the rules governing international trade transactions, technical regulations and standards for specific export market access, as well as on business development.
- Support the identification of and women's beneficial involvement in potential sectors/segments for the production and commercialization of higher value-added products through consultations with organizations of women producers and exporters and gendered analysis of the relevant value chains. This also necessitates research and development programmes to provide technological solutions for diversification in order to address issues of increased competition facing small-scale women producers and SMEs

CONCLUSION

Trade as an activity of economic exchange has a long history that far precedes its regulation within World Trade Organization (WTO) rules that we see today. Trade liberalisation entails the reduction of barriers to trade, such as import tariffs, in order to promote international trade and competition. The conventional wisdom simply assumed that trade liberalisation itself was the key factor that would automatically ensure the growth and development of poor countries. But there is an emerging consensus that trade liberalisation does not always reduce poverty and often increases inequality. Analysis of the gendered impacts of trade agreements underscores the critical links between trade and both the production and reproduction spheres. Moreover, as trade has an impact on gender equality, underlying gender inequality may have a decisive impact on the outcomes of trade policies by limiting productivity and growth.

The human rights approach has also provided a strategic entry point for gender advocates in governments, civil society and donor agencies to promote gender equality in and through trade. However, this approach is not always gendered and must be understood in conjunction with the gender and development (GAD) approach developed in the late 1990s. The GAD approach seeks to understand the gender roles and relations of unequal power which influence impacts of and responses to trade. There is need for the development of an alternative approach, which puts rights and understandings of gender and other power inequalities in the wider global context of developed and developing countries. Trade policies affect men and women differently due to gender inequalities in access to and control of economic and social resources and decision-making. Their impact is also mediated by the different roles that men and women have within societies in particular, the gendered division of labour. Trade liberalisation has no doubt led to an increase in employment opportunities for women. Earning an income externally to the household can lead to greater empowerment for women, both in the home and in the wider community. However, trade liberalisation can also lead to unemployment and the restructuring of labour markets a situation that tends to affect poor and marginalized groups of women more than men. A new and comprehensive approach is much emphasized to reduce gender inequalities by formulating suitable strategies with positive orientation for empowerment of women especially in developing countries.

REFERENCES

Ames, B., Brown, W., Devarajan, S. and Izquierdo, A. (2001), Macroeconomic Policy and Poverty Reduction, In *Poverty Reduction Strategy Sourcebook*, World Bank, Washington D.C.

Caliari, A. (2002), *Coherence between Trade and Financial Policies: Summary of Issues and Possible Research and Advocacy Agenda,* Background Paper, Available at http://www.coc.org/resources/articles/display.html?ID=326.

Carr, M., (ed.) (2004), *Chains of Fortune: Linking Women Producers and Workers with Global Markets*, Commonwealth Secretariat, London.

Elson, D., Evers, B. and Gideon, J. (1997), *Gender Aware Country Economic Reports: Concepts and Sources*, Genecon Unit, Graduate School of Social Sciences, Manchester University Press, Manchester.

FAO (2000), Synthesis of the Country Case Studies', in *Agriculture, Trade and Food Security, Vol. II: Country Case Studies*, Food and Agriculture Organization of the United Nations, Rome.

FIAS/IFC GEM GGA (2005), *Growth and Gender Assessment for Uganda: A Gender Perspective on Legal and Administrative Barriers to Investment,* Prepared for 'The Role of Gender: Assessing the Impact of the Business Environment on Women-Owned Businesses' Conference 29 November 2005, Available at http://www.bdsknowledge.org/dyn/be/docs/70/Session1.2EllisDoc.pdf

Fontana, M., Joekes, S. and Masika, R. (1998), *Global Trade Expansion and Liberalisation: Gender Issues and Impacts'*, BRIDGE Development Gender, Report No. 42, Institute of Development Studies, Brighton.

GERA Programme (2000), Demanding Dignity: Women Confronting Economic Reforms in Africa, In J. Kerr and D. Tsikata (eds.), North-South Institute/Third World Network-Africa, Ottawa.

Goldman, T. (2000), *Customs and Excise*, In Parliamentary Committee on the Quality of Life and Status of Women, CASE, and Idasa, Women's Budget Series: 2000 Issue, Cape Town.

ILRIG (2001), Integrating to Exclude: the Economic Integration of South Africa's Footwear Industry and the Consequent Marginalisation of its Workforce, In N. Newman, J. Pape and H. Jansen (eds.), *Is There an Alternative?* South African Workers Confronting Globalisation, ILRIG, Cape Town.

ITC (2003), Women in the Global Economy, *International Trade Forum Magazine No.4,* Available at http://www.tradeforum.org/news/fullstory.php/aid/625/In_India,_Integrating_the_Informal_Sector_into_t he_Global_Economy.html

Jackson, C. and Palmer-Jones, R. (1998), *Work Intensity, Gender and Well-being,* Discussion Paper No. 96, UN Research Institute for Social Development, Geneva.

Joekes, S. (1999), A Gender-analytical Perspective on Trade and Sustainable Development, In UNCTAD, *Trade, Sustainable Development and Gender*, UN Conference on Trade and Development, Geneva.

Kabeer, N. (2003), *Gender Mainstreaming in Poverty Eradication and the Millennium Development Goals: A Handbook for Policy-makers and other Stakeholders*, Commonwealth Secretariat-International Development Research Centre, London/ Ottawa.

Kabeer, N. (2000), *The Power to Choose: Bangladeshi Women and Labour Market Decisions in London and Dhaka*, Verso, London.

Klasen, S. (1999), *Does Gender Inequality Reduce Growth and Development? Evidence from Cross-country Regressions*, Background Paper for Engendering Development, World Bank, Washington DC.

Ladd, P. (2003), *Too hot to Handle? The Absence of Trade Policy from PRSPs*, Christian Aid, London, Available at www.christian-aid.org.uk.

McGee, R. and Brock, K. (2004), *Mapping Trade Policy: Understanding the Challenges of Civil Society Participation*, IDS Working Paper 225, Institute of Development Studies, Brighton.

Mukhopadhyay, S. and Sudarshan, R. (eds.) (2003), *Tracking Gender Equity Under Economic Reforms: Continuity and Change in South Asia*, Kali for Women and the International Development Research Centre, New Delhi/Ottawa.

Newman, C. (2001), *Gender, Time Use and Change: Impacts of Agricultural Export Employment in Ecuador*, Gender and Development Working Paper Series 18, World Bank, Washington D.C.

Quisumbing, A. (2003), What Have We Learned from Research on Intra-household Allocation, In A. Quisumbing (ed.), *Household Decisions, Gender and Development: A Synthesis of Recent Research*, International Food Policy Research Institute, Washington.

Randriamaro, Z. (2001), Financing for the Poor and Women: A Policy Critique, In B. Herman, F. Pietracci and K. Sharma (eds.), *Financing for Development: Proposals from Business and Civil Society, United Nations University (UNU) Policy Perspectives* 6: 25-33, UNU Press, New York.

Sachs, J. and Warner, A. (1995), Economic Reform and the Process of Global Integration, *Brookings Papers on Economic Activity* 1: 1-118.

Sengendo, M. and Tumushabe, G. (2003), *Market Access Information Provision and Needs for Female Farmers in Uganda's Horticultural and Fisheries Sector*, GERA Programme Phase II/ Third World Network-Africa (unpublished).

Sexton, S., Nair, S. and Kirbat, P. (2004), *A Decade after Cairo: Women's Health in a Free Market Economy,* Corner House Briefing 3, Available at http://www.thecornerhouse.org.uk/ item.shtml.

Smith, L. and Chavas, J. (1999), *Supply response of West African Agricultural Households: Implications of Intra-household Preference Heterogeneity,* Food Consumption and Nutrition Division Discussion Paper 69, International Food Policy Research Institute, Washington DC.

UNCTAD (2004), *Trade and Gender: Opportunities and Challenges for Developing Countries, UN Inter-Agency on Women and Gender Equality,* Task Force on Gender and Trade, Available at www.unctad.org.

UNDAW (2005), *Achievements, Gaps and Challenges in Linking the Implementation of the Beijing Platform for Action and the Millennium Declaration and Millennium Development Goals,* Report of the Expert Group Meeting, 7-10 February 2005, Baku, Azerbaijan, Available at http://www.un.org/ womenwatch/ daw/ egm/ bpfamd2005/ index.html.

UNDP (1995, 2000), *Human Development Report*, Oxford University Press, New York.

UNECA (2004), *Economic Report on Africa, Addis Ababa, Ethiopia*, Available at www.uneca.org.

UNIFEM (2005), *Progress of the World's Women 2005, Overview: Women, Work and Poverty,* New York, Available at www. unifem.org.

UNIFEM (2004), *Pathway to Gender Equality,* CEDAW, Beijing and the MDGs, New York.

UN Millennium Project (2005), *Investing in Development: A Practical Plan to Achieve the Millennium Development Goals,* Report to the UN Secretary-General, New York.

Vander Stichele, M. (1998), *Gender, Trade and the WTO: A Ghana Case Study,* Informal Working Group on Gender and Trade, Brussels.

Williams, M. (2004), *Current and Emerging Gender Issues in the Multilateral Trading System,* Background Document for the 7th Women's/Gender Affairs Ministerial Meeting (7WAMM) May 30 to June 2, the Fiji Islands.

Williams, M. (2003a), *Gender Mainstreaming in the Multilateral Trading System: A Handbook for Policymakers and other Stakeholders*, Commonwealth Secretariat, London.

Williams, M. (2003b), *Engendering African Governments, Participation in the Reform of PRSPs: How Effective, and how can this be in the Service of Gender Equality?* Commonwealth Secretariat, London.

Winters, A. (1999), Trade and Poverty: Is there a Connection? In WTO Special Studies No 5, *Trade, Income Disparity and Poverty*, World Trade Organization, Geneva.

World Bank (2001), *Engendering Development Through Gender Equality in Rights, Resources and Voice*, Policy Research Report, World Bank and Oxford University Press, *Washington*, D.C.

Zuckerman, E. and Garrett, A. (2003), *Do Poverty Reduction Strategy Papers Address Gender?* A Gender Audit of 2002 PRSPs, Gender Action, Available at www.genderaction.org

14

ACCESS TO MICRO-FINANCE FOR WOMEN ENTREPRENEURS IN INFORMAL SECTOR

KACHIRAJU S. KUMAR

INTRODUCTION

The informal sector plays an important role as a source of livelihood by providing jobs and reducing unemployment and underemployment. It bolsters entrepreneurial activity, but at the detriment of state regulations compliance, particularly regarding tax and labour regulations. It helps to alleviate poverty, although in many cases informal sector jobs are low-paid and the job security is poor. The size of the informal sector varies from the estimated 4-6 per cent in the high-income countries to over 50 per cent in the low-income countries. As witnessed, the role of informal sector in developing economies has been increasing during economic downturns and periods of economic adjustment and transition (ILO 2002 and Sethuraman 1981).

The International Labour Organization (ILO) introduced the concept of the informal sector. Informality is considered as a way of doing things characterized by (a) ease of entry, (b) reliance on indigenous resources, (c) family ownership, (d) small scale operations, (e) labour intensive and adaptive technology, (e) skills acquired outside of the formal sector, and

(g) unregulated and competitive markets. The International Symposium on the Informal Sector organized by the ILO (1999) proposed that the informal sector workforce can be categorized into three broad groups: (a) owner-employers of micro enterprises, which employ a few paid workers, with or without apprentices; (b) own-account workers, who own and operate one-person business, who work alone or with the help of unpaid workers, generally family members and apprentices; and (c) dependent workers, paid or unpaid, including wage workers in micro enterprises, unpaid family workers, apprentices, contract labour and paid domestic workers.

The informal sector has been given a number of interpretations by different authors. It is the non-structured sector that has emerged in the urban centres as a result of the incapacity of the modern sector to absorb new entrants. The so-called modern sector has not had the capacity to absorb all the new entrants to the labour market, especially in the developing countries. Thus, many new entrants find themselves engaged in the informal sector to have a means of survival. These activities, during the 1970s and even now, provide an alternative to high open unemployment. It is estimated that more than 50 per cent of the non-agricultural employment in Africa is found in the informal sector (ILO 2001).

The informal sector uses family and unpaid labour and relies on manual labour rather than on sophisticated machinery and equipment with flexibility in allowing people to enter and exit economic activities in response to market demand. It has the ability to improvise products from scrap materials and willing to operate businesses at times and locations convenient to customers with a tendency to locate smaller markets, out of the reach of the larger firms (McLaughlin 1990). It is also evident that micro enterprises only provide a means of subsistence through the production of goods and services on a small scale with lower quality and prices as small and medium enterprises are associated with higher levels of education of the entrepreneurs, higher levels of income and a longer time in business.

The informal sector describes economic activity that takes place outside the formal norms of economic transactions established by the state and formal business practices. Generally, the term applies to small or micro-business that is the result of individual or family self-employment. It includes the production and exchange of legal goods and services that involves the lack of appropriate business permits, violation of zoning codes, failure to report tax liability, non-compliance with labour regulations governing contracts and work conditions, and/or the lack of legal guarantees in relations with suppliers and clients. As such, it is conceptually, methodologically and theoretically difficult to define in terms of its precise nature, size and significance, leading some authors to criticize the term for lack of clarity (Peattie 1987).

Nevertheless, widespread agreement that the sector represents a growing proportion of economic activity, particularly in less developed countries (LDCs) has placed it at the center of debate about its role with respect to economic development. In fact the informal sector appears to provide at least some economic opportunities for the urban poor and particularly for women. It is not only providing services and commercial activities at a very low level of economic utility-not only means that the tertiary sector has often grown faster in many LDCs than the secondary sector but also creating a situation of whether regulatory norms should be enforced at the risk of reducing these opportunities.

The International Labour Office turned to the informal sector as a potential solution to unemployment in LDCs. While still seeing it as a collection of survival strategies held back by under-capitalization, lack of skills, and the small size of the enterprises, they argue that the informal sector is capable of absorbing employment if these negative conditions can be reversed (Sethuraman 1981).

The vast scale and rate of growth of the informal sector is presenting a challenge for governments of developing countries in recent years. The informal sector encompasses employment situations, which not only differ from those in the formal sector but also infringe upon established rules and laws. A challenge, as it absorbs a large and growing fraction of the labour force, and provides a safety net for the poor, is finding them excluded from formal employment and income opportunities.

The present research is an attempt to highlight the importance of micro-finance to women entrepreneurs, engaged in informal sector, whose creditworthiness is higher than men. Focus is laid on the need for suitable programmes that will ensure micro-finance to women engaged in informal sector.

WOMEN AS MICRO-ENTREPRENEURS IN THE INFORMAL SECTOR

Women as micro and small entrepreneurs have increasingly become a key target group for micro-finance programmes. Providing access to micro-finance is not only considered a precondition for poverty alleviation, but also for women's empowerment. Moreover, women are increasingly recognized to be better borrowers from financial institutions all over the world. But despite the proven positive impact of providing micro-finance services to female entrepreneurs in the informal sector, micro-finance is one among many other tools to address the multiple causes of poverty, unemployment and low incomes.

The micro-finance revolution started among rural women in Bangladesh in the 1970s. The revolution had its roots in the recognition that women needed credit and, more importantly, that they could use loans productively and responsibly. Poor women are being drawn into commercial economic activities for the first time, enabling them to take advantage of new opportunities.

It is indicated that micro-finance, with its combination of savings, loans, investment opportunities, insurance options and other financial services combined with group solidarity is considered a powerful instrument of social change, especially for women. Micro-finance has caused a shift in values and expectations that affect women's roles in society.

In Bangladesh, for example, a study of experience in a project aided by the International Fund for Agricultural Development has found that women involved in micro-finance not only change the way they manage household income, they also change their own roles and the roles of others in their families and communities.

Many women members of micro-finance groups no longer believe that they should dependent or that they should remain confined to the home. Through their involvement in micro-finance, many women become leaders, instigating change in social practices and relationships and mobilizing social action. Women's status, both in their homes and communities, is improved when they are responsible for loans and for managing savings. When they generate and control their own income, women gain a level of power that means they can make decisions independently and command more respect.

While the data about informal activities are somewhat unreliable, there is consensus that the informal sector is steadily growing in almost all developing countries. For example in Latin America, 8.4 of every ten new jobs created between 1990 and 1994 were in the informal sector. In Asia, the informal sector absorbs between 40 and 50 per cent of the urban labour force, and in Africa, the urban informal sector currently employs some 60 per cent of the urban labour force and will create more than 90 per cent of all additional jobs in this region (ILO 1997). The growing informalisation of the economy has caused a rise in the number of workingwomen. The participation rates of women in the informal sector are high with 80 per cent in Peru, 65 per cent in Indonesia, 72 per cent in Zambia, and 41 per cent in the Republic of Korea (Lim 1996).

Women are increasingly pushed into informal sector activities due to slow, or even negative, growth of formal sector employment opportunities combined with a rapid and significant growth in the urban labour force. Added to this, economic stabilization and restructuring programmes, and the quest for increased flexibility and deregulation of the economy have had detrimental effects on prospects of women in formal activities. For example, the reduction in public sector jobs has affected women more than men, because of their concentration in temporary and lower level jobs. Again the decline in formal sector wages, has forced many women to turn towards informal work.

Since the mid-1980s women as micro and small entrepreneurs have received increased attention and assistance by governments, international donors and NGOs. Micro-enterprises have been seen as having particular advantages for women because of their location in or near women's homes and links with the local markets. Supporting their entrepreneurship is seen as having important trickle down effects on wider poverty alleviation and gender inequality (Mayoux 1995).

With the growing role of female micro-entrepreneurs, women will need to rely on suitable strategies, looking at the constraints they face such as (a) lack of access to productive resources due to discriminations in property ownership and in employment (b) lack of time because of unequal gender division of labour in unpaid productive and reproductive activities (c) lack of skills due to lower levels of literacy and formal education (d) lack of access to labour as a result of norms of gender hierarchy and separation; (e) and lack of access to markets due to their exclusion from the most lucrative markets.

The lack of access to informal and formal credit by women micro and small entrepreneurs has been identified as the major constraint. ILO (2001) study indicates that 59% in Philippines, 76.4% in Bangladesh and 70% in Trinidad and Tobago face lack of capital, especially in the start-up period, as the problem most often mentioned by women micro entrepreneurs. It also confirmed that this problem is more severe for women than for men.

With informal sources of finance being relatively easy to access, women rely on moneylenders and pawnbrokers, friends and relatives and suppliers and shopkeepers. While these sources are providing the bulk of financial resources for female entrepreneurs and offer a number of potential advantages such as proximity between borrower and lender, immediacy of loan disbursement, small loan size, flexible repayment schedules and minimal collateral requirements, they can be costly and discriminatory. Formal financial institutions are less receptive and welcoming to female entrepreneurs. Their collateral requirements, bureaucratic loan application, disbursement procedures and the time and resources necessary to visit the banks virtually exclude poor women as clients. The provision of sustainable access to financial services for women has not only become a core component of many women's micro-enterprise programmes but also remains at the centre of the attention of governments, social partners, civil society organizations and international donors.

PROGRAMMES PROVIDING MICRO-FINANCE TO WOMEN ENTREPRENEURS

Since the mid 1970s, the mechanisms developed to provide women micro-entrepreneurs with access to financial services are diverse and offering alternatives to the formal banking system. These are also incorporating the advantages of informal savings and credit systems. The programmes providing finance to women entrepreneurs have an important feature such as close targeting of the most needy borrowers. In addition, the programmes have the characteristic of the decentralized loan delivery and management systems through intermediary institutions and group formation to ensure financial discipline and support systems to enhance productivity.

The following are different programmes that are providing women with access to financial services.

Social Programmes

These programmes are run by commercial banks, which provide borrowers with incentives from the government (for example: Integrated Rural Development Programme, India; Rural Development Banks, Bangladesh). Most commercial bank schemes have failed to reach large numbers of women borrowers, let alone women. Women's participation in formal small-scale enterprise lending programmes rarely exceeds 20 per cent.

Intermediary Programmes

These are generally run by NGOs offering micro-businesses a link to the formal banking system (for example: Women's World Banking; the original activities of Self-Employed Women Association (SEWA); Production Credit for Rural Women, Nepal; Institute for the Development of the Informal Sector, Peru). As most programmes have succeeded in reaching somewhat better off women, SEWA decided to set up its own poverty-oriented bank, because its members encountered too many difficulties in their dealings with banking procedures, application forms, opening hours attitudes of bank clerks etc.

Parallel Programmes

These provide financial services alongside other development and social programmes via non-bank institutions (for example: Working Women's Forum, India and Small Business Scheme of the National Christian Council of Kenya). Many of these programmes have succeeded in reaching women clients, heavily supported by donors.

Poverty-oriented Development Banks

These are generally started as intermediary or parallel programmes and then officially registered as banks (for example: SEWA Bank, India; Grameen Bank, Bangladesh). They have adapted systematic delivery systems and loan conditions to meet the specific needs of female clients.

Community Revolving Loan Funds

These are government and donor grants or loans which offer limited but useful services to women. If well managed, they can be sustainable. The major risk is erosion of funds due to default and inflation.

Savings and Credit Cooperatives and Unions

These are providing financial assistance through special schemes for women members (for example: Cooperative Union, Gambia). Participatory methods help to ensure that these organizations meet the real needs of members. They mobilize their own capital and are more or less democratic. Cooperatives can, however, be formalistic and financial services are not always readily available.

In fact, women have become the preferred clients of micro-finance institutions, as they tend to be better borrowers. Studies show that women borrowers' average delinquency rates tend to be lower than men's, especially for micro-loans (Almeyda 1996). Financial institutions lending to female entrepreneurs most often use collateral substitutes to overcome their lack of traditional collateral, such as property, equipment or capital. The best know examples are peer pressure (joint liability arrangements in lending to 'solidarity' groups) and probation (credit scoring). Both are conventional instruments in terms of ensuring repayment and have been used over a fairly long period (ILO 1996). However, micro-finance institutions should remain successful by offering primarily short-term working-capital loans, taking turnaround time for loan approval of less than 2 weeks, providing services close to borrowers' home or work, charging interest rates significantly above the rate of inflation and having lower salary levels than financially less viable programmes (Christen *et al.* 1995).

IMPACT OF MICRO-FINANCE ON WOMEN MICRO ENTREPRENEURS

The need for financing women enterprises has gained global attention due to the Micro-credit Summit, held in February 1997 in Washington. The aim is to ensure that 100 million of the world's poorest families, especially the women of those families, would receive credit for self-employment and other financial and business services by the year 2005 (ILO 1995). As a member of the UN Council of the Micro-credit Summit Campaign, ILO supports this goal although micro-finance is not a panacea. But the provision of micro-finance is one important instrument among others that will help female micro and small entrepreneurs to grow and develop.

It is believed that micro-finance will have a positive impact on women's livelihood in (i) leading to higher income that will help women to better perform their reproductive role as caretakers of the health, nutritional, and educational status of other household members, (ii) increasing women's employment in micro enterprises and in improving the productivity of women's income-generating activities, and iii) enhancing their self-confidence and status within the family as independent producers and providers of valuable cash resources to the household economy.

The plausibility of these assumptions is largely borne out by empirical evidence. Impact assessments provide evidence of the positive effects of micro-finance on the livelihood of women, especially in Asia:

- A study from Bangladesh confirms improvements in women's physical mobility, economic security, ability to make own purchases, freedom from family domination and violence, political and legal awareness and public participation as a result of a more stable integration into micro-finance circuits (Schuler and Hashemi 1994);
- A study of Grameen Bank suggests that women participants in credit programmes are more conscious of their rights, better able to resolve conflicts and have more control over decision making at the household and community levels (Chen 1996);
- Credit to women has positive effects on the schooling of girls, it increases women's asset holdings and is a significant determinant of total household expenditure (Pitt and Khandkar 1994);
- A study in Sri Lanka found that loans contributed to women's independent income and giving them more bargaining power in their relation with male family members (Hulme and Mosley 1996); and

- Enhanced women's empowerment, such as increased self-confidence and better cooperation with neighbours has also been observed in Thailand (MkNelly and Watetip 1993).

The findings for Africa give a less clear picture, in that there is a positive impact on self-confidence but little proof of increased access to credit, intra-household decision-making and individual assets ownership (Vengroff and Creevey 1994). In Latin America, a study in Ecuador found a significant increase in hourly income for women and in efficiency and productivity of their enterprises (Buvinic, Berger and Jaramillo 1989).

However, some studies have also detected negative impacts on women's income and employment, such as increased workloads (Vengroff and Creevey 1994) and higher social pressure to ensure loan repayment. Participation in credit schemes can lead to indebtedness that is unmanageable, simply because there are no sufficiently profitable income-earning activities in which to invest. In this situation, women may end up being even more dependent that they were before.

CONTROL OVER FINANCIAL RESOURCES

Women's control over financial resources is increasingly seen as a key factor in explaining these mixed results. While only a limited number of impact assessments exist that focus on this issue, the available evidence highlights that a significant part of women, who may have access to finance, may not have control over the loans contracted (Sebstad and Chen 1996). Again, about 63% of women's loans are actually invested by male relatives, while women bear the formal responsibility for repayment in a Bangladesh programme. It is also discovered that of 140 loans made by ACTIONAID to women, about 50% were used for men's productive activities. This situation confirmed that men try to control income from women's enterprises. According to a more recent study of women borrowers in the Grameen Bank, 10 of 40 women in the sample were passing on all or most of their loans to male family members under circumstances that gave them little control over the use of this capital (Todd 1996).

On the other hand, the loss of control over financial resources does not necessarily mean that women are worse off in terms of increased social and economic opportunities (Todd 1996). Even though women loose control over the use of their loans, their overall status in the household may improve due to their role as a financial mediator. But handing over loans to men may help to secure family stability by easing cash flow bottlenecks in the household. Women may also use credit as a bargaining chip to gain access to other opportunities offered by financial institutions, such as training, education and information.

However, women often have the best credit ratings. In Bangladesh, for example, women default on loans less often than men, and credit extended to women has a much greater impact on household consumption and quality of life for children. But, in many traditional societies, especially in South Asia and in parts of East and Central Africa, women have been excluded from the market economy. Women in East Africa are expected to do all the farm work and look after the family, while any cash income received is controlled mainly by men. But today, with micro-finance institutions spreading across large parts of Kenya and Uganda, it is widely accepted that rural women can play an important role in the rural economy.

It seems obvious that the impact of micro-finance services is higher when women actually control the financial resources acquired in their name. Increased control is likely to contribute to women's empowerment by facilitating women's entrepreneurship and assisting women in their reproductive tasks besides easing their repayment burden.

The discrepancy between nominal borrower status and effective control over loan transactions is also partly due to donor behaviour. This can materialize, for example, in a shift of refinancing from micro-finance organizations that emphasize women's social development and empowerment to others placing a premium on early and full financial sustainability; This also results in cutting back on support services, such as business management, skills training and education and information provision in order to cover costs. It could also be argued that in the long term, the insistence on financial sustainability may contribute to a 'more efficient and continuous supply of financial services that allow women micro entrepreneurs to take advantage of economic opportunities' (Almeyda 1996) by (i) stressing institutional viability, (ii) reducing cost due to increased efficiency in financial technologies, (iii) emphasizing market knowledge and (iv) using concepts of micro-finance, which cover both the enterprise and household sphere.

WOMEN ARE GOOD RISKS

Micro-finance has drawn millions of women into commercial economic activities enabling them to take advantage of new opportunities and develop new roles as cash income earners and economically active members of the community. It represents a shift away from feudal patron-client relationships towards income generating market economy with new social norms.

The impact of micro-finance on women and their organizations shows that the Millennium Development Goal to promote gender equality is key to achieving the target of halving extreme poverty and hunger by 2015 (Hulme and Mosley 1996). The ripples of women's micro-finance can build into waves of transformation, leading not only to greater self-confidence and new roles for women, but also to powerful institutions able to take on complex new tasks serving the whole of society. The women's groups intrinsic to micro-finance are now extending their activities well beyond financial services. In India, for example, self-help groups of indigenous women now manage community-based projects, including the contracting of minor irrigation construction and soil conservation works.

MICRO-FINANCE: A WAY OUT OF POVERTY

As many nations have pledged to help the poor women to overcome poverty, one must recognize that it is important to them to have the means to find their own solutions. Micro-finance is a powerful aid and it gives poor families a chance to improve their livelihoods through their own economic activities.

Often, the one important thing preventing the poor from raising their standard of living is lack of access to financial services that would help them start or expand their economic activity or prevent risks. Most women engaged in micro-enterprises reported that lack of capital was the biggest problem they face in their business. Among other things, it prohibits expansion or employing others. In the North Africa and Middle East region alone, there are 60 million poor people, but only 112,000 have access to financial services (Hulme and Mosley 1996).

The benefits that micro-finance brings to poor families go beyond increased income and employment. It also provides greater opportunity for children to go to school, for families to obtain health insurance, and for the poor to make choices that best serve their needs. For many women, micro-finance proves to be a powerful instrument of social change. More and more we see women from traditional societies being drawn into commercial economic activities. In many cases, this is due to a small loan or savings or other service provided by a credit union, women's cooperative, or peasant organizations, which allows them to start or maintain a business.

Despite popular notions that the poor do not have any use for financial services, they need saving, remittances, and other services and they do not represent a high credit risk. In fact, repayment rates are higher among clients of micro-finance institutions than those of commercial banks. Poor women often have the best credit ratings. Nevertheless, nearly half the people in the world do not have access to basic financial services simply because they are not available to them.

In order for the micro-finance institution to be able to answer to the needs of poor people, it is imperative that we help to build this sector of our economy. We must strive to increase the efficiency and sustainability of micro-finance programs and to encourage formal financial institutions to provide savings, remittances, loans, and other services to poor people. Micro-finance programmes may be an effective way to answer broader social issues while improving the lives of many poor families. Although micro-finance is not a 'magic pill' to cure poverty, however, it has the potential to help poor people lift themselves out of poverty.

POLICY RECOMMENDATION

There are certain constraints faced by female entrepreneurs in their access to micro-finance, support services that are required at many levels. At policy level it is necessary to undertake surveys to determine the needs, demands and debt capacity of women. It is also needed to introduce legal reforms to abolish gender differences in commercial and civil law. On finance side, there should be abolition of interest rate regimes by allowing non-bank financial institutions to take savings besides setting up of realistic capital requirements for non-bank financial institutions and formulating policies which are meant for gender-sensitization.

At the institutional level, supply side measures should address the constraints relating to track-record requirements, size requirement, equity requirement, etc., This should also include the creation of separate, gender-based parallel structures as self-sustaining financial institutions and gender-specific windows in financial institutions. The most important is the gender sensitization of existing financial institutions for the adoption of financial services that meet the needs of female micro-entrepreneurs and also accommodate their reproductive and productive roles.

To address constraints on the demand side, direct support measures can be taken in order to help women to satisfy the requirements made by financial institutions through the provision of education, enterprise development and training. Dissemination of important information about financial sector institutions and available micro-finance services and group-based savings and credit organizations, such as women's associations is also essential.

Governments, the social partners and other civil society organizations should respect and enforce basic principles for sustainable micro-finance, coordinate the activities and exchange the experiences in the area of micro-finance and gender. They should also allow for the participation of clients, especially female entrepreneurs, in the design and offering of financial services to micro and small enterprises.

CONCLUSION

Micro-finance is considered as one of the most essential tools in the development of women entrepreneurship in developing countries. It is not only the situation of lack of access to capital that constrains the development of micro-enterprises but also its use for viable activities as women often become burdened by the repayment obligation, especially as they use credit primarily for consumption purposes. The impact of providing micro-finance is greatest for persons that live above the poverty line, i.e. it is more cost-effective to provide the somewhat better-offs among the poor with micro-finance services.

The current enthusiasm for micro-finance needs to be examined cautiously, especially in looking at the limited outreach that micro-finance institutions possess. Some estimate the percentage of poor reached at only 2 per cent. Moreover, only about 5 per cent of all micro-finance institutions are judged to eventually become financially sustainable. The current danger is that too much money is being invested in too few institutions. International donors, pressed to increase their involvement in micro-finance, are already departing from established principles of sound assistance in micro-finance in the search for funding opportunities. However, women in micro and small enterprise need to be assisted by holistic strategies and comprehensive programmes that address women's lack of access to productive resources especially finance.

REFERENCES

Almeyda, G. (1996), *Money Matters*, Inter American Development Bank, New York.

Buvinic, M., M. Berger and C. Jaramillo (1989), Impact of a Credit Project for Women and Men Micro-entrepreneurs in Quito, Ecuador, In M. Berger and M. Buvinic (eds.), *Women's Ventures*, Kumarian Press, West Hartford.

Chen, M.A. (1996), *Beyond Credit: A Sub-sector Approach to Promoting Women's Enterprises*, Aga Khan Foundation, Ottawa.

Christen, B, Rhyne, E., Vogel, R. and C. McKean (1995), *Maximizing the Outreach of Microenterprise Finance: An Analysis of Successful Micro-finance Programs,* USAID, Washington.

Hulme, D., and P. Mosley (1996), *Fight against Poverty*, Macmillan, London.

ILO (1995), *Gender, Poverty and Employment: Turning Capabilities into Entitlements*, Geneva.

ILO (1996), *Collateral, Collateral Law and Collateral Substitutes,* Paper for the Donors' Working Group on Financial Sector Development, Social Finance Unit, Geneva.

ILO (1997), *World Labour Report,* Geneva.

ILO (1999), *World Labour Report,* Geneva.

ILO (2001), *Action to assist rural women: Gender analysis study*, Geneva.

ILO (2002), *Women and Men in the Informal Economy,* Geneva.

Lim, L.L. (1996), *More and better Jobs for Women*, An Action Guide, Geneva.

Mayoux, L. (1995), *From Vicious to Virtuous Circles? Gender and Micro-enterprise Development*, Occasional Paper No. 3, UNRISD, Geneva.

McLaughlin, S. (1990), *The Wayside Mechanic,* Centre for Institutional Education, University of Massachusetts, Massachusetts.

MkNelly, B. and Ch. Watetip (1993), *Impact evaluation of Freedom from Hunger's Credit with Education Program in Thailand,* Davis.

Peattie, Lisa A. (1987), An Idea in Good Currency and How it Grew: The Informal Sector, *World Development*, 15 (7): 851-860.

Pitt, M.M. and S.R. Khandker (1994), *Household and Intra-household Impacts of the Grameen Bank and Similar Targeted Credit Programs in Bangladesh*, World Bank, Washington DC.

Schuler, S.R. and S.M. Hashemi (1994), Credit Programs, Women's Empowerment, and Contraceptive Use in Rural Bangladesh, *Studies in Family Planning*, 25 (2): 65-76.

Sebstad, J. and G. Chen (19960, *Overview of Studies on the Impact of Microenterprise Credit*, AIMS, USAID, Washington.

Sethuraman, S.V. (1981), *The Urban Informal Sector in Developing Countries: Employment, Poverty and Environment,* ILO, Geneva.

Todd, H. (1996), *Women at the Center: Grameen Bank Borrowers after one Decade*, West view Press, Oxford.

Vengroff, R. and L. Creevey (1994), *Evaluation of Project Impact: ACEP Component of the Community Enterprise Development Project,* Report to USAID/Dakar, University of Connecticut, Storrs.

15

GENDER DISCRIMINATION IN WEST BENGAL

JAYABATI GANGOPADHYAY AND R.K. GHOSAL

INTRODUCTION

It is well recognized that in the recent literature of economic inequality the gender inequality has occupied a prominent position. In fact, the discrimination against the women in a society has raised the question of social and economic empowerment of women through their participation in the development process. Professor Amartya sen has also echoed his strong voice pertaining to the discrimination against women in the society and also questioned the different societal norms and conventions, which go against women. Alongside he has also emphasized the urgency of social, economic and political empowerment of the women through social consciousness (Dreze and Sen 2002). There cannot be any doubt whatsoever that the basic requirements for the empowerment of the women in the societies discrimination against women in our male dominated society is not only reflected in terms of gender inequality but it also more vividly pronounced in respect of discrimination of social and economic opportunities amongst the people. It is not necessarily true that the fruits of economic development would automatically percolate equally across the sexes. Further it is also unlikely to expect that the development would automatically be participatory irrespective of sex. Discrimination against women has in fact become our historical inheritance. So for the empowerment of women in our male dominated society what are crying needs, the improvement of female literacy rates, improvement in the economic role of women and emancipation of women from various castes, religions and prejudices prevailing in our society, formation of women agencies. These are likely to help in improving the capabilities of the women in our society. Now if one accepts female-male ratio as a common indicator of gender-discrimination then it is surprising enough to note that in almost all the states excepting Kerala these ratios remain well below unity and it has a tendency to fall. In this paper we have tried to examine the nature of the gender discrimination in West Bengal and its districts in terms of its various correlates. Although there is a vast literature on gender discrimination, the study on West Bengal and its districts is still scarce (Sen 1990).

THE STATUS OF WOMEN

It is a general belief that in many societies there is a preference for sons over daughters and hence this aspect has been discussed frequently in the literature. There is also an interesting study on the gender preference across the states in India and it is found that in India there are marked state and regional variations in gender preference. Its effect on contraceptive prevalence is far more complex than has been understood. Regions of strong gender preference do not necessarily show an adverse impact on contraceptive prevalence (Kulkarni 1999). Further, it is also observed that girls in poor countries are on an average provided with less education from their families and women on average have far fewer employment opportunities in the market. In fact, they face a variety of social restrictions on their movements. It is quite likely that poor women in poor countries are always working women. But they do not reduce their workload in home maintenance, childcare, food preparation etc. No substitute opportunities are open to them. They are to play vital role of being at once mother, wife and housekeeper. Out of these necessities they seek jobs. Within all these limitations their returns expected to be very low. This is true for West Bengal also. In this context, one obvious question can be arose that, is there any improvement in the status of women or is there any reduction in the degree of gender preference? To answer this we have to first analyse the data concerning the status of women in West Bengal both at the aggregate level and also at the disaggregate level during the period of our study. It is to be mentioned that due to non-availability of data for the period 1951-1971 and also for the year 2001, we will here analyse the above aspect only for the two periods i.e. for 1981 and 1991. For our purpose we consider total fertility rates, female literacy rates, female workforce participation rates and women's average age of marriage as four basic indicators for women's status. Table1 present the data relating to the Parameters measuring status of women in West Bengal during 1981-91.

Table 1
Status of Women in West Bengal during 1981-91

Status	1981	1991
TFR	3.10	3.61
FLR	30.26	46.56
FWPR	5.80	7.95
MA	–	17.21

Source: (1) Occasional Paper-I of 1997, Census of India, (2) Census reports of West Bengal 1981, 1991 (3) West Bengal state district profile 1991.

Key: TFR-Total Fertility Rate; FLR-Female Literacy Rate; FWPR-Female Workforce Participation Rates; MA- Women's Average Age of Marriage.

It is observed from the table that female literacy rate (%) in West Bengal has increased from 30.26% in 1981 to 46.56% in 1991. It has also been found that female workforce participation rates increases from 5.80% in 1981 to 7.95% in 1991. Generally it is hypothesized that higher female literacy rates along with higher female workforce participation rate which is associated with lower level of fertility rates, influences birth rates. But the analysis of our data that is currently available does not support the hypothesis. Here, it is evident that total fertility rate in West Bengal has increased from 3.1 in 1981 to 3.61 in 1991. It seems that preference for large family size would also dominate fertility choice. Thus one can plausibly say that female education does not play any vital role in influencing the status of women in West Bengal and we cannot say firmly that there is an improvement in the status of women even in the recent years. Now to have a clear insight about the nature and pattern of status of women in West Bengal during the recent years, let us consider the data on women's status at the district level, which is presented in Table 2.

Table 2
Disaggregate Data on Status of Women in West Bengal during 1981-1991

District	*1981*				*1991*			
	TFR	*FLR*	*FWFPR*	*MA*	*TFR*	*FLR*	*FWFPR*	*MA*
Bardhaman	2.7	33.80	6.23	-	3.59	51.46	7.61	17.21
Birbhum	3.2	24.20	5.54	-	3.81	37.17	8.05	16.89
Bankura	3.0	23.10	10.69	-	3.46	36.55	14.09	16.84
Medinipur	3.4	29.24	6.52	-	3.71	56.63	7.50	16.75
Haora	2.8	40.64	1.98	-	3.62	57.83	7.16	17.65
Hugli	2.9	38.65	6.13	-	2.86	56.90	2.99	17.49
24-Parganas	2.8	35.40	2.78	-	4.01	49.20	3.79	17.17
Kolkata	1.2	63.12	6.17	-	3.62	72.09	6.82	19.05
Nadia	3.8	29.28	3.22	-	3.70	44.42	4.32	16.70
Murshidabad	4.1	17.75	4.44	-	4.86	29.57	7.85	16.49
West Dinajpur	3.7	17.10	5.57	-	4.42	27.87	9.77	17.38
Malda	4.2	14.22	5.80	-	5.01	24.92	11.46	16.78
Jalpaiguri	3.7	20.40	11.10	-	3.86	33.20	12.04	17.83
Darjeeling	2.7	32.40	10.63	-	3.54	47.84	19.41	18.82
Cooch Behar	4.2	19.43	3.35	-	4.09	33.31	6.23	16.76
Puruliya	3.3	13.25	13.75	-	4.08	22.01	20.50	16.66
C.V.	23.50	44.94	61.99		13.67	33.00	53.40	

Source:(1) Occasional Paper-I of 1997, Census of India, (2) Census reports of West Bengal 1981, 1991 (3) West Bengal state district profile 1991

Key: TFR-Total Fertility Rates, FLR-Female Literacy Rate, FWPR- Female workforce participation rate, MA-Average age of marriage, C.V-Coefficient of Variation.

The table gives us an interesting message that there is an increase in the female literacy rates and female workforce participation rates in almost all the districts of the state during the period under consideration. But the pace of increase in female literacy rates and female workforce participation rates varies from district to district. It seems that increase in the levels of education for female obviously have some adverse impact on fertility rate. But our analysis of census data reveals somewhat different picture. At the district level too we find that there is an increasing tendency in the total fertility rate for almost all the districts of West Bengal during 1981-91. It gives us a paradoxical result. In this case also we find that the pace of increase in fertility rate varies from district to district. We measured the degree of variability in total fertility rate, female literacy rate and female workforce participation rate in West Bengal during 1981-91 in terms of coefficient of variation which reads the figures 23.50%, 13.67% for total fertility rates, 44.94%, 33.00% for female literacy rates, and 61.99%, 53.40% for female workforce participation rates for the years 1981 and 1991 respectively. It is surprising enough to note that the inter-district variability in respect of these three basic indicators of the status of women has decreased continuously during the period. Now to see whether there exists any negative association between the levels of education and women's status we can safely classify the districts in respect of status of women into two groups viz. districts having women's status higher than the state average level and districts with women's status below the state average level. This classification of districts is presented in Table 3.

The Table clearly depicts the fact that the districts e.g. Murshidabad, Malda, Cooch Behar, Jalpaiguri, Medinipur, Nadia and Purulia have experienced higher total fertility rate as compared to the state average level in 1981. In 1991 all these districts were in the same category except for the districts Medinipur, Jalpaiguri and Nadia. The Table also dispels an interesting message that the ranking of the districts in respect of total fertility rate, female literacy rate,

Table 3
Ranking of Districts regarding Women's Status in West Bengal during 1981-1991

Districts	*1981*			*1991*			
	Low TFR	*High FLR*	*High FWPR*	*Low TFR*	*High FLR*	*High FWPR*	*High MA*
Having high women's status	Bardhaman (2)	BArdhaman (5)	Bankura (3)	Hugli (1)	Kolkata (1)	Purulia (1)	Kolkata (1)
	Birbhum (6)	Medinipur (8)	Medinipur (5)	Bankura (2)	Haora (2)	Darjeeling (2)	Darjeeling (2)
	Bankura (5)	Haora (2)	Jalpaiguri (2)	Darjeeling (3)	Hugli (3)	Bankura (3)	Jalpaiguri (3)
	Haora (3)	Hugli (3)	Darjeeling (4)	Bardhamna (40)	Medinipur (4)	Jalpaiguri (4)	Haora (4)
	Hugli (4)	24-Par. (4)	Purulia(1)	Haora (5)	Bardhaman (5)	Malda (5)	Hugli (5)
	24-Parg. (3)	Kolkata(1)		Kolkata (5)	24-Par. (6)	West Dinajpur (6)	West Dinajpur (6)
	Kolkata (1)	Nadia (7)		Nadia (6)	Darjeeling (7)		
	Darjeeling (2)	Darjeeling (6)		Medinipur (7)	Nadia (8)		
				Birbhum (8)			
				Jalpaiguri (9)			
	High TFR	Low FLR	Low FWPR	High TFR	Low FLR	Low FWPR	Low MA
Having low women's status	Medini-pur (8)	Murshida-bad (13)	Bardha-man (96)	24-Parg.(10)	Birbhum (9)	Birbhum (7)	Bardha-man (7)
	Murshida-bad (11)	Birbhum (9)	Birbhum (11)	Purulia (11)	Bankura(10)	Murshida-bad (8)	24-Parg. (8)
	West Dinajpur (9)	Bankura (10)	Haora (16)	Cooch Behar (12)	Cooch Behar (11)	Bardhaman (9)	Birbhum (9)
	Malda (12)	West Dinajpur (14)	Hugli (8)	West Dinajpur (13)	Jalpaiguri (12)	Medinipur (10)	Bankura (10)
	Jalpaiguri (9)	Malda (15)	24-parg. (15)	Murshida-bad (14)	Murshida-bad (13)	Haora (11)	Malda (11)

Contd...

Districts	*1981*			*1991*			
	Low TFR	*High FLR*	*High FWPR*	*Low TFR*	*High FLR*	*High FWPR*	*High MA*
	Cooch Behar (12)	Jalpai-guri (11)	Kolkata (7)	Malda (15)	West Dinajpur (14)	Cooch Behar (13)	Cooch Behar (12)
	Purulia (7)	Cooch Behar (12)	Nadia (14)		Malda (15)	Nadia (14)	Medini-pur (13)
	Nadia (10)	Purulia (16)	Murshida-bad (12)		Purulia (16)	24-Parg.(15)	Nadia (14)
			West Dinajpur (10)			Kolkata (12)	Purulia (15)
			Malda (9)			Hugli (16)	Murshida-bad (16)
			Cooch Behar (13)				

female workforce participation rate and average age of marriage have changed over time, i.e. the relative position of the districts in respect of these parameters have changed over the period 1981-1991. Interestingly we find that lower rate of fertility does not always imply the higher rate of female literacy, female workforce participation rate and average age of marriage i.e. higher level of women's status. Some of the districts like Bardhaman, Birbhum, Bankura, Haora, Hugli, 24 Parganas, Kolkata etc. show lower total fertility rate, higher female literacy but lower female workforce participation rate in both periods. It seems that there may be some other socio-economic factors responsible for the improvement in women's status.

GENDER INEQUALITY

It is well known that overall sex ratio is a summary statistic, which reflects discrimination. To have a greater insight about the aspect of gender discrimination in West Bengal and its districts, we have also used this statistic. Besides this, we also consider gender differentials in literacy rates and child mortality rates (under five mortality rates), which are mute testimony to the marked difference between the levels of well being of men and women in West Bengal. These statistics are presented in Table 4. From the table it is evident that in West Bengal also women are on average less educated. But surprisingly it has been found that there is a sharp improvement in the overall sex ratio in West Bengal during 1981-91. In fact, it has increased from .911 in 1981 to .917 in 1991. The table also dispels another important message that child mortality rate for male was lower than that of female in 1981. But in 1991, the depiction became the reverse.

Further, to study regional variations in gender differentials in well being in West Bengal during 1981-91, we will look at the disaggregate data, which is presented in Table 4. Due to constrained of availability of data on income differences between the genders in West Bengal and its districts during 1981-1991, we are compelled to consider only the evidence on male-female literacy ratio, the sex-ratio and

Table 4
Gender Inequality in West Bengal and Its Districts

State / District	*Literacy*				*Sex ratio*		*Under-five mortality rate*			
	Male	*Female*	*Male*	*Female*			*Male*		*Female*	
	1981	*1991*	*1981*	*1991*	*1981*	*1991*	*1981*	*1991*	*1981*	*1991*
Bardhaman	-	71.12	33.80	51.46	.897	.809	95	79	99	67
Birbhum	-	59.26	24.20	37.17	.962	.946	143	121	140	112
Bankura	51.92	54.45	23.10	36.55	.964	.951	88	84	90	86
Medinipur	55.57	81.27	29.24	56.63	.951	.944	137	87	142	95
Haora	60.78	76.11	40.64	57.83	.873	.881	86	74	90	70
Hugli	57.99	75.77	38.65	56.90	.909	.917	86	64	85	65
24-Parganas	-	65.33	35.40	49.20	.909	.918	124	103	123	105
Kolkata	-	75.15	63.12	72.09	.741	.799	57	44	66	42
Nadia	43.75	60.05	29.28	44.42	.946	.936	142	99	139	112
Murshidabad	31.75	46.42	17.75	29.57	.959	.943	153	119	161	124
West Dinajpur	-	49.79	17.10	27.87	.938	.932	152	113	151	114
Malda	31.44	36.42	14.22	24.92	.949	.938	169	130	175	150
Jalpaiguri	-	-	20.40	33.20	.910	.927	145	117	140	104
Darjeeling	51.89	56.46	32.40	47.84	.888	.914	101	72	96	78
Cooch Behar	40.09	46.83	19.43	33.31	.935	.935	184	127	179	129
Puruliya	45.41	62.17	13.25	23.24	.957	.947	100	76	99	67
West Bengal			30.25	46.56	.911	.917	123	94	125	92

Source: Various census reports of West Bengal and, West Bengal state district profile [1991].

male-female under-five mortality rates for West Bengal and its districts during 1981-91.

The table gives us an interesting message that Bardhaman, Haora, Hugli, 24 Parganas, Kolkata, Nadia, Darjeeling have experienced an improvement in the overall sex-ratio during 1981-91 in this regard. It has also been found that in all the districts of West Bengal women are less educated than men, which is revealed from the gender differences in literacy rates during 1981-91. It implies that women are at a disadvantage in this regard as well. Considering another aspect of gender differential, i.e. under-five mortality rates during the period of our study it is evident that only five districts e.g. Bardhaman, Medinipur, Kolkata, Murshidabad and Malda have registered higher under-five mortality for women than men in 1981. But in 1991, the pictures became horrible. Ten districts of the state viz. Bankura, Medinipur, Hugli, 24 Parganas, Nadia, West Dinajpur, Murshidabad, Malda etc. have experienced higher under-five mortality for women than men.

Thus we find that the gender discrimination persists in an increasing order in almost all the districts in varying degrees. However, we do not find any relation between status of women and female literacy rate.

CONCLUSION

In this paper we have examined the nature and correlates of gender discrimination in West Bengal and its districts since 1980. We have also examined the nature of the cross-district variations in gender-inequality and the proximate factors behind it. The major conclusions, which emerge from our analysis, can be summarized as follows:

First, in the context of gender discrimination in West Bengal during 1981-1991, we find that it persists in an increasing order in almost all the districts of the state in varying degrees.

Second, we find that in West Bengal women are on average less educated than men, which is revealed from the gender differences in literacy rates during 1981-1991.

Third, the data on another aspect of gender-differential i.e. under-five mortality rates reveal that only five districts viz. Bardhaman, Medinipur, Murshidabad and Malda have registered higher under-five mortality for women than men in 1981. But in 1991, we find that seven districts of the state viz. Bankura, Medinipur, Hugli, 24 Parganas, Nadia, West Dinajpur, Malda etc. have experienced higher under five mortality for women than men.

Fourth, we find that some districts like Bardhaman, Haora, Hugli, 24 Parganas, Kolkata, Nadia and Darjeeling have experienced an improvement in the overall sex ratio during the period of our study.

Finally, we do not find any positive relationship between female literacy rate and the status of women. As female literacy is not the sole indicator of women's status, we find an unsatisfactory performance of other indicators (viz. age of marriage, total fertility rates, female workforce participation rate etc.) in this regard.

REFERENCES

Dreze. J and Sen. A (2002), *India, Development and Participation,* Oxford University Press.

Kulkarni, P.M. (1999), Gender Preference Contraceptive Prevalence: Evidence of Regional Variations, *Economic and Political Weekly*, October 16-23: 3058-3062.

Sen, I. (ed.) (1990), *A Space within the Struggle: Women's Participation in People's Movements,* Kali for Women, New Delhi.

INDEX